Foundations in Accountancy

FTX

FOUNDATIONS IN TAXATION
(United Kingdom)

P
R
A
C
T
I
C
E

&

R
E
V
I
S
I
O
N

K
I
T

> Welcome to BPP Learning Media's Practice & Revision Kit for FTX. In this Practice & Revision Kit, which has been reviewed by the **ACCA examining team**, we:
>
> - Include **Do you know?** Checklists to test your knowledge and understanding of topics
> - Provide you with **two** mock exams including the Specimen Exam

FOR EXAMS IN JUNE AND DECEMBER 2021

BPP LEARNING MEDIA

First edition January 2012
Tenth edition November 2020

ISBN 9781 5097 3443 6
Previous ISBN 9781 5097 2818 3

e-ISBN 9781 5097 3493 1

British Library Cataloguing-in-Publication Data
A catalogue record for this book
is available from the British Library

Published by

BPP Learning Media Ltd
BPP House, Aldine Place
London W12 8AA

www.bpp.com/learningmedia

Printed in the United Kingdom

Your learning materials, published by BPP Learning Media Ltd, are printed on paper sourced from sustainable, managed forests.

All our rights reserved. No part of this publication may be reproduced, stored in a retrieval system or transmitted, in any form or by any means, electronic, mechanical, photocopying, recording or otherwise, without the prior written permission of BPP Learning Media.

Contains public sector information licensed under the Open Government licence v3.0.

We are grateful to the Association of Chartered Certified Accountants for permission to reproduce past examination questions. The suggested solutions in the practice answer bank have been prepared by BPP Learning Media Ltd, except where otherwise stated.

©
BPP Learning Media Ltd
2020

A note about copyright

Dear Customer

What does the little © mean and why does it matter?

Your market-leading BPP books, course materials and e-learning materials do not write and update themselves. People write them: on their own behalf or as employees of an organisation that invests in this activity. Copyright law protects their livelihoods. It does so by creating rights over the use of the content.

Breach of copyright is a form of theft – as well as being a criminal offence in some jurisdictions, it is potentially a serious breach of professional ethics.

With current technology, things might seem a bit hazy but, basically, without the express permission of BPP Learning Media:

- Photocopying our materials is a breach of copyright

- Scanning, ripcasting or conversion of our digital materials into different file formats, uploading them to Facebook or emailing them to your friends is a breach of copyright

You can, of course, sell your books, in the form in which you have bought them – once you have finished with them. (Is this fair to your fellow students? We update for a reason.) But the e-products are sold on a single user licence basis: we do not supply 'unlock' codes to people who have bought them secondhand.

And what about outside the UK? BPP Learning Media strives to make our materials available at prices students can afford by local printing arrangements, pricing policies and partnerships which are clearly listed on our website. A tiny minority ignore this and indulge in criminal activity by illegally photocopying our material or supporting organisations that do. If they act illegally and unethically in one area, can you really trust them?

Contents

	Page
Finding questions	
Question index	v
Topic index	ix
Helping you with your revision	x
Using your BPP Practice & Revision Kit	xi
Passing the FTX exam	xii
Approach to examining the syllabus	xiii
The computer-based examination	xiv
Tackling Multiple Choice Questions	xv
Using your BPP products	xvi
Questions and answers	
Questions	3
Answers	91
Exam practice	
Mock exam 1 – Specimen Exam	
• Questions	187
• Answers	197
Mock exam 2	
• Questions	211
• Answers	223
Tax rates and allowances	235
Bibliography	241
Review form	

Question index

	Marks	Time allocation Mins	Page Question	Page Answer
Part A: Introduction to the UK tax system				
1 Multiple choice questions: Introduction to the UK tax system	–	–	5	91
Part B: Adjusted profit/loss computations for trades and professions				
2 Question with help: Adjustment of profit	–	–	8	91
3 Leon	15	18	9	92
4 Sarah	5	6	10	93
5 Question with help: Capital allowances	–	–	11	94
6 Jim	15	18	12	94
7 Amanda	15	18	12	96
8 Ian	10	12	13	97
9 Jackie	10	12	13	98
10 Owen	5	6	14	99
11 Donna	10	12	14	100
12 Question with help: Partnerships	–	–	14	101
13 Carol, Wendy and Bob	5	6	15	101
14 Peter, Sam and Martha	10	12	15	102
15 Norman	5	6	16	103
16 Danny	5	6	20	103
17 Multiple choice questions: Adjusted profit/loss computations for trades and professions	–	–	22	104
Part C: Income tax liability				
18 Question with help: Income tax liability	–	–	27	106
19 Fred	5	6	27	106
20 Linda	15	18	28	107
21 Mary	5	6	28	108
22 Valero	10	12	28	109
23 Patrick	15	18	29	110
24 Peppy	5	6	29	111
25 Beryl	5	6	30	112
26 Coral	15	18	30	113
27 Stephen	15	18	31	114

	Marks	Time allocation Mins	Page Question	Page Answer
28 Alison	10	12	31	116
29 Liam and Jordan	5	6	32	117
30 Declan	5	6	32	117
31 Nancy	5	6	32	118
32 Stuart	15	18	32	119
33 Doreen	5	6	33	120
34 Sonia	5	6	33	121
35 David	10	12	34	121
36 Jules	5	6	34	122
37 Jenny	15	18	34	123
38 Laslo	5	6	35	124
39 Simon	15	18	35	125
40 Amber	5	6	36	126
41 Hamish	15	18	36	126
42 Paul	10	12	36	127
43 Lin	5	6	37	128
44 Richard	5	6	37	129
45 Alisha	5	6	37	129
46 Barry	5	6	38	130
47 Multiple choice questions: Income tax liability	–	–	38	130
Part D: Capital gains tax				
48 Question with help: Capital gains tax liability	–	–	47	134
49 Silas	10	12	47	135
50 Jack	5	6	48	136
51 Ravi	10	12	48	137
52 Trudy	10	12	48	138
53 Ivan	5	6	51	138
54 Tony	5	6	51	139
55 Carla	5	6	51	140
56 Alberto	10	12	51	140
57 Sandra	5	6	52	141
58 Jessie	10	12	52	142
59 Eddie	10	12	52	142
60 Tanya	5	6	53	143

QUESTION INDEX

	Marks	Time allocation Mins	Page Question	Page Answer
61 Marion	10	12	53	144
62 Multiple choice questions: Capital gains tax	–	–	54	145
Part E: Corporation tax liabilities				
63 Question with help: Corporation tax	–	–	60	147
64 Taps Ltd	15	18	60	147
65 XYZ Ltd	15	18	61	149
66 Bush Ltd	10	12	62	150
67 Fires Ltd	10	12	63	151
68 Radiators Ltd	15	18	63	153
69 Broad Ltd	15	18	64	154
70 Rose Ltd	10	12	65	155
71 BDD Ltd	10	12	65	156
72 Cargo Ltd	10	12	66	157
73 Stem Ltd	10	12	66	158
74 Petal Ltd	5	6	67	159
75 Roof Ltd	5	6	67	160
76 Box plc	10	12	68	160
77 Andsnes Ltd	10	12	68	161
78 Jasmine plc	5	6	69	162
79 Question with help: Loss relief	–	–	69	163
80 Laurel Ltd	10	12	70	164
81 Caution Ltd	5	6	70	165
82 Waddle Ltd	10	12	70	165
83 Alphabetic Ltd	10	12	71	166
84 Peter Collins	10	12	71	167
85 Heaters Ltd	5	6	71	168
86 Flower plc	5	6	71	168
87 Multiple choice questions: Corporation tax liabilities	–	–	72	169

	Marks	Time allocation Mins	Page Question	Page Answer
Part F: Value added tax				
88 Question with help: Value added tax payable	–	–	78	171
89 Emma	10	12	79	172
90 Legg Ltd	10	12	79	172
91 AccountsRUs	10	12	80	173
92 City Merchandise	10	12	80	174
93 The Stuart Partnership	5	6	81	174
94 Ivor	5	6	81	175
95 Resolute plc	5	6	81	175
96 Bob	5	6	81	175
97 Martha and Dominic	5	6	82	176
98 Narrow Ltd	5	6	82	176
99 Celeste	5	6	82	177
100 Dana	5	6	82	177
101 Blue Ltd	5	6	83	178
102 Merrill	5	6	83	178
103 Multiple choice questions: Value added tax	–	–	84	179
Mock exams				
Mock exam 1 (Specimen Exam)	100	120	187	197
Mock exam 2	100	120	211	223

Topic Index

Listed below are the key FTX syllabus topics and the numbers of the questions in this Kit (excluding Mock Exams) covering those topics.

If you need to concentrate your practice and revision on certain topics or if you want to attempt all available questions that refer to a particular subject, you will find this index useful.

Syllabus topic	Question numbers
UK tax system	1
Adjustment of trading profit/loss	2, 3, 4, 6, 7, 17
Capital allowances	5, 6, 7, 17
Basis of assessment for self-employed	6, 7, 8, 9, 10, 17, 83
NICs for self-employed	17, 83
Relief for trading losses	11
Partnerships	12, 13, 14, 17
Tax returns for self-employed, partnerships	15, 16
Savings income	18, 20, 23, 26, 27, 28, 32, 37, 39, 41, 47
Employment income	19, 20, 21, 22, 23, 24, 25, 26, 27, 30, 31, 37, 39, 40, 41, 47
NICs for employed	29, 47, 87
Property income	26, 33, 34, 35, 36, 37, 38, 47
Income tax liability	18, 20, 23, 26, 27, 28, 32, 37, 39, 41, 47
Pension contributions	20, 22, 23, 26, 28, 32, 39, 42, 47
Income tax administration	22, 43, 44, 45, 46, 47
Chargeable gains – individuals	48, 49, 50, 51, 53, 54, 55, 56, 57, 58, 59, 60, 61, 62
Reliefs for gains	54, 55, 57, 60, 62
Tax returns for gains	52
Taxable total profits	63, 64, 65, 66, 67, 68, 69, 70, 71, 72, 73, 87
Corporation tax computation	63, 64, 65, 68, 69, 70, 71, 79, 84, 85, 87
Chargeable gains – companies	69, 74, 75, 76, 77, 78, 87
Relief for corporate losses	79, 80, 81, 82, 87
Corporation tax administration	79, 83, 85, 86, 87
Value added tax	88, 89, 90, 91, 92, 93, 94, 95, 96, 97, 98, 99, 100, 101, 102, 103

Helping you with your revision

BPP Learning Media – ACCA Approved Content Provider

As an ACCA **Approved Content Provider**, BPP Learning Media gives you the **opportunity** to use revision materials reviewed by the ACCA examining team. By incorporating the ACCA examining team's comments and suggestions regarding the depth and breadth of syllabus coverage, the BPP Learning Media Practice & Revision Kit provides excellent, **ACCA-approved** support for your revision.

These materials are reviewed by the ACCA examining team. The objective of the review is to ensure that the material properly covers the syllabus and study guide outcomes, used by the examining team in setting the exams, in the appropriate breadth and depth. The review does not ensure that every eventuality, combination or application of examinable topics is addressed by the ACCA Approved Content. Nor does the review comprise a detailed technical check of the content as the Approved Content Provider has its own quality assurance processes in place in this respect.

BPP Learning Media do everything possible to ensure the material is accurate and up to date when sending to print. In the event that any errors are found after the print date, they are uploaded to the following website: www.bpp.com/learningmedia/Errata.

Selecting questions

We provide signposts to help you plan your revision:

- A full **question index**
- A **topic index** listing questions that cover each part of the syllabus, so that you can locate the questions that provide practice on key topics, and see the different ways in which they might be tested.

Attempting mock exams

There are two mock exams that provide practice at coping with the pressures of the exam day. We strongly recommend that you attempt them under exam conditions. **Mock exam 1** is the Specimen Exam, updated for Finance Act 2020. **Mock exam 2** reflects the question styles and syllabus coverage of the exam.

Using your BPP Practice & Revision Kit

Aim of this Practice & Revision Kit

To provide the practice to help you succeed in the examination for FTX *Foundations in Taxation*.

To pass the examination you need a thorough understanding in all areas covered by the syllabus and study guide.

Recommended approach

- Make sure you are able to answer questions on **everything** specified by the syllabus and study guide. You cannot make any assumptions about what questions may come up in your exam. The examining team aims to discourage 'question spotting'.

- Learning is an **active** process. Use the **DO YOU KNOW**? Checklists to test your knowledge and understanding of the topics covered in FTX *Foundations in Taxation* by filling in the blank spaces. Then check your answers against the **DID YOU KNOW**? Checklists. Do not attempt any questions if you are unable to fill in any of the blanks – go back to your **BPP Interactive Text** and revise first.

- When you are revising a topic, think about the mistakes that you know that you should avoid by writing down **POSSIBLE PITFALLS** at the end of each **DO YOU KNOW?** Checklist.

- Once you have completed the checklists successfully, you should attempt the questions on that topic. Each section has a selection of **MUTIPLE CHOICE QUESTIONS** and **COMPULSORY WRITTEN QUESTIONS**. Make good use of the **HELPING HANDS** provided to help you answer the questions.

- There is a mark allocation for each compulsory written question. Each mark carries with it a time allocation of 1.2 minutes (including time for selecting and reading questions). A 15-mark question should therefore be completed in 18 minutes.

- Thirty percent of the exam consists of **Multiple Choice Questions (MCQs)**. You should attempt each bank of MCQs to ensure you are familiar with their styles and to practise your technique. Ensure you read **Tackling Multiple Choice Questions** on page xv to get advice on how best to approach them.

- Once you have completed all of the questions in the body of this Practice & Revision Kit, you should attempt the **MOCK EXAMS** under examination conditions. Check your answers against our answers to find out how well you did.

Passing the FTX exam

FTX *Foundations in Taxation* does not assume any prior knowledge of taxation. However, you are expected to understand the format of accounts for sole traders, partnerships and companies from Foundations in Accountancy Module FA2 *Maintaining Financial Records* and Module FFA *Financial Accounting*.

To access Foundations in Accountancy syllabuses, visit the ACCA website:

www2.accaglobal.com/students/fia

The exam

This is a computer-based exam. All questions in the exam are compulsory. This means you cannot avoid any topic, but also means that you do not need to waste time in the exam deciding which questions to attempt. There are 15 MCQs and eight longer questions in the examination. This means that the examining team is able to test most of the syllabus at each sitting, and that is what they aim to do. So you need to have revised right across the syllabus for this exam.

Topics to revise

There are certain topics that almost always come up and you must practise:

- Employment income
- Calculation of income tax
- Value added tax
- Calculation of corporation tax

Revision

This Practice & Revision Kit has been reviewed by the FTX examining team and contains the Specimen Exam. If you just worked through it to the end you would be very well prepared for the exam. It is important to tackle questions under exam conditions. Allow yourself just the number of minutes shown next to the questions in the index and don't look at the answers until you have finished. Then correct your answer and go back to the Interactive Text for any topic you are really having trouble with. Try the same question again a week later – you will be surprised how much better you are getting. Doing the questions like this will really show you what you know, and will make the exam experience less worrying.

Doing the exam

If you have honestly done your revision you can pass this exam. There are certain points which you must bear in mind:

- Read the question properly, particularly the longer questions. You don't want to waste time doing something that has not been asked for. It is worth reading a longer question through twice.

- Make sure you answer the question actually set, rather than the question you might wish had been set.

- Make sure you present your answer well to give it structure and to make it easier for the marker to identify where marks can be awarded. You can do this by using headings, short paragraphs, spaces between paragraphs and bullet points.

- Don't spend more than the allotted time on each question. If you are having trouble with a question leave it and carry on. You can come back to it at the end. If there is part of a question that you can't do, leave it and do the rest.

Approach to examining the syllabus

FTX is a two-hour exam. All questions will be compulsory and will assess all parts of the syllabus.

The two hour time allocation **does not** provide for any reading time.

The exam is structured as follows:

		No of marks
Section A	15 compulsory multiple choice questions of 2 marks each	30
Section B	Eight compulsory questions	
	Two questions (15 marks each)	30
	Two questions (10 marks each)	20
	Four questions (5 marks each)	20
Total		100

One of the 15-mark questions will focus on income tax and the other 15-mark question will focus on corporation tax. The remaining questions will examine topics from any area of the syllabus.

The computer-based examination

Computer-based examinations (CBEs) are available for the Foundations in Accountancy exams. The CBE exams for the first seven modules can be taken at any time, these are referred to as 'exams on demand'. The Option exams can be sat in June and December of each year, these are referred to as 'exams on sitting'. Computer based examinations must be taken at an ACCA CBE Licensed Centre.

Computer-based examinations must be taken at an ACCA CBE Licensed Centre.

How do CBEs work?

- Questions are displayed on a monitor.
- Candidates enter their answer directly onto the computer.
- Candidates have two hours to complete the examination.
- Candidates sitting exams on demand are provided with a Provisional Result Notification showing their results before leaving the examination room.
- The CBE Licensed Centre uploads the results to the ACCA (as proof of the candidate's performance) within 72 hours.
- Candidates sitting the Option exams will receive their results approximately five weeks after the exam sitting once they have been expert marked.
- Candidates can check their exam status on the ACCA website by logging into myACCA.

Benefits

- **Flexibility** as the first seven modules, exams on demand, can be sat at any time.
- **Resits** for the first seven modules can also be taken at any time and there is no restriction on the number of times a candidate can sit a CBE.
- **Instant feedback** for the exams on demand as the computer displays the results at the end of the CBE.

For more information on computer-based exams, visit the ACCA website:

www.accaglobal.com/gb/en/student/exam-entry-and-administration/computer-based-exams.html

Tackling multiple choice questions

MCQs are part of all Foundations in Accountancy exams. Of the total marks available in the exam, multiple choice questions (MCQs) comprise 30%.

The MCQs in your exam contain four possible answers. You have to **choose the option that best answers the question**. The incorrect options are called distracters. There is a skill in answering MCQs quickly and correctly. By practising MCQs you can develop this skill, giving you a better chance of passing the exam.

You may wish to follow the approach outlined below, or you may prefer to adapt it.

Step 1	Skim read all the MCQs and identify what appear to be the easier questions.
Step 2	Attempt each question – **starting with the easier questions** identified in Step 1. Read the question **thoroughly**. You may prefer to work out the answer before looking at the options, or you may prefer to look at the options at the beginning. Adopt the method that works best for you.
Step 3	Read the options and see if one match your own answer. Be careful with numerical questions as the distracters are designed to match answers that incorporate common errors. Check that your calculation is correct. Have you followed the requirement exactly? Have you included every stage of the calculation?
Step 4	You may find that none of the options match your answer: • Re-read the question to ensure that you understand it and are answering the requirement • Eliminate any obviously wrong answers • Consider which of the remaining answers is the most likely to be correct and select the option
Step 5	If you are still unsure make a note and continue to the next question.
Step 6	Revisit unanswered questions. When you come back to a question after a break you often find you are able to answer it correctly straight away. If you are still unsure have a guess. You are not penalised for incorrect answers, so **never leave a question unanswered!**

After extensive practice and revision of MCQs, you may find that you recognise a question when you sit the exam. Be aware that the detail and/or requirement may be different. If the question seems familiar read the requirement and options carefully – do not assume that it is identical.

Using your BPP products

This Practice & Revision Kit gives you the question practice and guidance you need in the exam. Our other products can also help you pass:

- **Interactive Text** introduces and explains the knowledge required for your exam
- **Passcards** provide you with clear topic summaries and exam tips

You can purchase these products by visiting www.bpp.com/learning-media.

Questions

Do you know? – Part A: Introduction to the UK tax system

Check that you can fill in the blanks in the statements below before you attempt any questions. If in doubt, you should go back to your BPP Interactive Text and revise first.

- The administrative function for the collection of tax is undertaken by ....

- Tax law is made by statute. Each year at least one .... is passed, incorporating proposals set out in one or more ....

- Some Acts of Parliament provide for the making of detailed regulations by ....

- .... set out how HMRC intends to apply the law.

- Tax appeals are heard by the ....

- Taxes charged on income are ....

- Direct taxes are those charged on ...., ..., and ....

- Indirect taxes are paid by .... to ....

Now consolidate your knowledge of Part A of the syllabus by attempting all the MULTIPLE CHOICE QUESTIONS in QUESTION 1.

Did you know? – Part A: Introduction to the UK tax system

Could you fill in the blanks? The answers are in bold. Use this page for revision purposes as you approach the exam.

- The administrative function for the collection of tax is undertaken by **Her Majesty's Revenue and Customs (HMRC)**.
- Tax law is made by statute. Each year at least one **Finance Act** is passed, incorporating proposals set out in one or more **budgets**.
- Some Acts of Parliament provide for the making of detailed regulations by **statutory instrument**.
- **Statements of practice** set out how HMRC intends to apply the law.
- Tax appeals are heard by the **Tax Tribunal**.
- Taxes charged on income are **revenue taxes**.
- Direct taxes are those charged on **income, gains,** and **wealth**.
- Indirect taxes are paid by **the consumer** to **the supplier**.

Now consolidate your knowledge of Part A of the syllabus by attempting all the MULTIPLE CHOICE QUESTIONS in QUESTION 1.

1 Multiple choice questions: Introduction to the UK tax system

Allow 2 minutes for each question.

1.1 Which of the following is the best description for the function of HM Treasury in the UK tax system?

   ○ It is responsible for raising revenue for the government through the tax system
   ○ It deals with taxpayer's queries
   ○ It provides legal advice
   ○ It has the administrative function for collection of tax (2 marks)

1.2 **Which TWO of the following are a source of tax law?**

   (i) Extra Statutory Concession A19
   (ii) Statutory Instrument 2008/2682
   (iii) Taxation of Chargeable Gains Act 1992
   (iv) Statement of Practice B1

   ○ (i) and (ii)
   ○ (i) and (iii)
   ○ (ii) and (iii)
   ○ (ii) and (iv) (2 marks)

1.3 Brody has appealed concerning an item of expenditure of £1,000 which has been disallowed in his income tax computation.

   Which body will hear his appeal?

   ○ First Tier Tax Tribunal
   ○ HM Revenue and Customs
   ○ HM Treasury
   ○ Upper Tax Tribunal (2 marks)

1.4 Which of the following is not a revenue tax?

   ○ Income tax
   ○ Corporation tax
   ○ National insurance
   ○ Capital gains tax (2 marks)

1.5 Which of the following is an indirect tax?

   ○ National insurance contributions
   ○ Value added tax
   ○ Capital gains tax
   ○ Corporation tax (2 marks)

Did you know? – Part B: Adjusted profit/loss computations for trades and professions

Check that you can fill in the blanks in the statements below **before** you **attempt any questions**. If in doubt, you should go back to your BPP Interactive Text and revise first.

- Depreciation must be added back to net trade profits as it is not deductible for tax purposes, instead relief is given via ……………………………………
- Profits taxed twice when a business starts are known as …………………………… profits and can be relieved ……………………………………………………
- Staff entertaining is …………………………… for tax purposes whilst customer entertaining is …………………………… for tax purposes.

TRY QUESTIONS 2, 3 AND 4

- Writing down allowances on the main pool are given at ………….%.
- The annual investment allowance for a 12-month period of account is £……………………

TRY QUESTION 5

- Where a person has been self-employed for many years, that person is assessable on a ……………… year basis
- The basis period for the first tax year runs from the date the trade starts to the next ……………
- Any overlap profits unrelieved when the trade ceases are deducted from ………………
- Self-employed individuals pay Class ……………… and Class ……………… National Insurance Contributions.

TRY QUESTIONS 6, 7, 8, 9 AND 10

- The three factors to take into account when making a loss relief claim are ……………, ……………, and ……………

TRY QUESTION 11

- Before sharing partnership profits among the partners we must first allocate …………………………… and/or ……………………………

TRY QUESTIONS 12, 13 AND 14

- A self-employed person with profits in excess of the VAT threshold is required to submit Form ……………… showing income and expenditure.

TRY QUESTIONS 15 AND 16

Now consolidate your knowledge of Part B of the syllabus by attempting all the MULTIPLE CHOICE QUESTIONS in QUESTION 17.

Do you know? – Part B: Adjusted profit/loss computations for trades and professions

Could you fill in the blanks? The answers are in bold. Use this page for revision purposes as you approach the exam.

- Depreciation must be added back to net trade profits as it is not deductible for tax purposes, instead relief is given via **capital allowances**.
- Profits taxed twice when a business starts are known as **overlap** profits and can be relieved **in the final tax year of trade**.
- Staff entertaining is **allowable** for tax purposes whilst customer entertaining is **not allowable** for tax purposes.

  TRY QUESTIONS 2, 3 AND 4

- Writing down allowances on the main pool are given at **18%**.
- The annual investment allowance for a 12-month period of account is **£1,000,000**.

  TRY QUESTION 5

- Where a person has been self-employed for many years, that person is assessable on a **current** year basis.
- The basis period for the first tax year runs from the date the trade starts to the next **5 April**.
- Any overlap profits unrelieved when the trade ceases are deducted from **the final tax year's taxable profits**.
- Self-employed individuals pay Class **2** and Class **4** National Insurance Contributions.

  TRY QUESTIONS 6, 7, 8, 9 AND 10

- The three factors to take into account when making a loss relief claim are **tax rate**, **timing**, and **preserving personal allowances**.

  TRY QUESTION 11

- Before sharing partnership profits among the partners we must first allocate **interest on capital** and/or **salaries**.

  TRY QUESTIONS 12, 13 AND 14

- A self-employed person with profits in excess of the VAT threshold is required to submit Form **SA103F** showing income and expenditure.

  TRY QUESTIONS 15 AND 16

Now consolidate your knowledge of Part B of the syllabus by attempting all the MULTIPLE CHOICE QUESTIONS in QUESTION 17.

2 Question with help: Adjustment of profit

George carries on a trade as a drapery wholesaler making up accounts to 31 January in each year.

His statement of profit or loss for the year ended 31 January 2021 showed the following results.

	£	£
Gross operating profit		82,594
Add bank interest received		2,000
		84,594
Less: wages	22,504	
rent, rates, light and heat	26,492	
repairs	7,206	
professional charges (1)	1,000	
other expenses (2)	3,962	
travelling and entertaining (3)	9,041	
impairment debts (4)	1,336	
depreciation	2,874	
		(74,415)
Net profit		10,179

Notes

		£
1	*Professional charges*	
	Debt collection – all trade debtors	150
	Accountancy	760
	Advice regarding trading agreement	90
		1,000
2	*Other expenses*	
	Chamber of Commerce subscription	40
	Other allowable expenses	3,922
		3,962
3	*Travelling and entertaining*	
	General travelling including travelling salespersons' car expenses	7,527
	Expenses of George's car	640
	Entertaining customers	874
		9,041
4	*Impairment debts*	
	Amounts written off – trade debtors	541
	Amounts written off – non-trade debtors	795
		1,336

The private use by George of his car is 25%.

Required

Compute the adjusted trading profit for income tax purposes based on this statement of profit or loss. You should start with the net profit figure of £10,179 and indicate by the use of zero (0) any items which do not require adjustment.

 **Approaching the answer**

Use this answer plan to construct your answer if you are stuck.

Step 1 You are asked to compute the adjusted trading profit. You should therefore start by setting out a pro forma, starting with the net profit.

Step 2 You should then work systematically through the statement of profit or loss. The question requires you to indicate by the use of zero (0) any items which do not require adjustment, so make sure you do this to gain the relevant marks.

Step 3 To deal with the car expenses you must bring together two pieces of information (the amount and the private use percentage) which are separated in the question.

Step 4 Finally, add up your adjusted profit computation.

3 Leon   18 mins

Leon operates a small unincorporated business. His most recent set of accounts was for the year ended 31 October 2020 and his statement of profit or loss showed the following results.

	Notes	£	£
Gross operating profit			110,000
Add interest received	1		240
rental income received	2		4,400
			114,640
Less expenses:			
wages and salaries	3	68,550	
lighting and heating	4	720	
depreciation		400	
bank overdraft interest		140	
donations	5	300	
legal fees	6	700	
motor car expenses	7	2,580	
miscellaneous expenses	8	930	
loss on sale of machinery		200	
			(74,520)
Net profit			40,120

Notes

1. The interest received is the amount due on cash deposited with a local building society.

2. The rental income represents the amount received on a small workshop let to another trader.

3. Wages and salaries comprise the following.

	£
Gross payments of salary to staff	33,868
Employer's national insurance contributions	1,590
Drawings by Leon	26,500
Payments to Emily (Leon's wife)	6,592
	68,550

Emily works 16 hours a week for 40 weeks a year. Other staff on similar contracts receive £9 per hour.

4. Leon and Emily live in a flat above the business premises. 60% of the total heating and lighting cost incurred is used in the flat and 40% in the business.

5   Donations during the year were made to the following:

	£
Oxfam – a registered charity (Gift aid)	200
Local nature reserve – a registered charity (for garden bench inscribed with Leon's business name)	100
	300

6   Legal fees comprise £400 for trade debt collection and £300 for legal work regarding the collection of the outstanding rent.

7   Motor car expenses comprise the following.

	£
Running costs (including petrol)	2,400
Parking fines – Leon	120
– Staff	60
(both fines occurred whilst the individuals were engaged on business activities)	
	2,580

HMRC has agreed that the motor car running costs are to be split 70% for private use and 30% for business use.

8   Miscellaneous expenses comprise the following.

	£
Internet services (all business)	700
Gifts to customers	
(bottles of whisky costing £11.50 each)	230
	930

9   Leon took goods from the inventory of the business for his own use. These goods had cost £1,400 and this amount is included in the purchases total, but has not been included in the sales total. The profit margin on these goods is 20% of the selling price.

Required

Calculate Leon's adjusted trading profit for the year ended 31 October 2020. You should start with the net profit figure of £40,120 and indicate by the use of zero (0) any items which do not require adjustment.

(15 marks)

4 Sarah   6 mins

Sarah is a sole trader making up accounts to 31 March each year. She decided to lease new business premises and paid a premium of £18,000 for the grant of a ten-year lease on 1 April 2020.

Required

Calculate the annual amount Sarah is able to deduct from her assessable trading profits in respect of the premium paid.   **(5 marks)**

5 Question with help: Capital allowances

Saruman is a sole trader, carrying on a small engineering business. He prepares accounts annually to 5 April. The following information is relevant to his capital allowances.

Main pool brought forward on 6 April 2020	£31,200
Tax written down value of motor car for Saruman's use on 6 April 2020	£600

The following events occurred during the year ended 5 April 2021.

Disposals:	20 April 2020	–	Plant £12,000 (original cost £10,000)
	21 May 2020	–	Motor car for Saruman's own use as shown above £920 (original cost £1,088)
	9 September 2020	–	Plant £800 (original cost £3,000)
Additions:	1 May 2020	–	New plant £25,000
	18 August 2020	–	New car for Saruman's use £19,000. The car has 100g/km CO_2 emissions

Private use of both of the cars is 25%.

Required

Calculate the capital allowances available to Saruman for the year ending 5 April 2021.

Approaching the answer

Use this answer plan to construct your answer if you are stuck.

Step 1	When tackling a capital allowances computation, the first step is to set out the headings of the columns clearly, leaving plenty of space for items that need individual treatment (such as assets with private use).
Step 2	Deal systematically with the additions and disposals, and calculate the total for each column before working out the capital allowances available.
Step 3	Remember to take the AIA where relevant and add any balance to the pool if necessary.
Step 4	Remember to adjust for private use where necessary.
Step 5	Where disposal proceeds exceed original cost, the deduction for capital allowances purposes is limited to the cost. This means that only £10,000 is deducted for the disposal on 20 April 2020.

6 Jim   18 mins

Jim's premium bicycle manufacturing business is owned by Olympic cyclist Jim who operates the business as a sole trader. Jim started business on 1 February 2021.

The first set of accounts was made up to 31 May 2022. The trading profit (after tax adjustments but before capital allowances) was £1,415,602. On 18 May 2022 the business spent £1,342,876 on new plant and machinery.

The second period of account was for the 12 months ended 31 May 2023 and showed a trading profit (before tax adjustments and capital allowances) of £1,660,000.

The accounts ended 31 May 2023 included the following items.

Expenditure

Depreciation £12,000.
£123,649 for building of a new warehouse for bicycles on 1 July 2022.

Receipts

£3,200 for interest on the business's bank account.

During the period 1 June 2022 to 31 May 2023 Jim took a bicycle which had cost £2,850 from inventory for his own personal use. He has not paid for this. No entry has been made in the accounts other than the cost of purchase. Jim's normal profit margin is 25% of the selling price.

Required

(a)   Calculate the tax adjusted profit for:

  (i)   The period ending 31 May 2022. You should start with the trading profit of £1,415,602.
        (3 marks)

  (ii) The year ending 31 May 2023. You should start with the trading profit of £1,660,000.
        (7 marks)

(b)   Calculate the first four years of assessable trading income (apportionment to be done in months).
      (5 marks)

Assume the tax rules and rates for 2020/21 apply in later years.

(Total = 15 marks)

Helping hand. Write down the basis periods for each tax year before trying to match them to profits.

7 Amanda   18 mins

Amanda started in business on 1 December 2020. She prepared her first set of accounts to 31 May 2021 and annually thereafter. Her first two sets of adjusted trading profits after capital allowances were:

Period ended 31 May 2021	£4,260
Year ended 31 May 2022	£8,190

During her accounting year ended 31 May 2023 Amanda had the following results.

	£	£
Gross profit		11,000
Bank interest received		450
		11,450
Electricity	810	
Accountant's fees	280	
Depreciation	120	
Drawings	640	
Car expenses	1,840	(3,690)
Net profit		7,760

Amanda works from home and 40% of the electricity costs relate to personal use. 40% of the car expenses relate to private use.

Capital allowances of £3,442 were claimed for the year ended 31 May 2023.

Required

(a) Calculate the adjusted trading profit after capital allowances for the year ended 31 May 2023. You should start with the net profit figure of £7,760 and indicate by the use of zero (0) any items which do not require adjustment. (7 marks)

(b) Calculate the assessable trading profits for the four tax years 2020/21 to 2023/24 inclusive. (6 marks)

(c) Calculate the overlap profits for the opening years of assessment. (2 marks)

Assume that the rules and rates of income tax in 2020/21 apply in later years.

(Total = 15 marks)

8 Ian — 12 mins

Ian started a business on 1 February 2019 and prepared his first set of accounts for the period ended 30 June 2019. Thereafter accounts were prepared annually to 30 June. Ian's first two accounting periods had adjusted profits as follows.

Five months to 30 June 2019	£18,000
Year to 30 June 2020	£30,000

Required

(a) Calculate Ian's assessable profits for the first three tax years of his business, clearly stating the basis periods that apply. (8 marks)

(b) Calculate the amount of overlap profits for all of the tax years covered in (a) above. (2 marks)

(Total = 10 marks)

9 Jackie — 12 mins

Jackie started her picture framing business on 1 May 2016. Due to falling profits she ceased to trade on 28 February 2021.

Her profits for the whole period of trading were as follows.

	£
1 May 2016 to 31 July 2017	18,000
1 August 2017 to 31 July 2018	11,700
1 August 2018 to 31 July 2019	8,640
1 August 2019 to 31 July 2020	6,800
1 August 2020 to 28 February 2021	4,100

Required

Calculate the total assessable profits for each of the tax years concerned. (10 marks)

Helping hand. Overlap profits can be relieved in the final tax year of trade.

10 Owen — 6 mins

Owen commenced trading as a sole trader on 1 October 2019. Owen decided to prepare accounts to 30 April each year. Owen's results for his first two periods of account are as follows.

	£
Period to 30 April 2020	21,000
Year ended 30 April 2021	72,000

Required

Calculate the assessable trading profits for the two tax years affected by the above accounting results, clearly stating the tax years and basis periods that apply, and state the basis of assessment for the following tax years.

Note. You are not required to calculate overlap profits. **(5 marks)**

11 Donna — 12 mins

Donna has been a self-employed trader for many years. She has the following gross income for the tax years 2019/20 to 2021/22.

	2019/20 £	2020/21 £	2021/22 £
Trading profit/(loss)	75,900	(85,000)	18,600
Property business income	2,100	3,800	2,000

Required

(a) **State the three factors that will influence an individual's choice of loss relief claims. (3 marks)**

(b) **Calculate Donna's taxable income for each of the tax years 2019/20, 2020/21 and 2021/22 on the assumption that she relieves the trading loss of £85,000 for the tax year 2020/21 on the most favourable basis.**

You should assume that the tax rates and allowances for the tax year 2020/21 apply throughout.

(7 marks)

(Total = 10 marks)

Helping hand. The three factors required for part (a) are stated in the syllabus.

12 Question with help: Partnerships

Clare and Justin had been trading in partnership for many years sharing profits and losses as to Clare one third and Justin two thirds. They prepared their accounts to 31 January each year.

Malcolm joined the partnership on 1 May 2020. From this date the profit and losses were shared equally.

Trading profits were as follows.

	£
Y/e 31.01.21	117,000
Y/e 31.01.22	72,000

Required

Calculate the amount on which each partner will be taxed in respect of the partnership profits for 2020/21.

 **Approaching the answer**

Use this answer plan to construct your answer if you are stuck.

Step 1	You should start by dividing the profits for each period of account between the partners in accordance with the profit sharing ratio for that period.
Step 2	Next work out how much profit should be taxed in each tax year. Clare and Justin will be taxed on a current year basis. Apply the opening year rules to Malcolm.

13 Carol, Wendy and Bob — 6 mins

Carol, Wendy and Bob have been in partnership for several years. Carol receives an annual salary of £10,000 and Bob receives 4% interest on the capital of £70,000 he has contributed. The balance of profits is shared in the ratio of 3:1:1 to Carol, Wendy and Bob respectively.

For the accounting year ended 31 January 2021 the partnership tax adjusted trading profit was £80,000.

Required

Calculate each partner's taxable income from the partnership for the accounting year ended 31 January 2021.

(5 marks)

14 Peter, Sam and Martha — 12 mins

Peter, Sam and Martha have been in partnership since early 2014. Due to a fall in demand for their services Martha decided to leave the partnership on 30 September 2020. Profits for the partnership for the two most recent accounting periods have been:

Year to 31 December 2019   £60,000
Year to 31 December 2020   £45,000

Up to 30 September 2020 each partner received a salary of £10,000 per year and shared the remaining profits as follows: Peter 40%, Sam 40% and Martha 20%. Following Martha's departure the salaries for Peter and Sam remained the same and the remaining profits were shared equally.

Martha had unrelieved overlap profits of £4,000 from the start of the partnership.

Required

(a) **Calculate the partnership profits for each partner for the year to 31 December 2019 and the year to 31 December 2020.** (7 marks)

(b) **Calculate the taxable profits for Martha for the tax years 2019/20 and 2020/21.** (3 marks)

(Total = 10 marks)

15 Norman — 6 mins

Norman has been in business for many years as a carpenter making up accounts to 5 April each year.

In the year to 5 April 2021, Norman had the following income and expenditure:

(a) Income from customers £90,000
(b) Materials used in business (wood, trimmings, paint etc) £20,000
(c) Van expenses £4,200
(d) Advertising £1,000

£840 of the van expenses related to Norman's private use of his van.

Required

Using the above information, state the figures that would be included from Box 15 to Box 47 inclusive on the self-employed full supplementary pages (shown on the next three pages) for Norman for 2020/21.

(5 marks)

Self-employment (full)

Tax year 6 April 2020 to 5 April 2021 (2020–21)

Please read the 'Self-employment (full) notes' to check if you should use this page or the 'Self-employment (short)' page.

For help filling in this form, go to www.gov.uk/taxreturnforms and read the notes and helpsheets.

Your name

Your Unique Taxpayer Reference (UTR)

Business details

1 Business name – unless it's in your own name

2 Description of business

3 First line of your business address – unless you work from home

4 Postcode of your business address

5 If the details in boxes 1, 2, 3 or 4 have changed in the last 12 months, put 'X' in the box and give details in the 'Any other information' box

6 If your business started after 5 April 2020, enter the start date DD MM YYYY

7 If your business ceased after 5 April 2020 but before 6 April 2021, enter the final date of trading

8 Date your books or accounts start – the beginning of your accounting period

9 Date your books or accounts are made up to or the end of your accounting period – read the notes if you have filled in box 6 or 7

10 If you used cash basis, money actually received and paid out, to calculate your income and expenses, put 'X' in the box

Other information

11 If your accounting date has changed permanently, put 'X' in the box

12 If your accounting date has changed more than once since 2015, put 'X' in the box

13 If special arrangements apply, put 'X' in the box

14 If you provided the information about your 2020–21 profit on last year's tax return, put 'X' in the box

Business income

15 Your turnover – the takings, fees, sales or money earned by your business

£

16 Any other business income not included in box 15

£

16.1 Trading income allowance – read the notes

£

SA103F 2020　　　　Page SEF 1　　　　HMRC 12/19

(Adapted from HMRC, 2020)

Business expenses

Please read the 'Self-employment (full) notes' before filling in this section.

Total expenses

If your annual turnover was below £85,000, you may just put your total expenses in box 31

Disallowable expenses

Use this column if the figures in boxes 17 to 30 include disallowable amounts

Box	Total expenses	Box	Disallowable expenses
17	Cost of goods bought for resale or goods used £ · 0 0	32	£ · 0 0
18	Construction industry – payments to subcontractors £ · 0 0	33	£ · 0 0
19	Wages, salaries and other staff costs £ · 0 0	34	£ · 0 0
20	Car, van and travel expenses £ · 0 0	35	£ · 0 0
21	Rent, rates, power and insurance costs £ · 0 0	36	£ · 0 0
22	Repairs and maintenance of property and equipment £ · 0 0	37	£ · 0 0
23	Phone, fax, stationery and other office costs £ · 0 0	38	£ · 0 0
24	Advertising and business entertainment costs £ · 0 0	39	£ · 0 0
25	Interest on bank and other loans £ · 0 0	40	£ · 0 0
26	Bank, credit card and other financial charges £ · 0 0	41	£ · 0 0
27	Irrecoverable debts written off £ · 0 0	42	£ · 0 0
28	Accountancy, legal and other professional fees £ · 0 0	43	£ · 0 0
29	Depreciation and loss or profit on sale of assets £ · 0 0	44	£ · 0 0
30	Other business expenses £ · 0 0	45	£ · 0 0
31	Total expenses (total of boxes 17 to 30) £ · 0 0	46	Total disallowable expenses (total of boxes 32 to 45) £ · 0 0

SA103F 2020   Page SEF 2

(Adapted from HMRC, 2020)

Net profit or loss

| 47 | **Net profit** – if your business income is more than your expenses (if box 15 + box 16 minus box 31 is positive) £ · 0 0 | 48 | **Or, net loss** – if your expenses are more than your business income (if box 31 minus (box 15 + box 16) is positive) £ · 0 0 |

Tax allowances for vehicles and equipment (capital allowances)

There are 'capital' tax allowances for vehicles, equipment and certain buildings used in your business (do not include the cost of these in your business expenses). Please read the 'Self-employment (full) notes' and use the examples to work out your capital allowances.

49	**Annual Investment Allowance** £ · 0 0
50	**Capital allowances at 18% on equipment, including cars with lower CO2 emissions** £ · 0 0
51	**Capital allowances at 6% on equipment, including cars with higher CO2 emissions** £ · 0 0
52	**Zero-emission goods vehicle allowance** £ · 0 0
53	**The Structures and Buildings Allowance** (you must hold a valid allowance statement – read the notes for details on how much you can claim per year) £ · 0 0
54	**Electric charge-point allowance** £ · 0 0

55	**100% and other enhanced capital allowances** £ · 0 0
56	**Allowances on sale or cessation of business use (where you've disposed of assets for less than their tax value)** £ · 0 0
57	**Total capital allowances (total of boxes 49 to 56)** £ · 0 0

Box 58 is not in use

| 59 | **Balancing charge on sales of assets or on the cessation of business use (including where Business Premises Renovation Allowance has been claimed) for example, where you've disposed of assets for more than their tax value** £ · 0 0 |

Calculating your taxable profit or loss

You may have to adjust your net profit or loss for disallowable expenses or capital allowances to arrive at your taxable profit or your loss for tax purposes. Please read the 'Self-employment (full) notes' and fill in the boxes below that apply.

60	**Goods and services for your own use** £ · 0 0
61	**Total additions to net profit or deductions from net loss (box 46 + box 59 + box 60)** £ · 0 0
62	**Income, receipts and other profits included in business income or expenses but not taxable as business profits** £ · 0 0

63	**Total deductions from net profit or additions to net loss (box 57 + box 62)** £ · 0 0
64	**Net business profit for tax purposes (if box 47 + box 61 minus (box 48 + box 63) is positive)** £ · 0 0
65	**Net business loss for tax purposes (if box 48 + box 63 minus (box 47 + box 61) is positive)** £ · 0 0

SA103F 2020   Page SEF 3

(Adapted from HMRC, 2020)

16 Danny — 6 mins

On 6 October 2020, Danny joined a partnership. The existing partners were Charlie and Elliot. Profits were shared equally between the partners both before and after Danny joined the partnership.

The partnership makes up accounts to 31 December each year. In the year to 31 December 2020, the partnership made a profit of £126,000 and in the year to 31 December 2021, it made a profit of £90,000.

Required

(a) Calculate Danny's taxable profit for the tax year 2020/21. (2 marks)

(b) State the entries that would made in the relevant boxes from Box 3 to Box 16 inclusive of the short supplementary partnership page (shown on the next page) for Danny for 2020/21. (3 marks)

(Total = 5 marks)

Partnership (short)
Tax year 6 April 2020 to 5 April 2021 (2020–21)

Your name

Your Unique Taxpayer Reference (UTR)

Complete a 'Partnership' page for each partnership of which you were a member and for each partnership business.
For help filling in this form, go to www.gov.uk/taxreturnforms and read the notes and helpsheets.

Partnership details

1. Partnership reference number

2. Description of partnership trade or profession

3. If you became a partner after 5 April 2020, enter the date you joined the partnership DD MM YYYY

4. If you left the partnership after 5 April 2020 and before 6 April 2021, enter the date you left

5. If the partnership used cash basis, money actually received and paid out, to calculate its income and expenses, put 'X' in the box – read the notes

Your share of the partnership's trading or professional profits

Please refer to the Partnership Statement to complete these pages and if you need any help, read the 'Partnership (short) notes'.
If you want to enter a loss, or an adjustment needs to be taken off, put a minus sign (–) in the box next to the £ sign.

6. Date your basis period began DD MM YYYY

7. Date your basis period ended DD MM YYYY

8. Your share of the partnership's profit or loss
– from box 11 or box 12 on the Partnership Statement
£

9. If your basis period is not the same as the partnership's accounting period, enter the adjustment needed to arrive at the profit or loss for your basis period
£

10. Adjustment for change of accounting practice
– from box 11A on the Partnership Statement
£

11. Averaging adjustment – only for farmers, market gardeners and creators of literary or artistic works
£

12. Foreign tax claimed as a deduction – only if Foreign Tax Credit Relief is not being claimed on the 'Foreign' pages
£

13. Overlap relief used this year
£

14. Overlap profit carried forward
£

15. If box 8 includes any disguised remuneration income, put 'X' in the box – from box 12A on the Partnership Statement

16. Adjusted profit for 2020–21 – see the working sheet in the notes
£

17. Losses brought forward from earlier years set off against this year's profit (up to the amount in box 16)
£

18. Taxable profits after losses brought forward (box 16 minus box 17)
£

19. Any other business income not included in the partnership accounts
£

20. Your share of total taxable profits from the partnership's business for 2020–21 (box 18 + box 19)
£

SA104S 2020 Page SP 1 HMRC 12/19

(Adapted from HMRC, 2020)

17 Multiple choice questions: Adjusted profit/loss computations for trades and professions

Allow 2 minutes for each question.

17.1 Norman is a sole trader and has accounting profits for the year ended 31 December 2020 of £160,000. Included within this figure is:

- £3,000 legal fees for acquiring a new 15-year lease of his business premises
- £180 car parking fines incurred by Norman whilst on business trips
- £40 interest for late payment of his previous year's income tax

How much must be added back to the accounting profit when calculating the tax-adjusted profit figure for the year ended 31 December 2020?

- ○ £3,180
- ○ £3,220
- ○ £220
- ○ £3,040 **(2 marks)**

17.2 Emily started trading on 1 January 2020. She decided to prepare accounts to 31 October each year.

What are the period(s) of overlap?

- ○ 1 January 2020 to 5 April 2020
- ○ 1 November 2020 to 5 April 2021
- ○ 1 January 2020 to 5 April 2020 and 1 November 2020 to 31 December 2020
- ○ 6 April 2020 to 31 December 2020 and 6 April 2021 to 31 October 2021 **(2 marks)**

17.3 George ceased trading on 31 March 2021. His taxable trading income was:

Y/e 31.12.20	£5,600
P/e 31.03.21	£4,500

George had £2,300 of unused overlap profits.

What is his taxable trading income for 2020/21?

- ○ £10,100
- ○ £7,800
- ○ £3,300
- ○ £2,200 **(2 marks)**

17.4 Mark is self-employed. He makes up his accounts to 31 March each year, and for the year ended 31 March 2021, his taxable trading income was £55,000.

What are the Class 4 NICs payable by Mark for 2020/21?

- ○ £3,745
- ○ £3,904
- ○ £4,095
- ○ £4,950 **(2 marks)**

17.5 Vassos has been trading for many years preparing accounts to 5 April.

The only asset in the business for capital allowances purposes was a car with CO_2 emissions of 100 g/km which Vassos uses 75% for business purposes. The tax written down value of the car at 6 April 2020 was £7,000. On 1 September 2020 Vassos sold the car for £6,000 which was less than its original cost.

What are the maximum capital allowances available to Vassos for the year ended 5 April 2021?

- ○ £1,000
- ○ £750
- ○ £1,260
- ○ £135 **(2 marks)**

17.6 Leo and Frew have been in partnership for many years. Kathy joined the partnership on 1 January 2021, with profits being shared equally between the three partners. The partnership had a trading profit of £60,000 for the year ended 31 December 2021.

What profits will Kathy be assessed on for 2020/21?

- ○ £5,000
- ○ £15,000
- ○ £20,000
- ○ £60,000 **(2 marks)**

17.7 **Which of the following items of expenditure will William be allowed to deduct in calculating his tax-adjusted trading profit before capital allowances?**

- ○ The cost of improving the central heating in his offices
- ○ The cost of installing air conditioning in his workshop
- ○ The cost of initial repairs to a recently acquired second-hand office building which was not usable until the repairs were carried out
- ○ The cost of redecorating his showroom **(2 marks)**

17.8 Richard has been a sole trader for many years making up his accounts to 31 July each year. He ceased to trade on 31 December 2020. Richard's most recent adjusted profits for tax purposes have been:

Year to 31 July 2019	£16,000
Year to 31 July 2020	£14,000
Five months to 31 December 2020	£7,000

He has unused overlap profits for earlier years amounting to £4,000.

What is Richard's taxable trading profit figure for the tax year 2020/21?

- ○ £17,000
- ○ £7,666
- ○ £21,000
- ○ £3,000 **(2 marks)**

17.9 Ella commenced trading on 1 January 2020 making up her first accounts for the 18-month period ended 30 June 2021.

What is Ella's basis period for 2020/21?

- ○ 1 July 2020 to 30 June 2021
- ○ 6 April 2020 to 5 April 2021
- ○ 1 January 2020 to 31 December 2020
- ○ 1 January 2020 to 5 April 2021 **(2 marks)**

17.10 Cherry commenced business as a sole trader on 1 January 2020 and prepared her first set of accounts for the period ended 28 February 2021. In the 14-month period ended 28 February 2021 her adjusted profit for tax purposes was £21,000. Her second set of accounts will be for the year ended 28 February 2022 when the tax-adjusted profits are expected to be £24,000.

What are Cherry's trading profits for the tax year 2020/21?

- ○ £21,000
- ○ £18,000
- ○ £18,500
- ○ £21,250 (2 marks)

17.11 Harry is a sole trader and has deducted the following items of expenditure in the statement of profit or loss for his most recent accounting period:

Depreciation	£2,000
Legal fees in acquiring a new ten-year lease	£1,000
Entertainment of: staff	£2,800
clients	£4,300

How much should be added back to Harry's net profit to arrive at his adjusted taxable profit?

- ○ £9,100
- ○ £10,100
- ○ £7,300
- ○ £6,300 (2 marks)

17.12 Louella is a sole trader and acquired a car for both business and private purposes on 1 June 2020. The car has a CO_2 emission rate of 125 grams per kilometre and cost £20,000. The private mileage for Louella's accounting period ended 31 March 2021 represented 25% of the total mileage for that year.

What is the maximum amount of capital allowances that Louella can claim in respect of the car for the tax year 2020/21?

- ○ £3,600
- ○ £2,700
- ○ £900
- ○ £1,200 (2 marks)

17.13 Diksha is a sole trader and had a tax adjusted profit of £37,000 for the tax year 2020/21. In addition, Diksha receives property income of £6,000 each tax year.

How much is Diksha's class 4 national insurance contribution (NIC) liability for the tax year 2020/21?

- ○ £2,475
- ○ £3,330
- ○ £3,015
- ○ £3,870 (2 marks)

17.14 James bought a factory from a developer on 1 June 2020 for £400,000 incurring legal fees of £10,000. He started to use the factory immediately for the purpose of his trade.

What is James' entitlement to structures and buildings allowances for the year ended 31 December 2020?

- ○ £12,000
- ○ £7,000
- ○ £7,175
- ○ £12,300 (2 marks)

Do you know? – Part C: Income tax liability

Check that you can fill in the blanks in the statements below before you attempt any questions. If in doubt, you should go back to your BPP Interactive Text and revise first.

- Income must be included in the correct column of the tax computation as either .... , ... or .... income.

- All individuals are entitled to a tax free amount known as the .... However, this is reduced (possibly to zero) if the individual has adjusted net income in excess of ....

- Basic rate taxpayers are entitled to a savings income nil rate band of £........................ and higher rate taxpayers are entitled to a savings income nil rate band of £........................

- All taxpayers are entitled to a dividend nil rate band of £........................

- The tax rate bands are applied first to .... income, then to .... income and then to .... income.

- The percentage used to calculate the benefit for use of a petrol or diesel company car is based on ....

- The additional benefit for use of company accommodation purchased for over £75,000 is usually based on ....

- Relief for contributions to an occupational pension is given by deducting the gross contribution from ...., whilst relief for personal pension contributions is given to higher rate taxpayers by ....

- Employees pay Class .... NI contributions and employers pay Class .... and on benefits they pay Class ....

  TRY QUESTIONS 18, 19, 20, 21, 22, 23, 24, 25, 26, 27, 28, 29, 30, 31 AND 32

- Property income is usually computed for an individual using the .... basis.

- The relief available for renting out a room in your house to a lodger is known as ....

- If property is let furnished, relief for expenditure on furniture is given by ....

- Three advantages of a property being treated as a furnished holiday let are:
  - ....
  - ....
  - ....

  TRY QUESTIONS 33, 34, 35, 36, 37 AND 38

- The maximum pension contribution a non-earner can make to their personal pension and receive tax relief is £........................

- The maximum tax relievable amount that an individual (and/ or their employer) can pay into their pension in any one year without incurring an income tax charge is known as the ....

  TRY QUESTIONS 39, 40, 41 AND 42

- An individual leaving employment receives a form ....

- Form .... gives details of an employee's taxable pay in a tax year, whilst the form that gives details of an employee's benefits in a tax year is the ....

- An individual must normally submit their tax return by .... after the end of the tax year if they do so online or by .... if they wish to file a paper return.

  TRY QUESTIONS 43, 44, 45 AND 46

Now consolidate your knowledge of Part C of the syllabus by attempting all the MULTIPLE CHOICE QUESTIONS in QUESTION 47.

Did you know? – Part C: Income tax liability

Could you fill in the blanks? The answers are in bold. Use this page for revision purposes as you approach the exam.

- Income must be included in the correct column of the tax computation as either **non-savings**, **savings** or **dividend** income.

- All individuals are entitled to a tax free amount known as the **personal allowance**. However, this is reduced (possibly to zero) if the individual has adjusted net income in excess of **£100,000**.

- Basic rate taxpayers are entitled to a savings income nil rate band of **£1,000** and higher rate taxpayers are entitled to a savings income nil rate band of **£500**.

- All taxpayers are entitled to a dividend nil rate band of **£2,000**.

- The tax rate bands are applied first to **non-savings** income, then to **savings** income and then to **dividend** income.

- The percentage used to calculate the benefit for use of a petrol or diesel company car is based on CO_2 **emissions**.

- The additional benefit for use of company accommodation purchased for over £75,000 is usually based on **cost**.

- Relief for contributions to an occupational pension is given by deducting the gross contribution from **earnings** whilst relief for personal pension contributions is given to higher rate taxpayers by **increasing the basic rate limit**.

- Employees pay Class **1 (employee)** NI contributions and employers pay Class **1 (employer)** and on benefits they pay Class **1A**.

  TRY QUESTIONS 18, 19, 20, 21, 22, 23, 24, 25, 26, 27, 28, 29, 30, 31 AND 32

- Property income is usually computed for an individual using the **cash** basis.

- The relief available for renting out a room in your house to a lodger is known as **rent a room relief**.

- If property is let furnished, relief for expenditure on furniture is given by **replacement furniture relief**.

- Three advantages of a property being treated as a furnished holiday let are:
  - **Profits are earnings for pension purposes**
  - **Business asset for business asset disposal relief**
  - **Capital costs of furniture are deductible when paid (cash basis) or capital allowances available (accruals basis)**

  TRY QUESTIONS 33, 34, 35, 36, 37 AND 38

- The maximum pension contribution a non-earner can make to their personal pension and receive tax relief is **£3,600**.

- The maximum tax relievable amount that an individual (and/ or their employer) can pay into their pension in any one year without incurring an income tax charge is known as the **annual allowance**.

  TRY QUESTIONS 39, 40, 41 AND 42

- An individual leaving employment receives a form **P45**.

- Form **P60** gives details of an employee's taxable pay in a tax year, whilst the form that gives details of an employee's benefits in a tax year is the **P11D**.

- An individual must normally submit their tax return by **31 January** after the end of the tax year if they do so online or by **31 October** if they wish to file a paper return.

  TRY QUESTIONS 43, 44, 45 AND 46

Now consolidate your knowledge of Part C of the syllabus by attempting all the MULTIPLE CHOICE QUESTIONS in QUESTION 47.

18 Question with help: Income tax liability

In 2020/21, Julie has the following income.

	£
Salary (amount before tax)	53,320
Building society interest	4,915
Lotto winnings	250
Dividends	1,500

During the tax year, Julie pays eligible interest of £800 on a loan to buy machinery for use in her employment.

Required

What is Julie's tax liability for 2020/21? If £7,500 of tax has been deducted from her salary under PAYE, how much more tax must she pay? Your answer should identify by the use of zero (0) any item which is not taxable.

Approaching the answer

Step 1	Set up a pro forma computation with columns for non-savings income, savings income and dividend income and a total column.
Step 2	Fill in the figures provided in the question to calculate total income, remembering to exclude any exempt income.
Step 3	Deduct eligible interest to compute net income.
Step 4	Deduct the personal allowance to calculate taxable income.
Step 5	Apply the bands and tax rates to the taxable income to calculate income tax liability. Don't forget that a higher rate taxpayer is entitled to a savings income nil rate band of £500 and all taxpayers are entitled to a dividend nil rate band of £2,000.
Step 6	Deduct PAYE and tax deducted at source to calculate tax payable.

19 Fred — 6 mins

Fred is an employee of a company and received the following benefits during the tax year 2020/21:

- Use of a house. The house was purchased by the company in 2016 for £305,000 and first occupied by Fred in 2018 when the market value was £315,000. The annual rateable value for 2020/21 was £3,150.

- Loan of furniture. It had a market value of £8,000 when first provided in 2018. The company removed the furniture on 30 June 2020 and Fred used his own furniture from that date.

Required

Calculate, for the purposes of income tax, the total value of the benefits provided to Fred in the tax year 2020/21. **(5 marks)**

20 Linda — 18 mins

Linda works for a company receiving an annual salary of £50,000.

Linda received a bonus of £8,000 in February 2021 relating to the company's year to 31 December 2020. She also received a bonus of £2,000 in May 2021 relating to a special project undertaken in March 2021.

For the tax year 2020/21 Linda's employer deducted £10,600 income tax (under PAYE) from Linda's income.

Linda also received the following income during the tax year 2020/21.

Dividends from UK companies	£3,000
Bank interest	£2,000
National savings certificate interest	£600
National savings investment account interest	£400

All the above sums were the amounts received.

Linda paid professional subscriptions of £200 to an HM Revenue and Customs (HMRC) approved professional body relevant to her employment.

Linda is a member of the company's occupational pension scheme. In the tax year 2020/21 the company paid £2,400 into the scheme on Linda's behalf. Linda, herself, contributed £1,800.

Linda also owns a buy-to-let property and has rental income (net of expenses) of £3,000 in the tax year 2020/21.

Required

Calculate the income tax payable by Linda for the tax year 2020/21. Your answer should identify by the use of zero (0) any item which is not taxable at all or not taxable in 2020/21. **(15 marks)**

21 Mary — 6 mins

Mary works for AB (UK) Ltd. During the tax year 2020/21 she had use of a diesel car which did not meet the RDE2 standard. The car had a CO_2 emission rate of 121 grams per kilometre and a recommended list price of £15,000. It was first provided to Mary on 6 September 2020 for both her private and business use.

The company pays for all the running costs of the car, which amounted to £1,800 for the period to 5 April 2021.

Mary was required to contribute £10 per month towards the cost of private fuel.

Required

Calculate the total value of benefits provided to Mary for the purposes of income tax, for the tax year 2020/21.

(5 marks)

22 Valero — 12 mins

Valero works for PQT plc. During the tax year 2020/21, Valero was given the following benefits:

- A loan to help him purchase a yacht. PQT plc advanced him £40,000 on 6 April 2020 and charged him interest at the rate of 0.5% per annum. Valero repaid £8,000 of the loan on 6 July 2020, but the remaining £32,000 remains outstanding.

- Use of a home cinema system. This was first provided to Valero to use at home on 6 April 2017, the date it was purchased by PQT plc at a cost of £4,000. The system was gifted to Valero outright on 5 April 2021, when it was worth £900.

- Occupational pension contributions amounting to £4,000 during 2020/21. These were paid by PQT plc, on Valero's behalf.

Required

(a) Calculate the total value of benefits provided to Valero for the purposes of income tax, for the tax year 2020/21. Your answer should identify by the use of zero (0) any item which is not taxable.
(9 marks)

(b) State which HM Revenue and Customs (HMRC) form PQT plc is required to complete to report these benefits and the date by which it should be submitted. (1 mark)

(Total = 10 marks)

23 Patrick — 18 mins

Patrick has worked for CDE Ltd since 2017 and he has provided you with the following information regarding his income and outgoings for the tax year 2020/21.

Income

- A gross salary of £158,850
- Profit from a sole trader business of £20,000
- Dividends received from UK companies of £4,000
- Interest credited to his bank account of £3,000
- Interest received from national savings certificates of £400
- Premium bond prizes received of £1,500

Expenditure

- Pension contributions paid to CDE Ltd's HMRC registered occupational pension scheme of £400 per month
- A donation of £800 (net) paid to a UK registered charity in August 2020 under the gift aid scheme

Tax, amounting to £53,400, for 2020/21 was deducted from Patrick's employment income under PAYE.

Required

Calculate the income tax payable by Patrick for the tax year 2020/21. Your answer should identify by the use of zero (0) any item which is not taxable. (15 marks)

24 Peppy — 6 mins

Peppy works for Pepster Ltd. During the tax year 2020/21 Peppy was provided with a car, which has a recommended list price of £28,000. The car has a CO_2 emission rate of 128 grams per kilometre and is petrol driven.

The car was first made available to Peppy on 1 July 2020 and is used for both business and private purposes. Peppy paid £6,000 towards the initial cost of the car and £40 per month for the private use of the car.

Pepster Ltd does not provide fuel for Peppy's private use.

Required

Calculate, for the purposes of income tax, the total value of the benefits provided to Peppy in the tax year 2020/21. (5 marks)

Helping hand. Look very carefully at the dates for which the benefit is provided – if the benefit is not provided for the whole of the tax year, how do you deal with this?

FTX FOUNDATIONS IN TAXATION

25 Beryl   6 mins

Beryl works in the London office of VXZ Ltd. On 1 August 2020 she was transferred permanently to VXZ Ltd's Newcastle office, which is nearly 300 miles away. As a result Beryl moved house to the Newcastle area. During the tax year 2020/21 Beryl received the following benefits from VXZ Ltd.

- Medical treatment. Beryl was absent from work for the whole of November 2020 due to a back injury. VXZ Ltd paid £450 for a course of physiotherapy, recommended in writing by the company's doctor, to enable Beryl to resume work.

- Staff suggestion scheme award. Beryl was awarded £4,500 (which reflected the financial importance of the suggestion) under VXZ Ltd's staff suggestion scheme for suggesting a new method of recruiting staff.

- Mileage allowance. Beryl used her own car for both business and private purposes. She drove a total of 15,000 miles during the tax year 2020/21 of which 10,000 miles were for visits to business clients, 2,000 miles were for journeys to and from work and the remaining 3,000 miles were for private journeys. Beryl's company paid her 55p a mile for every business mile.

- To help with Beryl's move to Newcastle, VXZ Ltd paid Beryl £10,000 in July 2020 towards her relocation costs.

- A place in VXZ Ltd's workplace nursery in Newcastle for Beryl's 4 year old daughter at a cost of £5,000.

- A flower display, which cost VXZ Ltd £40, to welcome Beryl to her new house.

- An interest-free loan of £15,000 to enable Beryl to undertake building works on her new house. The loan was made on 1 August 2020 and the whole amount was outstanding at 5 April 2021.

Required

Calculate, for the purposes of income tax, the total value of the benefits provided to Beryl in the tax year 2020/21. Your answer should indicate by the use of zero (0) any exempt benefits.

(5 marks)

26 Coral   18 mins

Coral works for Zoom Ltd and has provided you with the following information regarding her income and outgoings for the tax year 2020/21.

Income

- A gross salary of £99,000
- A bonus of £7,000 received in May 2020
- Benefits with a taxable value for income tax purposes of £2,500
- Dividends of £3,000 received from UK companies in August 2020
- Bank interest of £1,100 credited to her UK bank account in December 2020
- Building society interest of £360 credited to her Individual Savings Account (ISA) in March 2021
- A Lotto prize of £2,400
- Rental income of £4,800. This is the total taxable amount received in the tax year 2020/21 from a house owned jointly with her husband.

Expenditure

- A total amount of £120 paid to a UK charity under a payroll deduction scheme, administered by Zoom Ltd
- Personal pension contributions amounting to £4,000 (net) paid to a HM Revenue and Customs (HMRC) registered pension provider
- Professional subscriptions of £180 to a HMRC approved professional body relevant to Coral's employment

Tax, amounting to £28,640, was deducted from Coral's employment income under PAYE for the tax year 2020/21.

Required

Calculate the income tax payable by Coral for the tax year 2020/21. Your answer should identify by the use of zero (0) any item which is not taxable. **(15 marks)**

27 Stephen — 18 mins

Stephen has worked for Wood plc for the last three years receiving an annual salary of £50,730. For the tax year 2020/21 Wood plc deducted £7,900 income tax (under PAYE) from Stephen's income.

In addition to his salary Stephen received the following benefits from Wood plc for the whole of the tax year 2020/21.

- Use of a diesel engine company car which does not meet the RDE2 standard, with a CO_2 emission rate of 106 grams per kilometre and a recommended list price of £22,000. Stephen used the car 40% for private purposes and 60% for business purposes. Stephen pays for his own fuel when using the car for private purposes but pays the company £250 per month for the use of the car.
- Medical insurance which cost the company £750 in the tax year 2020/21 but would have cost Stephen £950 if he had arranged the cover himself.
- Use of a computer, which had cost the company £1,600 in August 2018. Stephen does not use the computer for business purposes.
- A cake costing £35 on the occasion of his birthday.

During 2020/21 Stephen received the following amounts of interest:

	£
Building society interest	1,375
Interest from National Savings and Investments Certificate	100

In the tax year 2020/21 Stephen received UK dividends amounting to £1,200.

Required

Calculate the income tax payable by Stephen for the tax year 2020/21. Your answer should identify by the use of zero (0) any item which is not taxable. **(15 marks)**

Helping hand. Can you spot the items which are not taxable?

28 Alison — 12 mins

Alison started in business as a sole trader on 1 July 2020 and had the following results:

	£
6 month period ended 31 December 2020	7,500
Year ended 31 December 2021	18,000

Alison also had a part-time job and received a salary of £14,500 in 2020/21 (PAYE deducted £400).

During 2020/21 Alison received £1,375 of building society interest and UK dividends of £3,400. She also won a premium bond prize of £50.

Required

Calculate the income tax payable by Alison for the tax year 2020/21. Your answer should identify by the use of zero (0) any item which is not taxable. **(10 marks)**

29 Liam and Jordan   6 mins

Liam is employed by Hallow Ltd and earns a salary of £4,300 per month in 2020/21.

Jordan is self-employed. Her tax adjusted profits for the year ended 31 December 2020 are £56,000.

Required

Calculate the national insurance contributions (NIC) payable by Liam (using a monthly basis) and Jordan respectively for the tax year 2020/21. (5 marks)

30 Declan   6 mins

Declan, an employee, received the following benefits during the tax year 2020/21.

- The use of a hybrid company car with a list price of £80,000. The employer only paid £72,000 as the car was sold on a special promotion. The car had been used throughout the tax year 2020/21 for both business and private purposes. The car has CO_2 emissions of 42 grams per kilometre and electric range of 50 miles. The company also provided fuel for private use. Declan contributed £10,000 towards the cost of the car and £100 monthly for private use. He did not make any contribution towards fuel costs.
- A computer, with a value of £800 when first provided in January 2019, was made available to Declan for his private use throughout the tax year 2020/21. The computer was not used for business purposes.

Required

Calculate, for the purposes of income tax, the value of each of the benefits provided to Declan for the tax year 2020/21. (5 marks)

31 Nancy   6 mins

Nancy is employed by Anton Ltd. She received the following benefits during the tax year 2020/21.

- A loan of £20,000 had been advanced in January 2020 to help Nancy purchase a holiday cottage. Nancy repaid £6,000 of this loan on 31 December 2020 but the balance of £14,000 is still outstanding. The company charged Nancy 1% interest throughout the tax year 2020/21.
- Her employer paid Nancy incidental expenses amounting to £12 per night for 60 days overseas business travel, and £4 per night for 40 days UK business travel, during the tax year 2020/21.

Required

Calculate, for the purposes of income tax, the value of each of the benefits provided to Nancy for the tax year 2020/21. Your answer should identify by the use of zero (0) any item which is not taxable. (5 marks)

32 Stuart   18 mins

Stuart has been in partnership with Fahrid for many years. During the accounting years ending 31 May 2020 and 31 May 2021 the partnership had tax adjusted trading profits of £115,250 and £121,000 respectively. The profits are always split 60% to Stuart and 40% to Fahrid. Stuart borrowed £10,000 from a local bank in January 2020 to help purchase plant and machinery for use in the partnership. Interest is charged at a rate of 8% per year. The full amount of the loan is still outstanding.

Stuart paid £1,600 net to a personal pension plan during the tax year 2020/21.

Stuart received the following investment income during the tax year 2020/21.

Interest from a National Savings and Investments certificate	£1,800
Interest from a National Savings and Investments investment account	£1,665
Premium bond prizes	£250
Dividends	£5,000

The above amounts are the actual amounts received or credited to the account.

Stuart made payments on account amounting to £12,000 relating to his income tax liability for 2020/21.

Required

Calculate the payment that Stuart should make by 31 January 2022 in respect of his income tax liability for 2020/21. Your answer should identify by the use of zero (0) any item which is not taxable.

Note. You should ignore capital allowances. (15 marks)

33 Doreen — 6 mins

Doreen has rented out a fully furnished house for many years. The house does not qualify as furnished holiday accommodation. She had the following income received and expenditure paid.

Rental income	£1,200 per month from 6 April 2020 to 5 March 2021 when Doreen sold house
Security deposit	£2,400 paid by last tenant on 6 April 2019, £300 used by Doreen for cleaning due to the poor state the property was left in, remainder returned to tenant
Replacement furniture	Sofa costing £1,500 (larger than the original). Replacing original type would have cost £1,280. Original sofa scrapped with nil value

Required

Calculate Doreen's property income for the tax year 2020/21. (5 marks)

34 Sonia — 6 mins

In the tax year 2020/21 Sonia rented out a fully furnished property for a monthly rental of £1,000. The full amount was received during the tax year, with the exception of £1,000 due for March 2021, which was received in June 2021.

Sonia paid the following expenses in the tax year 2020/21 in connection with the property.

	£
Insurance for 1 January 2020 to 31 December 2020	300
Insurance for 1 January 2021 to 31 December 2021	360
Agent's fees	600
Replacement table	750

The replacement table was similar to the original table. The original table was sold to a furniture dealer for £50.

Required

Calculate Sonia's property income for the tax year 2020/21 if she elects for the accruals basis to apply.

(5 marks)

35 David — 12 mins

You have received the following letter from a client.

> 3 October 2020
>
> Dear Hilary
>
> A friend of mine says she takes in lodgers, who stay for about a year, but she doesn't have to pay any tax on the rent she collects. I'd like to do the same. Can you tell me how this tax dodge works?
>
> Yours sincerely
>
> David

Required

Draft paragraphs to be included in a reply to this letter. (10 marks)

Helping hand. Before you start, plan your answer. Think about who you are writing to. Your reply must be phrased in appropriate non-technical terms so that the recipient will easily understand it.

36 Jules — 6 mins

Jules purchased a holiday home in 2020, which qualifies for the special tax advantages for furnished holiday accommodation.

Required

Explain THREE tax advantages of a property qualifying as furnished holiday accommodation.

Note. You are not required to explain the qualifying conditions. **(5 marks)**

37 Jenny — 18 mins

Jenny, an employee of Newco Ltd, who returned to the UK at the end of April 2020, having spent the previous six months on holiday overseas, has asked you to calculate her income tax payable for the tax year 2020/21. She has provided the following information.

(a) She started work with Newco Ltd on 1 May 2020 with an annual salary of £32,700. She received a salary increase of 4% from 1 January 2021.

(b) A bonus of £12,090 in respect of the company's half-year to 30 September 2020 was received in December 2020 and a bonus of £5,500 in respect of the company's year to 31 March 2021 was received in May 2021.

(c) Jenny was provided with a hybrid car by Newco Ltd on 1 May 2020. The car was available for private use throughout the rest of the tax year 2020/21. The list price of the car was £12,450 and it had CO_2 emissions of 40g/km and an electric range of 25 miles.

(d) UK dividends of £10,000 were received in January 2021.

(e) Bank interest of £1,100 was received in December 2020.

(f) Premium bond prizes of £250 and £50 were received in May 2020 and November 2020 respectively.

(g) An amount of £160 was paid to a registered UK charity under the gift aid scheme in November 2020.

(h) Newco Ltd deducted income tax under PAYE totalling £5,565 from Jenny's earnings.

(i) Property income of £1,658 from letting out her flat in April 2020.

Required

Calculate the income tax payable by Jenny for the tax year 2020/21. Your answer should identify by the use of zero (0) any item which is not taxable. **(15 marks)**

38 Laslo — 6 mins

Laslo rented out a fully furnished property at a monthly rent of £400 from 6 July 2020. The full amount of rent due has been received during 2020/21 except that the rent due on 6 March 2021 was not received until 6 April 2021. Expenses consisted of:

	£
Insurance paid 6 July 2020 (for the period 6 July 2020 to 5 June 2021)	360
Cost of new furniture bought 1 July 2020	2,500
Cost of building new garden wall 1 December 2020	1,800

The tenant damaged an armchair which was part of the new furniture bought on 1 July 2020. Laslo replaced the chair with an identical model at a cost of £342 on 1 February 2021.

The property was not available for letting prior to 6 July 2020.

Required

Calculate the property income for Laslo for the tax year 2020/21. **(5 marks)**

39 Simon — 18 mins

Simon is a manager working for Able plc.

In 2020/21 Simon received a gross salary of £70,000 and on 16 February 2021 he received a bonus of £26,760 based on Able plc's results for the year ended 31 December 2020. Simon contributes 5% of his gross salary (excluding bonuses) into Able plc's HMRC registered occupational pension scheme every year.

Able plc deducted income tax (under PAYE) of £25,300 from Simon's salary in 2020/21.

Simon also let out a room in his house during the whole of 2020/21. The rent payable was £750 a month. Simon incurred additional expenses in relation to the letting of £1,200. Simon has elected to use rent a room relief.

Simon's other income for 2020/21 was:

Bank interest	£4,500
Dividends from UK companies	£1,000
Dividends from shares held in an Individual Savings Account (ISA)	£270

Simon paid £320 (net) to a UK registered charity under the Gift Aid scheme and a £390 annual fee to an HMRC approved relevant professional body, required for his position in the company, in 2020/21.

Required

Calculate the income tax payable by Simon for the tax year 2020/21. Your answer should identify by the use of zero (0) any item which is not taxable. **(15 marks)**

40 Amber — 6 mins

Amber is employed by Younger plc. Amber received the following benefits in 2020/21:

- Use of a company-owned house. The house was used permanently by Amber and her family from 6 October 2020. The house had been purchased by the company for £120,000 in May 2010 and had a market value when Amber moved in of £215,000. The annual rateable value of the house was £8,000 and Amber paid £600 a month to the company for the use of the property. Amber paid for all of the household expenses. The house is not classed as job-related.
- Workplace parking. Amber was provided with a free car parking space in a public car park adjacent to her place of work. This cost the company £540 for the year ending 5 April 2021.
- General business expenses. Amber received an amount of £6 a day for 80 days of business trips in the UK and £9 a day for 60 days of business trips abroad. All of these trips required overnight stays away from home and the amounts paid were used to cover the costs of incidental expenses such as newspapers and telephone calls home.

Required

Calculate the taxable benefits for the tax year 2020/21. Your answer should identify by the use of zero (0) any item which is not taxable. **(5 marks)**

41 Hamish — 18 mins

Hamish is an employee. Hamish received a salary of £180,000 in the tax year 2020/21. In addition to his salary, the only other income Hamish received in the tax year 2020/21 was:

Dividends from a UK company	£3,000
Interest from the Abfax building society	£2,000
Premium bond prize	£100

The following information is also relevant to the tax year 2020/21.

Gift aid donation paid	£1,200
Occupational pension scheme contributions paid by Hamish	£14,000
Occupational pension scheme contributions paid by Hamish's employer	£8,000
Income tax deducted (under PAYE) from Hamish's salary	£59,000

Required

Calculate the income tax payable by Hamish for the tax year 2020/21. Your answer should identify by the use of zero (0) any item which is not taxable. **(15 marks)**

42 Paul — 12 mins

Paul wants to start making contributions to a pension plan. His employers have advised him that they have a HMRC registered occupational pension scheme that he can join. However, a friend has told him that both he and his employer can contribute to a personal pension plan instead. He has asked you, as his tax advisor, for information on the two forms of pension scheme. You have arranged a meeting with Paul to discuss the information he requires.

Required

Write brief notes, to be used at a meeting with Paul, explaining the following points.

- The maximum contributions allowed per year
- The method(s) of him obtaining relief
- The tax effects, if any, of the company making contributions to the plans on his behalf

Note. Your answer should only cover the above points. You are not required to mention the rules on receiving benefits on retirement. **(10 marks)**

QUESTIONS

43 Lin — 6 mins

Lin, a sole trader, paid the following amounts of tax for the tax year 2019/20.

Income tax	£16,000
Class 4 national insurance contributions	£3,000

For the tax year 2020/21 Lin's final income tax and class 4 national insurance contribution liabilities are expected to be as follows.

Income tax	£19,300
Class 4 national insurance contributions	£3,500

Required

In respect of Lin's 2020/21 income tax and class 4 national insurance contribution liabilities, state the due dates of payment, together with the amounts payable on each date.

Note. You should ignore any payments on account for the tax year 2021/22. **(5 marks)**

44 Richard — 6 mins

Richard works for Zoom plc but will leave his job at the end of May 2021.

Richard has already found another job with Tape Ltd, which he will start on 1 June 2021.

Required

(a) **State what form Zoom plc must issue to Richard, how many parts of the form there are and what Richard will do with the parts.** **(2 marks)**

(b) **Briefly explain how the form will be used to ensure that PAYE is operated correctly by T Ltd on Richard's earnings.** **(3 marks)**

(Total = 5 marks)

45 Alisha — 6 mins

Alisha works for JKL plc and is about to complete her 2020/21 self-assessment tax return.

Required

(a) **State which form gives details of Alisha's total taxable earnings and tax deducted for the tax year 2020/21, and by which date she must receive a copy of this form from JKL plc.** **(2 marks)**

(b) **State which form gives details of the cash equivalents of Alisha's benefits received for the tax year 2020/21, and by which date she must receive a copy of this form from JKL plc.** **(2 marks)**

(c) **State the latest date by which Alisha must submit an electronic tax return for the tax year 2020/21 to HM Revenue and Customs (HMRC).** **(1 mark)**

(Total = 5 marks)

46 Barry — 6 mins

Barry is a new client whom you met today. On 6 April 2019, he started in business as a sole trader and prepared his first set of accounts to 5 April 2020. Barry had not previously filed a self-assessment tax return and has not been contacted by HM Revenue and Customs (HMRC) about his tax affairs.

Barry is also concerned that HMRC might carry out a compliance check since he will be filing his first tax return.

Required

(a) State the date by which Barry should have notified HMRC of his chargeability to income tax for the tax year 2019/20 and the maximum penalty which could be imposed for late notification.

(2 marks)

(b) State the date by which HMRC can start a compliance check into Barry's return, once it has been submitted, and briefly explain the basis on which returns are selected for checking. **(3 marks)**

(Total = 5 marks)

47 Multiple choice questions: Income tax liability

Allow 2 minutes for each question.

47.1 Which of the following types of income is chargeable to income tax?

- ○ Dividends from a UK company
- ○ Income received from an Individual Savings Account
- ○ £10 of Lottery winnings
- ○ Interest on National Savings Certificates

(2 marks)

47.2 In 2020/21, Roberto had employment income of £106,000. This was his only income in 2020/21.

What is the restriction in the personal allowance available to Roberto in 2020/21?

- ○ £0
- ○ £3,000
- ○ £6,000
- ○ £9,500

(2 marks)

47.3 Angela works for Kat Ltd as a part-time salesperson at a salary of £6,000 a year. On 30 June 2020, she received a bonus of £3,000 in respect of Kat Ltd's trading results for the year ended 31 December 2019. She expects to receive a bonus of £3,500 in June 2021 in respect of Kat Ltd's results for the year ended 31 December 2020.

What is Angela's employment income for 2020/21?

- ○ £6,000
- ○ £9,375
- ○ £9,000
- ○ £9,500

(2 marks)

47.4 Marcus is employed by Able plc. He is provided with a car available for private use for 2020/21. The car has CO_2 emissions of 118g/km. The car has a diesel engine which does not meet the RDE2 standard. No private fuel is provided.

What is the percentage to be used to calculate the car benefit?

- ○ 23%
- ○ 26%
- ○ 30%
- ○ 31%

(2 marks)

47.5 Harry is a salesman who works in the Cardiff office one day a week and spends the rest of his time visiting customers.

Robin is a mechanic who works two days a week at the Cardiff depot and three days a week at the Bristol depot.

Chris works for a bank in Southampton but has been sent to work in Cardiff for 18 months.

The cost of travelling from home to Cardiff is allowable for:

- ○ Harry
- ○ Robin
- ○ Chris
- ○ None of them (2 marks)

47.6 Lucy is employed by Holt plc. She uses her own car for business purposes and is reimbursed 35p per mile by her employer. In 2020/21, Lucy travelled 8,000 miles on business.

What is the employment income consequence of the reimbursement for business mileage?

- ○ £2,800 taxable benefit
- ○ £(800) allowable deduction
- ○ £800 taxable benefit
- ○ £(3,600) allowable deduction (2 marks)

47.7 Anna was paid an annual salary of £12,000 paid monthly during 2020/21. In addition, she received a bonus of £1,000 in December 2020, and her employer provided her with a TV for which the taxable benefit is £400.

On what amounts are National Insurance contributions payable?

- ○ Class 1 employee's and employer's contributions on £13,000 only
- ○ Class 1 employee's contributions on £13,000, Class 1 employer's contributions on £13,400
- ○ Class 1 employee's contributions on £13,400, Class 1 employer's contributions on £13,000, Class 1A contributions on £400
- ○ Class 1 employee's contributions on £13,000, Class 1 employer's contributions on £13,000, Class 1A contributions on £400 (2 marks)

47.8 Penny is a part-time shop assistant. For the tax year 2020/21 her employer included Penny in the company medical insurance scheme which had cost the employer £800 per employee. Penny receives no other benefits from her employer.

Which form, if any, does Penny's employer use to report this benefit to HM Revenue and Customs (HMRC) and by when must this form reach HMRC?

- ○ P11D – 6 July 2021
- ○ P45 – 5 April 2021
- ○ P60 – 31 May 2021
- ○ Tax-free benefit – no form required (2 marks)

47.9 John was provided by his employer with a computer for private use on 1 November 2020. The market value of the computer when first provided to an employee for private use was £3,600 and had a market value of £2,000 when provided to John for private use.

What is the value of the benefit that must be shown on the benefits form completed by his employer for 2020/21?

- ○ £400
- ○ £720
- ○ £300
- ○ £167 (2 marks)

47.10 Jim is an employee of July Ltd. Jim receives cash earnings of £27,000 and a car benefit amounting to £3,000 in the tax year 2020/21.

How much class 1 employee's national insurance (NI) does Jim suffer in respect of the tax year 2020/21?

- A £2,100
- B £2,513
- C £3,240
- D £2,460

(2 marks)

47.11 Ian's employer provides him with a diesel powered motor car which meets the RDE2 standard, together with fuel for private use. The motor car has an official CO_2 emission rate of 149g/km.

For 2020/21 what is the percentage that will be used when calculating Ian's car and fuel benefits?

- ○ 32%
- ○ 33%
- ○ 36%
- ○ 37%

(2 marks)

47.12 Lee was provided by his employer with the use of free accommodation for the whole of the tax year 2020/21. It was not deemed to be job related.

The accommodation cost Lee's employer £131,000 in February 2017 and has an annual value of £6,000.

What is Lee's additional benefit in respect of the accommodation for the tax year 2020/21?

- ○ £1,395
- ○ £7,260
- ○ £2,948
- ○ £1,260

(2 marks)

47.13 Bill earns £40,000 a year working for Pear plc. During the tax year 2020/21 Bill received £12 per night incidental expenses allowance from Pear plc in respect of 14 nights working overseas.

How much of this expense allowance is taxable?

- ○ £0
- ○ £168
- ○ £98
- ○ £28

(2 marks)

47.14 Peter has taxable income (after deducting his personal allowance) for the tax year 2020/21 as follows.

Non-savings income	£4,800
Savings income	£3,500

What is Peter's tax liability (before the deduction of any tax deducted at source) for the tax year 2020/21?

- ○ £960
- ○ £1,420
- ○ £1,460
- ○ £1,620

(2 marks)

47.15 Sally has been the only employee of a sole trader for many years and earns a salary of £60,000 per year.

What are the employer's class 1 national insurance contributions (NIC) for the tax year 2020/21?

- ○ £1,887
- ○ £7,067
- ○ £5,887
- ○ £3,067

(2 marks)

47.16 **Which of the following is not business travel for the purpose of an income tax expense claim?**

- ○ Travel to visit a client
- ○ Travel from home to a temporary place of work
- ○ Travel to and from a permanent place of work
- ○ Travel to visit a trade fair relevant to the employer's business (2 marks)

47.17 Jimmy is an employee earning £36,000 a year, payable in equal monthly amounts. The NIC employee limits for each month are £792 and £4,167. In December 2020 he received a bonus of £8,000.

What were Jimmy's class 1 employee's national insurance contributions (NIC) for December 2020?

- ○ £1,225
- ○ £542
- ○ £405
- ○ £1,409 (2 marks)

47.18 Queenie received the following property income during 2020/21.

(i) Annual rental of £6,300 (payable in advance) from a furnished flat first let on 6 August 2020. Allowable general expenses of £700 were paid in the let period.

(ii) £5,500 from letting a furnished room in her own home.

What amount of taxable property income does Queenie have for 2020/21?

- ○ £3,600
- ○ £4,300
- ○ £5,600
- ○ £11,100 (2 marks)

47.19 Brian granted a ten-year lease on a property to a tenant for a premium of £20,000.

On what amount of the premium will Brian be assessed to income tax?

- ○ Nil
- ○ £3,600
- ○ £16,400
- ○ £20,000 (2 marks)

47.20 David earned £3,500 from part time work during 2020/21.

What is the maximum pension contribution that David could have made during 2020/21 on which there would have been tax relief?

- ○ £0
- ○ £3,500
- ○ £3,600
- ○ Unlimited contribution (2 marks)

47.21 Chloe is an employee receiving an annual salary and benefits. She also receives bank interest during the year ended 5 April 2021. She has no other income or gains.

What date must Chloe retain her records until, for 2020/21?

- ○ 31 January 2023
- ○ 5 April 2023
- ○ 31 January 2027
- ○ 5 April 2027 (2 marks)

47.22 Smith is a sole trader. He has been in business for many years.

On which dates were/are Smith's payment on accounts and balancing payment due for 2020/21?

- ○ Payments on account 31 January 2021 and 31 July 2021, balancing payment 31 January 2022
- ○ Payments on account 31 July 2020 and 31 January 2021, balancing payment 31 July 2021
- ○ Payments on account 31 January 2022 and 31 July 2022, balancing payment 31 January 2023
- ○ Payments on account 31 July 2021 and 31 January 2022, balancing payment 31 July 2022

(2 marks)

47.23 Paul rents out a flat which is fully furnished. The house does not qualify as a furnished holiday letting. Paul paid the following expenses in relation to the letting:

	£
New chairs for garden (not previously provided) bought July 2020	600
Replacement cooker (upgrade, similar cooker to original would have cost £750, no scrap value for old cooker) bought September 2020	900

What is the amount of allowable expenses that Paul can claim to compute his property income for 2020/21?

- ○ £1,500
- ○ £1,350
- ○ £750
- ○ £600

(2 marks)

47.24 John's income tax liabilities and Class 4 NICs for 2019/20 and 2020/21 are as follows,

	2019/20 £	2020/21 £
Income tax	10,000	12,500
Class 4 NIC	2,000	2,500
	12,000	15,000

When will John pay his tax liability for 2020/21?

- ○ The full amount of £15,000 will be paid on 31 January 2022
- ○ Payments on account of £7,500 will be made on 31 January and 31 July 2021, with nothing payable on 31 January 2022
- ○ Payments on account of £6,000 will be made on 31 January and 31 July 2021, with the balance of £3,000 being paid on 31 January 2022
- ○ Payments on account of £5,000 will be made on 31 January and 31 July 2021, with the balance of £5,000 being paid on 31 January 2022

(2 marks)

47.25 Lewis granted a 11-year lease on a property to a tenant for a premium of £30,000.

On what amount of the premium will Lewis be assessed to income tax?

- ○ £23,400
- ○ £6,000
- ○ £30,000
- ○ £24,000

(2 marks)

47.26 **How long must a sole trader keep and retain all records required to make and deliver correct tax returns?**

- ○ One year after the 31 January following the tax year
- ○ Two years after the end of tax year
- ○ Five years after the 31 January following the tax year
- ○ Six years after the end of the tax year

(2 marks)

47.27 Ryan has a trading loss of £80,000 for the tax year 2020/21. Due to carelessness he enters £88,000 on his tax return and makes a loss relief claim for £88,000 against his property income for the tax year 2020/21.

The property income would otherwise have been taxed at 40%.

What is the maximum penalty that could be charged by HM Revenue and Customs (HMRC) in respect of the error?

- ○ £3,200
- ○ £960
- ○ £2,240
- ○ £2,400 (2 marks)

47.28 Howard works for Quill plc and has use of a company van for both business and private purposes from 6 August 2020 to 5 April 2021. The van has CO_2 emissions of 105g/km and has a list price of £13,000. Petrol is provided by Quill plc for all purposes and Howard is not required to make any payment towards private use fuel.

What are the total benefits taxable on Howard in respect of private use of the van and van fuel for the tax year 2020/21?

- ○ £4,156
- ○ £2,327
- ○ £2,771
- ○ £6,000 (2 marks)

47.29 Ciara was given a hybrid car by her employer for business and private use on 5 December 2020. The list price of the car was £34,000 but the employer only paid £32,000 after a fleet discount. The CO_2 emissions of the car are 45 grams per kilometre and the electric range is 45 miles. Ciara pays all fuel costs.

What are the total benefits taxable on Ciara in respect of private use of the car for the tax year 2020/21?

- ○ £2,040
- ○ £640
- ○ £1,170
- ○ £680 (2 marks)

47.30 Manfred is an employee earning £28,000 per annum. Throughout the tax year 2020/21 Manfred lived in job related accommodation. In the tax year 2020/21 Manfred's employer paid the following amounts in respect of the accommodation:

Electricity	£400
Gas	£600
Redecoration	£3,000
New roof tiles	£2,000

What is Manfred's taxable benefit in respect of the accommodation expenses for the tax year 2020/21?

- ○ £6,000
- ○ £4,000
- ○ £2,800
- ○ £1,000 (2 marks)

47.31 Madison lives in a large six-bedroom house. In the tax year 2020/21, he let two of the rooms out to students for £8,250 per annum each. The expenses incurred in letting these rooms amounted to a total of £3,600 per annum. Madison has elected to use rent a room relief.

What is Madison's property income assessment for the tax year 2020/21?

- ○ £12,900
- ○ £9,000
- ○ £1,500
- ○ £5,400

(2 marks)

47.32 Hulin is an employee. On 6 October 2020 Hulin's employer gave him the use of a home cinema system for the remainder of the tax year 2020/21. His employer retained ownership of the system. The system had cost the company £1,800 but had a market value of £1,600 when provided to Hulin. The system had not been used by any other employee.

What is the taxable benefit figure relating to Hulin's use of the home cinema system for the tax year 2020/21?

- ○ £360
- ○ £320
- ○ £160
- ○ £180

(2 marks)

Do you know? – Part D: Capital gains tax

Check that you can fill in the blanks in the statements below before you attempt any questions. If in doubt, you should go back to your BPP Interactive Text and revise first.

- The calculation of a basic chargeable gain is .... less ....
- To determine which shares are being sold we apply the .... rules.
- If a chattel is sold for more than £.................... the gain is restricted to 5/3rds (............................... less £....................).
- Capital gains tax is charged at ....% on residential property gains and at ....% on other gains not qualifying for business asset disposal relief if the taxpayer is a higher rate taxpayer.
- The tax free amount of gains any individual may make in a tax year is known as the ....
- Current year losses must be set off .... the annual exempt amount and brought forward losses must be set off .... the annual exempt amount.
- If a trader sells an asset used in a trade and replaces it with another asset that will be used in a trade within .... year before or .... years after the disposal the trader may be able to claim .... relief.
- The maximum amount of gains eligible for business asset disposal relief in an individual's lifetime is ....
- If an asset is sold for less than it is worth (not a bargain at arm's length) the proceeds figure in the gains computation will be ....

TRY QUESTIONS 48, 49, 50, 51, 52, 53, 54, 55, 56, 57, 58, 59, 60 AND 61

Now consolidate your knowledge of Part D of the syllabus by attempting all the MULTIPLE CHOICE QUESTIONS in QUESTION 62.

Did you know? – Part D: Capital gains tax

Could you fill in the blanks? The answers are in bold. Use this page for revision purposes as you approach the exam.

- The calculation of a basic chargeable gain is **proceeds** less **cost**.
- To determine which shares are being sold we apply the **matching** rules.
- If a chattel is sold for more than £**6,000** the gain is restricted to 5/3rds (**gross proceeds** less £**6,000**).
- Capital gains tax is charged at **28%** on residential property gains and at **20%** on other gains not qualifying for business asset disposal relief if the individual is a higher rate taxpayer.
- The tax free amount of gains any individual may make in a tax year is known as the **annual exempt amount**.
- Current year losses must be set off **before** the annual exempt amount and brought forward losses must be set off **after** the annual exempt amount.
- If a trader sells an asset used in a trade and replaces it with another asset that will be used in a trade within **1** year before or **3** years after the disposal the trader may be able to claim **rollover** relief.
- The maximum amount of gains eligible for business asset disposal relief in an individual's lifetime is **£1,000,000**.
- If an asset is sold for less than it is worth (not a bargain at arm's length) the proceeds figure in the gains computation will be **the market value**.

TRY QUESTIONS 48, 49, 50, 51, 52, 53, 54, 55, 56, 57, 58, 59, 60 AND 61

Now consolidate your knowledge of Part D of the syllabus by attempting all the MULTIPLE CHOICE QUESTIONS in QUESTION 62.

48 Question with help: Capital gains tax liability

John had the following transactions in the year ended 5 April 2021.

(a) On 5 July 2020 he sold his holiday cottage in Scotland for £100,600. The legal and advertising expenses of the sale were £800.

John had purchased the property for £22,000 and had incurred costs of £8,000 for the building of an extension.

The property had never been John's main residence.

(b) On 14 September 2020 he sold 4,000 shares in JVD Products plc for £40,000, his transactions in these shares being as follows.

6 June 1991 purchased 5,000 shares cost £10,000
12 May 2008 purchased 2,800 shares cost £12,000
18 September 2020 purchased 500 shares cost £4,500

Business asset disposal relief is not available on this disposal.

(c) On 27 October 2020 he sold an oil painting for £5,000. John had purchased the painting for £6,800.

John had taxable income of £23,900 in 2020/21.

Required

Compute the capital gains tax liability of John for the tax year 2020/21.

Approaching the answer

Step 1	It is important to set out a CGT calculation in the right way. Also, when there are several disposals as in this question, work through each disposal one at a time.
Step 2	Remember that there are share matching rules.
Step 3	Remember to look out for chattels qualifying for special treatment.
Step 4	Deduct the losses and the annual exempt amount to compute taxable gains. Remember to deduct these from residential property gains first.
Step 5	Work out how much of the taxable gains falls within the basic rate band and apply the 18% rate of CGT to residential property gains. Apply the 28% rate of CGT to the remaining residential property gains and 20% to the other gains.

49 Silas   12 mins

Silas made the following disposals of capital assets during the tax year 2020/21.

26 June 2020: Six hectares of land were sold for £30,000 with expenses of selling amounting to £1,700. The six hectares had been part of a much larger field, which had been purchased in May 2006 for £80,000. The market value of the remaining part of the field on 26 June 2020 was £190,000.

14 January 2021: A painting, which had cost £10,000 in June 2011, was destroyed in a fire. Silas received £18,000 from an insurance company and immediately reinvested £15,000 in a replacement painting.

Neither of these assets had been used in a business and the land is not residential property.

Silas had a capital loss of £100 brought forward as at 6 April 2020. Silas had taxable income of £50,000 in 2020/21.

Required

(a) Calculate the capital gain (if any) arising on each of the above disposals. (6 marks)

(b) Calculate the capital gains tax payable by Silas for the tax year 2020/21 and state the date by which payment must be made. (4 marks)

(Total = 10 marks)

50 Jack — 6 mins

Jack runs a small business, and decided that his workshop was no longer suitable. As a consequence Jack sold his original workshop and purchased a new building. The original workshop was used solely for business purposes and the new workshop is also used solely for business purposes.

The original workshop had cost £80,000 in August 2008 and was sold for £190,000 in February 2021. The new building cost £175,000 in January 2021.

Jack always claims any available capital gains reliefs. This was his only disposal in 2020/21.

Required

(a) Calculate Jack's taxable gain for 2020/21. (4 marks)
(b) State the base cost of the replacement building. (1 marks)

(Total = 5 marks)

51 Ravi — 12 mins

Ravi made the following disposals of capital assets in the tax year 2020/21.

14 July 2020: 10,000 shares were sold for £28,000. These had been purchased as follows:

4,000 shares for £8,180 on 16 May 2006
3,000 shares for £9,600 on 14 August 2008
3,500 shares as a result of a 1 for 2 rights issue for £2.00 each in June 2012

18 August 2020: A painting was sold for £7,500. It had been purchased for £3,500 in November 2008.

2 February 2021: A vintage car was sold for £42,000. It had cost £13,000 in September 2009.

Required

Calculate Ravi's chargeable gains for the tax year 2020/21. (10 marks)

52 Trudy — 12 mins

Trudy gave 14,000 shares in Bud plc, a listed UK company, to her daughter Stephanie on 19 March 2021. The shares had originally cost Trudy £8,000 in June 2010.

On 19 March 2021 Bud plc's shares were quoted on the Stock Exchange Daily Official List at £1.90–£2.00.

The disposal of these shares did not qualify for gift relief.

Trudy had allowable losses of £2,400 carried forward from 2019/20.

Required

(a) Calculate Trudy's taxable gain for the tax year 2020/21. (6 marks)

(b) State the entries that would made in the relevant boxes from Box 23 to Box 54 inclusive of the capital gains summary (shown on the next two pages) for Trudy for 2020/21. (4 marks)

(Total = 10 marks)

Listed shares and securities Please read the notes before filling in this section.

23 Number of disposals

24 Disposal proceeds
£ . 0 0

25 Allowable costs (including purchase price)
£ . 0 0

26 Gains in the year, before losses
£ . 0 0

27 Losses in the year
£ . 0 0

28 If you are making any claim or election, put the relevant code in the box

29 If, during 2020-21, you submitted Real Time Transaction returns for the disposal of listed shares or securities, put the overall gain or loss in the box – include the individual amounts of gains in box 26 and losses in box 27
£ . 0 0

30 Tax on gains in box 29 already paid
£ . 0 0

Unlisted shares and securities Please read the notes before filling in this section.

31 Number of disposals

32 Disposal proceeds
£ . 0 0

33 Allowable costs (including purchase price)
£ . 0 0

34 Gains in the year, before losses
£ . 0 0

35 Losses in the year
£ . 0 0

36 If you are making any claim or election, put the relevant code in the box

37 If, during 2020-21, you submitted Real Time Transaction returns for the disposal of unlisted shares or securities, put the overall gain or loss in the box – include the individual amounts of gains in box 34 and losses in box 35
£ . 0 0

38 Tax on gains in box 37 already paid
£ . 0 0

39 Gains exceeding the lifetime limit for Employee Shareholder Status shares
£ . 0 0

40 Gains invested under Seed Enterprise Investment Scheme and qualifying for relief
£ . 0 0

41 Losses used against income – amount claimed against 2019-20 income
£ . 0 0

42 Amount in box 41 relating to Share Loss Relief in 2019-20 to which Enterprise Investment Scheme or Seed Enterprise Investment Scheme Relief is attributable
£ . 0 0

43 Losses used against income – amount claimed against 2018-19 income
£ . 0 0

44 Amount in box 43 relating to Share Loss Relief in 2018-19 to which Enterprise Investment Scheme or Seed Enterprise Investment Scheme Relief is attributable
£ . 0 0

SA108 2020   Page CG 2

(Adapted from HMRC, 2020)

Losses and adjustments Please read the notes before filling in this section.

Losses set against 2020-21 capital gains

45 Losses brought forward and used in-year
£   · 0 0

46 Income losses of 2020-21 set against gains
£   · 0 0

2020-21 capital losses – other information

47 Losses available to be carried forward
£   · 0 0

48 Losses used against an earlier year's gain
£   · 0 0

Investors' Relief and Business Asset Disposal Relief

49 Gains qualifying for Investors' Relief
£   · 0 0

50 Gains qualifying for Business Asset Disposal Relief
£   · 0 0

Tax adjustments to 2020-21 capital gains

51 Adjustments to Capital Gains Tax
£ –   · 0 0

52 Additional liability for non-resident or dual resident trusts
£   · 0 0

Non-resident Capital Gains Tax (NRCGT) on UK property or land and indirect disposals
Please read the notes before filling in this section.

52.1 For direct disposals of UK residential property or properties, put the total gains chargeable to NRCGT in the box
£   · 0 0

52.2 For direct disposals of non-residential UK properties or land, or indirect disposals of any UK properties or land, put the total gains chargeable to NRCGT in the box
£   · 0 0

52.3 If any of the gains in box 52.2 are from indirect disposals, put 'X' in the box

52.4 Tax on gains in boxes 52.1 and 52.2 already paid
£   · 0 0

52.5 Total losses available against NRCGT gains for the year
£   · 0 0

SA108 2020   Page CG 3

(Adapted from HMRC, 2020)

53 Ivan — 6 mins

Ivan had capital gains of £31,300 on the disposal of quoted shares and a capital loss of £8,000 in the tax year 2020/21. Ivan also had a capital loss of £7,000 brought forward as at 6 April 2020. Business asset disposal relief is not available on the disposal of the quoted shares.

Ivan had taxable income of £36,500 in 2020/21.

Required

Calculate Ivan's capital gains tax payable for the tax year 2020/21. (5 marks)

54 Tony — 6 mins

Tony sold his unincorporated business, which he had owned for several years, in February 2021.

He sold the entire business, which consisted of two business assets, a factory and a plot of land used for parking staff vehicles. The factory had cost £200,000 and was sold for £800,000 and the land had cost £213,000 and was sold for £180,000.

Tony has not previously sold any other business assets. His only other chargeable gain in 2020/21 was £12,300 arising from the disposal of shares held as an investment. Tony always claims any available capital gains reliefs. Tony has taxable income of £50,000 in 2020/21.

Required

Calculate Tony's capital gains tax payable for 2020/21. (5 marks)

55 Carla — 6 mins

Carla is a sole trader. On 19 December 2020 she sold an asset, which had always been used in her business, to her friend Becky for £80,000. The asset had cost Carla £70,000 in May 2009 and it had a market value of £100,000 on the day of the sale.

Required

(a) **Calculate Carla's chargeable gain on the disposal of the asset, assuming that both Carla and Becky make any beneficial claims to reduce the tax payable immediately on the sale. Your answer must clearly identify the amount of any relief claimed.** (4 marks)

(b) **State the base cost of the asset for Becky.** (1 mark)

(Total = 5 marks)

56 Alberto — 12 mins

Alberto made the following disposals of capital assets during the tax year 2020/21.

19 July 2020: A painting was sold for £3,000. The painting had been purchased, when it was mistakenly thought to be a rare portrait, for £9,000.

22 January 2021: 6,000 shares in EFG Ltd were sold for £38,500. Alberto had purchased 4,000 shares in September 2007 for £5,600. EFG Ltd had made a 1 for 1 bonus issue to its shareholders in May 2009.

Alberto had unused capital losses of £35,000 brought forward from the tax year 2019/20.

Required

(a) **Calculate the capital gains/losses arising on each of the above disposals.** (6 marks)
(b) **Calculate Alberto's taxable gains for the tax year 2020/21.** (4 marks)

(Total = 10 marks)

57 Sandra — 6 mins

Sandra has run a small manufacturing business for several years.

On 16 August 2020 she sold a factory, which had always been used in her business, for £220,000, realising a gain of £80,000.

On 10 June 2020 Sandra had invested £210,000 in fixed plant and machinery, which was to be used in her business.

Sandra wishes to claim all available capital gains tax reliefs.

Required

(a) Calculate Sandra's chargeable gain on the disposal of the factory. (2 marks)
(b) State when any deferred gain from (a) will become chargeable. (3 marks)

(Total = 5 marks)

58 Jessie — 12 mins

Jessie made the following disposals of assets in the tax year 2020/21.

15 May 2020:	A vintage car was sold for £44,000. This had been purchased for £28,000.
17 July 2020:	A field was sold for £210,000. This had been purchased for £105,000.
14 September 2020:	A painting was sold for £8,200 (net of expenses of £200). This had cost £3,100 plus £300 expenses.
19 January 2020:	A building was sold for £140,000. This had cost £160,000.

Jessie had taxable income of £44,000 in 2020/21. None of the assets were used in a business and the building was not residential property.

Required

Calculate Jessie's capital gains tax payable for the tax year 2020/21. (10 marks)

59 Eddie — 12 mins

Eddie made the following disposals of capital assets in the tax year 2020/21.

15 April 2020:	An antique table was sold for £3,000. The table had originally been purchased in June 2009 for £8,000. Eddie incurred selling expenses of £300.
17 August 2020:	A 20% share of a painting was sold for £28,000. The original painting had been purchased for £60,000 and the remaining 80% share had a current market value of £140,000. Eddie incurred selling expenses of £500.

Eddie had unused capital losses of £2,300 brought forward from the tax year 2019/20. He had taxable income of £60,000 in 2020/21.

Required

Calculate the capital gains tax payable by Eddie for the tax year 2020/21 and state the due date of payment. (10 marks)

60 Tanya — 6 mins

Tanya purchased a house in London on 1 March 1993 and sold it on 28 February 2021. Tanya had the following pattern of occupation and absences during her ownership of the property.

Event	Period	Detail
1	1 March 1993 to 31 August 2001	Lived in the house
2	1 September 2001 to 31 August 2005	Employed in Scotland
3	1 September 2005 to 31 August 2008	Lived in the house
4	1 September 2008 to 31 August 2014	Travelled abroad
5	1 September 2014 to 30 November 2014	Lived in the house
6	1 December 2014 to 28 February 2021	Lived with her mother and never returned to her own house

During Tanya's absences the house was left empty.

Tanya has never owned any other property and has always treated this house as her main residence.

Required

(a) Using the table format shown below state, with reasons, in respect of Tanya's entire period of ownership, each period covered by, or not covered by, private residence relief (PRR).

Event	Exempt years	Chargeable years	Reason
1			
2			
3			
4			
5			
6			

(b) State the due date for any capital gains tax payable by Tanya on the disposal of her home.

(5 marks)

61 Marion — 12 mins

Marion disposed of the following capital assets in the tax year 2020/21:

15 May 2020	A painting was sold for £7,500. Expenses of sale amounted to £1,300. The painting had originally cost Marion £2,800 in May 2009. The purchase costs amounted to £400.
19 August 2020	An antique desk was sold for £32,200. The desk had been purchased in September 2010 for £6,400. There were no expenses of sale or purchase.

Marion's taxable income (for income tax purposes) after deduction of the personal allowance for the tax year 2020/21 was £30,900.

Required

Calculate the capital gains tax payable by Marion for the tax year 2020/21. (10 marks)

62 Multiple choice questions: Capital gains tax

Allow 2 minutes for each question

62.1 Which of the following is an exempt asset for CGT purposes?

- ○ A vintage Bentley motor car worth £70,000
- ○ A shop used by a sole trader in his business
- ○ A painting sold for proceeds of £50,000
- ○ Shares in an unquoted trading company (2 marks)

62.2 Todd sold a house in November 2020. Todd has always rented out the house. His chargeable gain on sale was £25,200. Todd has taxable income of £50,000 in 2020/21.

What is Todd's capital gains tax liability on the sale assuming that he has no other disposals in 2020/21?

- ○ £2,580
- ○ £7,056
- ○ £3,612
- ○ £2,322 (2 marks)

62.3 Leanne is a sole trader. She sold a shop in July 2020 for £80,000, realising a chargeable gain of £25,000. Leanne used the proceeds to buy a new shop for £70,000 and used the remainder as working capital.

How much of the gain on the first shop is eligible for rollover relief?

- ○ £10,000
- ○ £21,875
- ○ £15,000
- ○ £25,000 (2 marks)

62.4 Ellen purchased a Victorian vase for £1,500. In October 2020 she sold the vase for gross proceeds of £7,000. There were no expenses of sale.

What is Ellen's chargeable gain?

- ○ Nil
- ○ £1,000
- ○ £1,667
- ○ £5,500 (2 marks)

62.5 Ian has been running a trading business for many years. In November 2020 he sold the business realising gains of £177,000. Ian makes a claim for business asset disposal relief. This is his first claim for the relief and he has no other chargeable assets. Ian has taxable income of £45,000 in 2020/21.

What is Ian's CGT liability on the sale of the business?

- ○ £32,940
- ○ £16,470
- ○ £17,700
- ○ £46,116 (2 marks)

62.6 George purchased a house on 1 January 2005 and lived in it until 31 December 2013. On 1 January 2014 George went to live with his parents and the house was unoccupied until it was sold on 30 June 2020. The gain on sale was £250,000.

What is the gain chargeable to capital gains tax on the sale after private residence relief?

- ○ £81,897
- ○ £30,172
- ○ £250,000
- ○ £168,103 (2 marks)

62.7 On 27 January 2021 Yolanda sold 10,000 ordinary shares in B plc. She had originally purchased 12,000 shares in B plc on 2 May 2006, and purchased another 8,000 shares on 10 February 2021.

How will Yolanda's disposal of 10,000 shares be matched with her acquisitions?

- ○ Against 10,000 of the shares purchased on 2 May 2006
- ○ Against 5,000 of the shares purchased on 10 February 2021 and then against 5,000 of the shares purchased on 2 May 2006
- ○ Against 10,000 of the total shareholding of 20,000 shares
- ○ Against the 8,000 shares purchased on 10 February 2021 and then against 2,000 of the shares purchased on 2 May 2006 **(2 marks)**

62.8 Rarshad sold her sole trader design business in August 2020 making a gain of £1.5m. She had run the business for many years. Rarshad makes a claim for business asset disposal relief. This is her first claim for the relief. The only other disposal that Rarshad made in 2020/21 was of an investment asset (not residential property), realising a gain of £12,300. She had taxable income of £100,000 in 2020/21.

What is her CGT liability for 2020/21?

- ○ £200,000
- ○ £150,000
- ○ £151,230
- ○ £300,000 **(2 marks)**

62.9 **Which of the following are exempt from capital gains tax for an individual?**

- (i) Damages for personal injury
- (ii) Qualifying corporate bonds (QCBs)
- (iii) Gilt-edged securities
- (iv) Receipts of compensation for destroyed or lost assets
- (v) Goodwill

- ○ (i), (ii) and (v)
- ○ (ii), (iii) and (iv)
- ○ (i), (ii) and (iii)
- ○ (i), (iii) and (v) **(2 marks)**

62.10 A factory, which had always been used as a business asset, was sold on 14 May 2020 resulting in a gain of £60,000. A depreciating asset, also used as a business asset, was purchased on 12 August 2020 using all the proceeds from the sale of the factory. The gain of £60,000 was held over. The depreciating asset will continue to be used as a business asset until it is sold on 14 October 2030.

When would the heldover gain of £60,000 become chargeable to capital gains tax?

- ○ 12 August 2020
- ○ 14 May 2030
- ○ 12 August 2030
- ○ 14 October 2030 **(2 marks)**

62.11 An individual taxpayer has chargeable gains of £17,200 and allowable capital losses of £3,000 in the tax year 2020/21. He also has allowable capital losses of £4,000 brought forward from the tax year 2019/20.

What is the correct use of these amounts for the tax year 2020/21?

- ○ £17,200 – £3,000 (current year loss) – £12,300 (annual exempt amount) – £4,000 (brought forward loss)
- ○ £17,200 – £3,000 (current year loss) – £12,300 (annual exempt amount) – £1,900 (brought forward loss)
- ○ £17,200 – £4,000 (brought forward loss) – £900 (current year loss) – £12,300 (annual exempt amount)
- ○ £17,200 – £4,000 (brought forward loss) – £3,000 (current year loss) – £12,300 (annual exempt amount)

(2 marks)

62.12 In December 2020 a sole trader disposed of his business, which he had owned for the last ten years, realising a gain of £180,000. The sole trader had no other capital gains and no income in the tax year 2020/21.

Assuming that business asset disposal relief is claimed, how much capital gains tax is payable for the tax year 2020/21?

- ○ £33,540
- ○ £18,000
- ○ £46,956
- ○ £16,770

(2 marks)

62.13 **By what date must capital gains tax on non-residential gains for the tax year 2020/21 be paid to avoid incurring interest and penalties and what would be the penalty (if any) if the tax was paid two weeks late?**

- ○ 31 December 2021, no penalty
- ○ 31 December 2021, penalty 5% of unpaid tax
- ○ 31 January 2022, no penalty
- ○ 31 January 2022, penalty 5% of unpaid tax

(2 marks)

62.14 Alyson has two chargeable gains in the tax year 2020/21:

£10,000 – amount qualifying for business asset disposal relief
£14,200 – residential property gain

Alyson has taxable income of £11,000 in the tax year 2020/21.

How much capital gains tax must Alyson pay for the tax year 2020/21?

- ○ £1,532
- ○ £1,190
- ○ £2,142
- ○ £1,342

(2 marks)

62.15 Anil disposes of a residential property which he had never lived in on 31 December 2020 realising a gain of £160,000. Anil has taxable non-savings income of £75,000 in 2020/21.

How much capital gains tax must Anil pay and what is the due date for payment?

- ○ £44,800 payable on 31 January 2022
- ○ £41,356 payable on 30 January 2021
- ○ £44,800 payable on 30 January 2021
- ○ £41,356 payable on 31 January 2022

(2 marks)

62.16 Sid purchased ten hectares of land for £80,000 incurring £2,000 in acquisition expenses. In June 2020 Sid sold six hectares for £90,000 incurring £4,000 in selling expenses. The market value of the remaining four hectares was £40,000.

What is the allowable cost figure for the purposes of calculating the capital gain on the disposal of the six hectares?

- ○ £56,769
- ○ £55,385
- ○ £54,603
- ○ £55,968

(2 marks)

Do you know? – Part E: Corporation tax liabilities

Check that you can fill in the blanks in the statements below before you attempt any questions. If in doubt, you should go back to your BPP Interactive Text and revise first.

- The rate of corporation tax for financial year 2020 is ....%.

- If a company has a long period of account of, say, 15 months this must be split into two accounting periods: the first of .... months, the second of .... months.

- A company claims capital allowances on a company car with CO_2 emissions of 90g/km provided to its managing director who uses the car 60% of the time for private use. This is the only item of plant or machinery that the company owns. The writing down allowance available is ....

- Interest received by a company is taxed as .... income.

  TRY QUESTIONS 63, 64, 65, 66, 67, 68, 69, 70, 71, 72 AND 73

- Companies are given relief for inflation on chargeable gains through the indexation allowance between the month of .... and the earlier of the month of .... and ....

  TRY QUESTIONS 74, 75, 76, 77, AND 78

- A company with a continuing business can make a claim to set the loss against its current period total profits and then carry it back against total profits for a maximum of ...... months.

- A company can use a loss in the last 12 months of trading by carrying it back for a maximum of ...... months.

- A company can carry forward a trading loss and usually set it against .... in future accounting periods.

  TRY QUESTIONS 79, 80, 81 AND 82

- Companies that are .... pay tax in quarterly instalments.

  TRY QUESTIONS 83, 84, 85 AND 86

Now consolidate your knowledge of Part E of the syllabus by attempting all the MULTIPLE CHOICE QUESTIONS in QUESTION 87.

QUESTIONS

Did you know? – Part E: Corporation tax liabilities

Could you fill in the blanks? The answers are in bold. Use this page for revision purposes as you approach the exam.

- The rate of corporation tax for financial year 2020 is **19**%.

- If a company has a long period of account of, say, 15 months this must be split into two accounting periods: the first of **12** months, the second of **3** months.

- A company claims capital allowances on a company car with CO_2 emissions of 90g/km provided to its managing director who uses the car 60% of the time for private use. This is the only item of plant or machinery that the company owns. The writing down allowance available is **the tax written down value × 18%**.

- Interest received by a company is taxed as **interest** income.

    TRY QUESTIONS 63, 64, 65, 66, 67, 68, 69, 70, 71, 72 AND 73

- Companies are given relief for inflation on chargeable gains through the indexation allowance between the month of **acquisition** and the earlier of the month of **disposal** and **December 2017**.

    TRY QUESTIONS 74, 75, 76, 77, AND 78

- A company with a continuing business can make a claim to set the loss against its current period total profits and then carry it back against total profits for a maximum of **12** months.

- A company can use a loss in the last 12 months of trading by carrying it back for a maximum of **36** months.

- A company can carry forward a trading loss and usually set it against **total profits** in future accounting periods.

    TRY QUESTIONS 79, 80, 81 AND 82

- Companies that are **large** pay tax in quarterly instalments.

    TRY QUESTIONS 83, 84, 85 AND 86

Now consolidate your knowledge of Part E of the syllabus by attempting all the MULTIPLE CHOICE QUESTIONS in QUESTION 87.

63 Question with help: Corporation tax

Abel Ltd, a UK trading company, produced the following results for the year ended 31 March 2021.

	£
Income	
Adjusted trading profit	244,000
Rental income	15,000
Bank deposit interest accrued (non-trading investment)	5,000
Chargeable gains: 25 September 2020	35,000
28 March 2021	7,000
(There were capital losses of £8,000 brought forward at 1 April 2020)	
Payments	
Qualifying charitable donation	7,000

Required

Compute the corporation tax payable by Abel Ltd for the above accounting period.

Approaching the answer

Step 1	In working out a company's taxable total profits, we must bring together all income and gains as total profits. Then deduct qualifying charitable donations to find taxable total profits. You must therefore start by setting out the standard layout for computing taxable total profits, and inserting all relevant figures from the question.
Step 2	Once you have found the taxable total profits, you can apply the rate of tax to compute the corporation tax liability.

64 Taps Ltd   18 mins

Taps Ltd is a UK registered company. For its 12-month accounting period ended 31 March 2021 Taps Ltd has provided you with the following information.

- Trading profit of £1,960,000, fully adjusted for tax purposes but before capital allowances.

- Non-trading interest of £20,000 was received from another UK company for the year ended 31 March 2021. In addition, a further £2,000 owed at 31 March 2021 was received in May 2021.

- Bank interest of £1,800 was paid to a UK bank for the year ended 31 March 2021. The interest was in respect of a loan taken for non-trade purposes. A further £300 due at 31 March 2021 has still not been paid.

- Rental income of £15,000 was receivable for the period from 1 December 2020 to 31 March 2021 from the letting of a of a small warehouse which was surplus to the company's business requirements. £2,000 of the rent for the period was not paid by the tenant until 5 April 2021.

- Gain on disposal of plot of land, held as an investment, in December 2020. The land was sold for gross proceeds of £211,040 and the cost of sale were £3,200. The land had been acquired in May 2013 for a cost of £78,000 and the cost of purchase were £2,000. The indexation factor between May 2013 and December 2017 is 0.112 and between May 2013 and December 2020 is 0.167.

- A qualifying charitable donation of £4,000 was paid in September 2020.

- On 1 April 2020 the balance on the main pool for capital allowance purposes was £197,000.

- The following items of plant and machinery were purchased and sold in the year to 31 March 2021.
  - Plant was purchased for £1,018,000 on 1 May 2020.
  - A car for the director's use was purchased for £40,000 on 1 December 2020. The car, which has 115g/km CO_2 emissions, is used 30% for private purposes.
  - Plant, which had cost £63,000 in May 2017, was sold for £60,000 on 2 February 2021.
- Taps Ltd had a trading loss of £258,700 brought forward on 1 April 2020. The company claims loss relief to the fullest extent as early as possible.

Required

(a) Calculate the maximum capital allowances that Taps Ltd can claim for the year ended 31 March 2021.

(5 marks)

(b) Calculate the corporation tax payable by Taps Ltd for the year ended 31 March 2021, assuming that the maximum capital allowances are claimed. (10 marks)

(Total = 15 marks)

65 XYZ Ltd   18 mins

XYZ Ltd is a UK registered company. During its eight-month accounting period from 1 May 2020 to 31 December 2020 the company had the following trading results.

	Notes	£	£
Operating profit			1,930,000
Loan interest	1		20,000
			1,950,000
Expenses:			
Legal expenses	2	20,000	
Administration costs	3	92,000	
Loan interest	4	5,000	
Depreciation		32,000	
Motoring expenses	5	28,700	
Wages		412,500	
Donations and subscriptions	6	2,500	
Staff pension contributions	7	30,000	(622,700)
Profit before taxation			1,327,300

Notes

1. The loan interest income is in respect of 5% loan stock purchased in 2016 as a long-term investment. The amount shown includes an accrued figure of £2,000 for an amount still owed to the company at 31 December 2020.

2. The legal expenses comprise:

	£
Costs of defending breach of contract claim	6,000
Fine for breaking the Health and Safety at Work Act	10,000
Legal fees for preparing staff contracts	4,000

3. Included within the administration costs are:

	£
Gifts of 300 Christmas food hampers to customers	11,500
Entertainment of staff	2,600

4. The loan interest paid is in respect of a loan of £100,000 borrowed to finance the purchase of fixed plant and machinery used in XYZ Ltd's trade. The loan was obtained in 2016. The total amount due for the period ended 31 December 2020 is as shown in the accounts.

5   Motoring expenses include:

	£
Parking fines incurred by employees on company business	300
Director's car expenses of which 40% is in respect of private journeys	2,400
Lease payments for the car (CO_2 emissions 120g/km) used by the commercial manager for the eight-month period	6,000

6   The donations and subscriptions were £2,000 to a national charity, and £500 to the local Chamber of Commerce.

7   The pension contributions are in respect of contributions paid during the period to a HM Revenue and Customs (HMRC) registered occupational pension plan for the company's employees.

8   Capital allowances for the eight-month accounting period from 1 May 2020 to 31 December 2020 have been calculated as £115,000.

9   XYZ Ltd was not a large company for the purpose of quarterly instalment payments in its year ended 30 April 2020.

Required

(a) Calculate XYZ Ltd's adjusted trading profit for the eight-month period ended 31 December 2020. State any items that do not require adjustment. You should start with the net profit figure of £1,327,300 and indicate by the use of zero (0) any items which do not require adjustment.
(10 marks)

(b) Calculate XYZ Ltd's corporation tax liability for the eight-month period ended 31 December 2020, and state the due date for payment. (3 marks)

(c) State the due date by which XYZ Ltd must file its corporation tax return for the eight-month period ended 31 December 2020 and the amount of the penalty that would be chargeable if the return is filed two months late (assuming that this is the first late return made by XYZ Ltd). (2 marks)

(Total = 15 marks)

66 Bush Ltd   12 mins

Bush Ltd prepares accounts to 31 March every year. The company had the following results in the accounting period ended 31 March 2021:

	£	£
Operating profit		295,000
Loan stock interest income		21,000
Property business income		9,000
Dividend income		18,000
Compensation received for damaged stock		15,000
		358,000
Expenses:		
Directors' remuneration	50,000	
Wages and salaries	80,000	
Depreciation	12,000	
Entertainment of		
– Staff	26,500	
– Clients	14,800	
Legal fees in respect of		
– Renewing a 60-year lease	4,500	
– Debt collecting	3,400	
Qualifying charitable donation	2,600	
Patent royalties (trade related)	13,400	
Loss on sale of a van	1,200	(208,400)
Net profit before taxation		149,600

Required

Calculate Bush Ltd's adjusted trading income for the year ended 31 March 2021. You should start with the net profit figure of £149,600 and indicate by the use of zero (0) any items which do not require adjustment.
(10 marks)

QUESTIONS

67 Fires Ltd — 12 mins

Fires Ltd prepares its accounts to 31 March every year. Fires Ltd is registered for value added tax (VAT) and all of its sales are standard rated.

Fires Ltd had the following transactions in capital assets during the accounting year ended 31 March 2021.

Purchases:
2 May 2020   A machine for £1,226,400
6 August 2020   A computer for £7,200
14 October 2020   A car for £16,000 (CO_2 emissions 125g/km)

Disposal:
16 September 2020   A machine, which had originally cost £24,000, was sold for £26,000.

All the above figures are **inclusive** of VAT.

The tax written down value of Fires Ltd's main pool on 1 April 2020 was £120,000.

The car purchased on 14 October 2020 is used 40% for private purposes and 60% for business purposes by the company's managing director.

The computer is to be treated as a short-life asset.

Required

Calculate the maximum capital allowances that Fires Ltd can claim for the year ended 31 March 2021.

The standard rate of VAT is 20% and applies to all transactions.   **(10 marks)**

68 Radiators Ltd — 18 mins

Radiators Ltd is a UK company. In the accounting year ended 31 March 2021, Radiators Ltd had the following income and expenditure.

Income and gains:
Adjusted trading profit (before capital allowances)	£1,164,840
Interest from a UK bank	£8,000
Rental income received	£17,500
Chargeable gains	£24,000

Expenditure:
Qualifying charitable donation	£4,560
Interest paid	£3,000

The interest paid is the accrued amount for the year to 31 March 2021 and was in respect of a loan used to purchase an investment.

The rental income relates to the letting of a retail shop which was previously used by Radiators Ltd in its business. The shop was let on 1 August 2020 at a rental of £2,500 per month. The rental payment for March 2021 was not received until 10 April 2021. In addition to the monthly rental, the tenant paid a premium of £12,000 for the seven year lease when the tenancy commenced.

The tax written down value on the main pool brought forward on 1 April 2020 was £150,000. Radiators Ltd purchased new machinery for £1,010,000 on 11 August 2020. It sold machinery for £25,000 on 14 January 2021. The machinery sold in January 2020 cost £22,000 in December 2017.

The chargeable gains of £24,000 include the gain that arose on the sale of the machinery in January 2021.

Required

Calculate the corporation tax payable by Radiators Ltd for the year ended 31 March 2021 and state the due date for payment. Ignore VAT.   **(15 marks)**

69 Broad Ltd — 18 mins

Broad Ltd is a UK resident company. During its accounting year ended 31 March 2021 Broad Ltd made a net trading profit of £1,640,000. Included in this figure (which has not yet been adjusted for tax purposes) were:

Income:	£
Bank interest (Note 1)	4,300
Profit on the sale of a non-current asset (Note 2)	102,000
Expenses:	
Loan stock interest (Note 3)	5,000
Qualifying charitable donation	10,000
Legal fees (Note 4)	10,000
Payments for loss of office (Note 5)	230,000

Notes

1. The bank interest was the total amount due for the year in respect of amounts deposited.

2. The profit on the sale of a non-current asset was on the sale of an office building for £140,000 in May 2020. The chargeable gain on the sale has been calculated to be £63,568.

3. The loan stock interest represents the amount payable on an issue of £100,000 5% loan stock in 2016, used to purchase a new item of plant, which is used in the trade.

4. The legal fees comprise £8,000 for obtaining a 60-year lease on a new factory and £2,000 for preparing staff employment contracts.

5. The payments for loss of office are in respect of redundancy payments made to ensure the business continues.

6. The balance on the main plant and machinery pool for capital allowances purposes on 1 April 2020 was £455,556. There were no purchases or disposals of plant and machinery during the year ended 31 March 2021.

7. Broad Ltd had a capital loss of £16,600 brought forward at 1 April 2020.

8. Broad Ltd paid its corporation tax by instalments for the year ended 31 March 2020.

Required

(a) Calculate the trading profit adjusted for tax purposes for Broad Ltd for the year ended 31 March 2021. You should start with the net profit figure of £1,640,000 and indicate by the use of zero (0) any items which do not require adjustment. (7 marks)

(b) Calculate the taxable total profits and the corporation tax payable by Broad Ltd for the year ended 31 March 2021. (5 marks)

(c) Explain why Broad Ltd must pay its corporation tax by instalments, calculate the amount of each instalment and state the date of each instalment. (3 marks)

(Total = 15 marks)

QUESTIONS

70 Rose Ltd   12 mins

Rose Ltd has always prepared accounts to 31 March annually. In early 2020 Rose Ltd decided to change its accounting reference date to 31 May and produced accounts for the 14 months ended 31 May 2021.

The results for the 14-month period ended 31 May 2021 were as follows.

	£
Adjusted trading profit (before capital allowances)	420,000
Chargeable gain – 14 December 2020	102,380
Capital loss – 2 May 2021	(10,000)
Qualifying charitable donation – paid 30 April 2021	(22,000)

The tax written-down value brought forward on the main plant and machinery pool as at 1 April 2020 was £91,000. A new machine was purchased on 14 June 2020 for £25,000.

Required

Calculate the corporation tax payable by Rose Ltd for the two accounting periods ended 31 May 2021.

(10 marks)

Note. You should assume that the rates of tax and allowances for the Financial Year 2020 remain the same for the Financial Year 2021.

71 BDD Ltd   12 mins

BDD Ltd is a UK-registered company which has prepared accounts to 30 April each year. The company decided to change its accounting date to 31 December and made up accounts for the eight-month period to 31 December 2020.

The tax written down values of the main plant and machinery pool and the special rate pool at 1 May 2020 were £290,000 and £16,000 respectively. The special rate pool consisted of a car.

The following purchases and disposals of capital items were made by the company during the period ended 31 December 2020:

31 May 2020	New machinery bought for £668,000
12 June 2020	Machinery sold for £14,000 (original cost £12,000)
25 August 2020	Plant bought for £15,000 (election made to be treated as short life asset)

In addition, the special rate pool car, which had originally cost £20,340, was traded in on 31 December 2020 for £8,000 against the cost of a new car, for which a further £27,000 was paid by the company. The new car has CO_2 emissions of 125g/km.

Required

Calculate the maximum capital allowances claimable by BDD Ltd for the eight-month period ended 31 December 2020. Ignore VAT.   **(10 marks)**

72 Cargo Ltd — 12 mins

Cargo Ltd is a trading company. In its year to 31 March 2021 the company had the following transactions in non-current assets.

Purchases:	16 May 2020	Plant	£15,000
	14 June 2020	Machinery	£7,000
	18 August 2020	A car for a director's use	£26,000
Sales:	17 July 2020	Plant (original cost £48,000)	£18,000
	20 August 2020	A special rate pool car (original cost £15,500)	£7,000

The car purchased on 18 August 2020 was used 20% for business and 80% privately. It has 125g/km CO_2 emissions.

In addition to the above the company had traded in an old car for a newer model on 2 November 2020. The old car had cost £11,500 in January 2017 and had a trade in value of £3,000. The company paid an additional £6,000 cash for the new model. Both cars were used 100% for business purposes and have CO_2 emissions of 100g/km.

The balance of the pools as at 1 April 2020 were:

Plant and Machinery	£248,000
Special rate pool	£8,000

Required

Calculate the maximum capital allowances available to Cargo Ltd for the year ended 31 March 2021. Ignore VAT. (10 marks)

Helping hand. Think about the car with private use carefully. Will the private use affect the capital allowances computation for the company?

73 Stem Ltd — 12 mins

Stem Ltd, a UK company, made the following purchases and disposals of capital items during its nine-month accounting period ending 31 December 2020.

Purchases:
25 June 2020 — A machine for £365,500
4 August 2020 — A machine for £367,650
7 October 2020 — A machine (N1)
2 December 2020 — A car for £20,000 (N2)

Disposals:
14 October 2020 — Plant for £6,000 (original cost £4,000)

Notes

1. The machine acquired on 7 October 2020 was purchased on a hire purchase agreement with 24 monthly payments of £1,500 starting in October 2020. The machine would have cost £30,350 to purchase outright.

2. The car has CO_2 emissions of 113 grams per kilometre.

The tax written down value of Stem Ltd's main pool brought forward on 1 April 2020 was £220,000.

Stem Ltd has agreed a contract with a building company to construct a brand new factory for use in its trade during its year ended 31 December 2021. The building is likely to be completed and brought into use by Stem Ltd by 1 November 2021 and will include the following items of expenditure:

Cost of the land	–	£200,000
Building construction costs	–	£1,200,000
Integral features, eg air conditioning, electrical and lighting systems	–	£500,000
Legal and professional fees	–	£25,000

Required

(a) Calculate the maximum capital allowances that Stem Ltd can claim for the nine-month period ended 31 December 2020. Ignore VAT. **(10 marks)**

(b) Outline the tax relief available to Stem Ltd in the year ended 31 December 2021 for each item of expenditure on the new factory. No calculations are required. **(5 marks)**

(Total = 15 marks)

74 Petal Ltd   6 mins

Petal Ltd sold 3,000 shares in Bud Ltd on 19 October 2020 for £21,000.

Petal Ltd had purchased shares in Bud Ltd as follows.

14 June 2007	1,000 shares for £3,000
17 July 2011	3,000 shares for £10,000

Indexation factors are:

June 2007 to July 2011	0.132
June 2007 to December 2017	0.341
June 2007 to October 2020	0.407
July 2011 to December 2017	0.185
July 2011 to October 2020	0.242

Required

Calculate the chargeable gain on Petal Ltd's disposal of shares in Bud Ltd.   **(5 marks)**

> **Helping hand.** For the share pool, you need three columns – one for the number of shares, one for cost and one for indexed cost.

75 Roof Ltd   6 mins

Roof Ltd has been in business for many years making up accounts to 31 March each year. On 1 December 2020, Roof Ltd sold an unwanted office block for proceeds (net of disposal costs) of £477,000. Roof Ltd had purchased the office block for £192,000 in September 2004. The office block was extended at a cost of £71,000 in May 2008.

Indexation factors are:

September 2004 to December 2017	0.478
September 2004 to December 2020	0.556
May 2008 to December 2017	0.293
May 2008 to December 2020	0.361

Required

Calculate the capital gain on the disposal of the office block in December 2020.   **(5 marks)**

76 Box plc   12 mins

Box plc makes up accounts to 31 March each year. In its 12-month period ending 31 March 2021 it has the following transactions in capital assets.

26 May 2020

20,000 shares in Crate plc sold for £124,000. These shares had been purchased as follows.

26 May 2000	13,000 shares for	£24,000
24 October 2006	5,000 shares for	£27,500
22 May 2020	2,000 shares for	£12,000

21 August 2020

A painting, which had been hanging in the managing director's office, was sold for £5,800. It had been purchased for £8,000 in October 2006.

Indexation factors are:

May 2000 to October 2006	0.174
October 2006 to December 2017	0.388
October 2006 to May 2020	0.436

Required

Calculate the total chargeable gains for Box plc for the year ending 31 March 2021.   (10 marks)

77 Andsnes Ltd   12 mins

Andsnes Ltd, a UK trading company, made the following disposals in the year ended 31 March 2021.

(a) On 15 May 2020 it sold a warehouse for £120,000. The company had bought the warehouse for £65,000 on 10 July 2009. The company had invested £100,000 in another warehouse on 1 May 2019. Both warehouses have been used since acquisition solely for the purposes of the company's trade.

(b) On 18 June 2020 it sold a plot of land for £69,000. It had bought it for £20,000 on 1 April 2011 and had spent £4,000 on defending its title to the land in July 2013. The land had been held as an investment and had not been used for trade purpose.

(c) On 19 December 2020 the company sold a vase used to decorate the boardroom for £4,900. The vase had cost £2,500 in May 2013.

Indexation factors are:

July 2009 to December 2017	0.303
July 2009 to May 2020	0.348
April 2011 to December 2017	0.186
April 2011 to June 2020	0.231
July 2013 to December 2017	0.114
July 2013 to June 2020	0.154
May 2013 to December 2017	0.112
May 2013 to December 2020	0.171

Required

Compute Andsnes Ltd's chargeable gains to be included in its taxable total profits for the year ended 31 March 2021.   (10 marks)

> **Helping hand.** Is rollover relief available to defer the gain arising on the sale of the warehouse? Look carefully at the dates to see whether the acquisition of the second warehouse is within the qualifying period.

78 Jasmine plc — 6 mins

Jasmine plc prepares accounts to 31 December each year.

On 10 March 2020, Jasmine plc bought a warehouse for use in its business for £520,000.

On 31 August 2020, Jasmine plc sold a factory, which it had used in its business, for £560,000. The factory had been bought in September 2010 and had cost Jasmine plc £275,000.

Required

Calculate Jasmine plc's chargeable gain for the year ended 31 December 2020, assuming that it claims any available reliefs.

Note. The indexation factor for September 2010 to December 2017 is 0.234 and for September 2010 to August 2020 is 0.298. **(5 marks)**

79 Question with help: Loss reliefs

Galbraith Ltd is a company with results as follows.

	Year ended 31 March		
	2021 £	2022 £	2023 £
Trading profit/(loss) (as adjusted for taxation)	125,000	(697,000)	80,000
Bank interest accrued (non-trading investment)	263,000	185,000	24,000
Chargeable gains	60,360	0	3,000
Qualifying charitable donation paid	40,000	57,000	30,000

Required

(a) **Calculate the corporation tax liabilities for the three years after claiming maximum loss relief at the earliest possible times, showing any unrelieved qualifying charitable donations. Assume the rate of corporation tax for Financial Year 2020 applies in later years.**

(b) **In respect of the corporation tax for the accounting period ended 31 March 2023, state when this will be due for payment and state the filing date for the return.**

Approaching the answer

Step 1 — In Requirement (a) you are alerted to the likelihood of encountering losses. First, set out the pro-forma showing the trading profit figures with a zero for any loss making periods. Set out the loss memorandum.

Step 2 — Insert the other figures that make up total profits into your pro-forma and then deduct losses from total profits. Questions usually require loss relief to be claimed as quickly as possible. Remember that loss relief carried back against total profits requires losses to be set off first against total profits of the loss-making accounting period. Remember that in the current period and on carry back, losses are set off before qualifying charitable donations, so qualifying charitable donations may become unrelieved. Any remaining losses are carried forward, and a claim can be made to set the whole or part of the remaining loss against total profits.

Step 3 — Remember that certain companies are required to pay their anticipated corporation tax liability by quarterly instalments. Does this apply to Galbraith Ltd?

80 Laurel Ltd — 12 mins

Laurel Ltd's results for recent periods of trading are as follows.

	Y/e 31.12.19 £	Y/e 31.12.20 £	Y/e 31.12.21 £
Trading profit/(loss)	44,000	(73,800)	95,200
Property business profit	9,400	6,600	6,500
Chargeable gain/(loss)	5,100	(7,500)	6,000
Qualifying charitable donations paid	(800)	(1,000)	(1,200)

Required

(a) State two factors that will influence a company's choice of loss relief claims. **(2 marks)**

(b) Assuming that Laurel Ltd claims relief for its trading losses as early as possible, calculate the company's taxable total profits for each of the years ended 31 December 2019, 2020 and 2021. Your answer should also clearly identify any unrelieved qualifying charitable donations and the amount of any unrelieved losses as at 31 December 2021.

(8 marks)

(Total = 10 marks)

81 Caution Ltd — 6 mins

Caution Ltd had the following results for the accounting periods up to the cessation of trade on 31 March 2021:

	Y/e 31.03.18 £	Y/e 31.03.19 £	Y/e 31.03.20 £	Y/e 31.03.21 £
Trading profits	105,000	60,000	27,000	(120,000)
Property business income	0	0	0	16,000

Required

Show how the loss of the year ended 31 March 2021 is relieved. **(5 marks)**

82 Waddle Ltd — 12 mins

Waddle Ltd commenced trading on 1 April 2019. The company's results for its first two periods of trading are as follows:

	Y/e 31.03.20 £	Y/e 31.03.21 £
Trading profit/(loss)	(18,000)	5,300
Property business income	3,950	4,500
Chargeable gain/(loss)	(1,000)	3,200
Qualifying charitable donations	(200)	(1,050)

Waddle Ltd claims current year loss relief, and then carry forward loss relief in the most beneficial manner.

Required

(a) Calculate Waddle Ltd's taxable total profits for the years ended 31 March 2020 and 2021. **(9 marks)**

(b) Identify the amount of any unrelieved trading loss as at 31 March 2021. **(1 mark)**

(Total = 10 marks)

QUESTIONS

83 Alphabetic Ltd — 12 mins

(a) Alphabetic Ltd makes up annual accounts to 30 September and is a large company for the purposes of payment of corporation tax. The company paid four quarterly instalments of corporation tax of £156,000 each in respect of the accounting period to 30 September 2020. These were paid on 14 April 2020, 14 July 2020, 14 October 2020 and 14 January 2021. It subsequently transpired that the actual liability for the period was £800,000 and the balance of £176,000 was paid on 1 July 2021.

Required

State the amounts on which interest will be charged in respect of the above accounting period and the dates from which it will run. (4 marks)

(b) **You are required to state:**

 (i) The fixed rate penalties for failing to submit a corporation tax return on time.
 (3 marks)

 (ii) The tax-geared penalties for failing to submit a corporation tax return on time.
 (3 marks)

Your answers should indicate under what circumstances these penalties are triggered.

(Total = 10 marks)

84 Peter Collins — 12 mins

Peter Collins is starting a roadside café business. He is considering whether to carry on the business as a sole trader or through a company.

Required

List five differences in the way in which a person trading as a sole trader is treated for tax and National Insurance purposes compared to operating through a company. (10 marks)

85 Heaters Ltd — 6 mins

Heaters Ltd is a large company for the purposes of payment of corporation tax. In the 12-month accounting period ended 31 March 2021 Heaters Ltd had a corporation tax liability of £380,000.

Required

State the dates and amounts of corporation tax due in respect of Heater Ltd's accounting period ended 31 March 2021. (5 marks)

86 Flower plc — 6 mins

Flower plc prepares accounts to 31 March each year. For the year ended 31 March 2021, Flower plc had taxable total profits amounting to £1,800,000 on which corporation tax of £342,000 was payable. Flower plc had taxable total profits of £2,000,000 in the year ended 31 March 2020.

Required

State the due dates of payment in respect of Flower plc's year ended 31 March 2021, and the amount of corporation tax payable on each date. (5 marks)

87 Multiple choice questions: Corporation tax liabilities

Allow 2 minutes for each question

87.1 PJX Ltd commenced trading on 1 January 2019 and prepared its first set of accounts for the 18-month period ended 30 June 2020. Thereafter PJX Ltd prepared accounts annually to 30 June.

What is PJX Ltd's second chargeable accounting period?

- ○ 1 July 2019 to 30 June 2020
- ○ 1 July 2020 to 30 June 2021
- ○ 1 January 2020 to 30 June 2020
- ○ 1 January 2020 to 31 December 2020 (2 marks)

87.2 In May 2020, HJD Ltd sold a motor car for £15,000. The motor car had a CO_2 emission rate of 160g/km and had cost the company £14,000 in August 2017. 20% of the motor car's usage had been for private purposes by a company director.

As at 1 April 2020, the tax written down value on HJD Ltd's special rate pool for capital allowance purposes was £12,500.

Assuming that no other assets are purchased or sold by HJD Ltd in the year ended 31 March 2021, what is the balancing charge on the special rate pool as a result of the sale of the motor car?

- A £2,500
- B £1,500
- C £2,000
- D £1,200 (2 marks)

87.3 K Ltd sells a factory for £200,000. The indexed gain on sale was £70,000. The company acquires another factory 15 months later for £187,500.

What is the amount of rollover relief which K Ltd can claim?

- ○ £12,500
- ○ £32,500
- ○ £37,500
- ○ £57,500 (2 marks)

87.4 Y Ltd had the following results for the year ended 31 March 2021:

	£
Trading income	175,000
Interest income	28,000
Chargeable gains	12,000

As at 1 April 2020 the company had trading losses brought forward of £180,000. The company always claims loss relief to the fullest extent possible and as early as possible.

What are Y Ltd's taxable total profits for the year ended 31 March 2021?

- ○ £28,000
- ○ £35,000
- ○ £40,000
- ○ £65,000 (2 marks)

87.5 C Ltd submitted its corporation tax return for the year ended 31 December 2020 on 1 February 2022. This is the first late submission it has made.

What is the fixed penalty due for late submission?

- ○ £100
- ○ £200
- ○ £500
- ○ £1,000 (2 marks)

87.6 P Ltd lets out an unused building on 1 January 2021 for a period of 21 years for a premium of £60,000.

How much of the premium is assessed as property income in P Ltd's taxable total profits for the year ending 31 March 2021?

- ○ £34,800
- ○ £60,000
- ○ £36,000
- ○ £24,000 (2 marks)

87.7 X Ltd has included a deduction in its accounting profit of £3,200 in respect of the annual leasing cost for a car, which has a recommended list price of £16,000 and CO_2 emissions of 120g/km. The lease of the car started on 1 April 2020 and the car has been used for the whole of the 12-month period ended 31 March 2021.

When preparing the adjusted profit for tax purposes what is the allowable deduction in respect of the leasing cost in the year ended 31 March 2021?

- ○ £0
- ○ £480
- ○ £2,720
- ○ £3,200 (2 marks)

87.8 Z Ltd, which prepares accounts to 30 June 2020, rents out a furnished property for an annual rent of £13,200. The tenant pays monthly in arrears and is late paying the June 2020 payment, not making payment until 14 July 2020. Z Ltd has allowable general letting expenses of £1,750. Z Ltd also spent £440 on replacement furniture.

How much must it include in its taxable total profits as its property business income?

- ○ £12,100
- ○ £11,010
- ○ £11,450
- ○ £9,910 (2 marks)

87.9 ABC Ltd is not a large company and prepares accounts to 31 December every year.

By which dates must ABC Ltd file its tax return and pay its corporation tax for the accounting period ended 31 December 2020?

	Return date	*Tax payable date*
○	31 January 2021	31 January 2021
○	31 December 2021	1 October 2021
○	31 January 2021	30 September 2021
○	31 December 2021	31 January 2021

(2 marks)

87.10 XYZ Ltd sold an unwanted factory for £640,000 on 15 March 2021. XYZ Ltd had paid £120,000 for the factory on 2 January 2012. XYZ Ltd incurred expenses of £8,000 in buying the factory and £6,000 in selling the factory.

The indexation factor for the period January 2012 to December 2017 is 0.168 and from January 2012 to March 2021 is 0.229.

What is XYZ Ltd's chargeable capital gain arising on the above disposal?

- ○ £485,840
- ○ £484,496
- ○ £490,496
- ○ £476,688 (2 marks)

87.11 A company has the following expenses in its statement of profit or loss:

Legal fees for the purchase of a new building	£800
Legal fees for defending an action for faulty goods	£1,500
Entertainment of staff (the company has 20 employees)	£3,200

How much must be added back to the company's profit before tax when computing the tax adjusted trading profit?

- ○ £2,300
- ○ £800
- ○ £4,000
- ○ £5,500

(2 marks)

87.12 A company makes up accounts to 31 December annually. For the years ended 31 December 2018 and 31 December 2019 taxable total profits (after deduction of a £1,000 qualifying charitable donation in each year) have been £30,000 and £25,000 respectively. For the year ended 31 December 2020 the company made an adjusted trading loss of £40,000 and had other taxable income of £10,000 and made no qualifying charitable donation.

What is the maximum amount of the loss that the company can claim to carry back to previous years?

- ○ £40,000
- ○ £29,000
- ○ £26,000
- ○ £25,000

(2 marks)

87.13 **Which of the following statements is true about company losses?**

- ○ Property business losses of a company can only be carried forward and used against property business profits of future accounting periods
- ○ Capital losses can always be used against capital gains of the previous accounting period
- ○ Trade losses can be carried forward but only used against trading profits of the same trade in future accounting periods
- ○ On cessation, trade losses can be carried back against total profits for 36 months

(2 marks)

87.14 Star Ltd prepares accounts to 31 December. On 30 September 2021, Star Ltd disposed of a factory which it had used in its trade for proceeds of £600,000. It had acquired the (newly constructed) factory from the developer on 1 June 2020 for £500,000.

What chargeable gain will be included in Star Ltd's corporation tax computation for the year ended 31 December 2021?

Assume FY21 rates and allowances are the same as FY20.

- ○ £80,000
- ○ £100,000
- ○ £120,000
- ○ £108,750

(2 marks)

87.15 On 14 November 2020, Green plc sold a factory for £290,000 and made a chargeable gain (after indexation allowance) of £120,000. The factory had always been used in Green plc's business. On 10 January 2021, Green plc used the proceeds to purchase some fixed plant and machinery for £310,000 which it immediately used in its business. Green plc has claimed to defer the gain of £120,000. Green plc plans to use this plant and machinery until 15 February 2031 when it will be sold.

On which date will the gain deferred become chargeable?

- ○ 15 February 2031
- ○ 14 November 2030
- ○ 10 January 2021
- ○ 10 January 2031 **(2 marks)**

87.16 PLA Ltd has the following results for the year ended 31 March 2021:

Adjusted trading profit	£90,000
Property business income	£14,000
Chargeable gains	£7,000

PLA Ltd has an unused capital loss of £8,000 and a property business loss of £22,000 brought forward as at 1 April 2020. It always makes claims to relieve losses as early as possible.

What are PLA Ltd's taxable total profits (TTP) for the year ended 31 March 2021?

- ○ £81,000
- ○ £97,000
- ○ £90,000
- ○ £82,000 **(2 marks)**

Do you know? – Part F: Value added tax

Check that you can fill in the blanks in the statements below before you attempt any questions. If in doubt, you should go back to your BPP Interactive Text and revise first.

- VAT payable is the total of .... VAT less .... VAT.
- The VAT fraction which we use to calculate standard rate VAT on a VAT inclusive figure is ....
- VAT may be reclaimed on amounts unpaid and written off after .... months.
- The date goods are made available or delivered to the customer is known as the basic ....
- VAT may be reclaimed on fuel for private use so long as output VAT is provided for using ....
- Irrecoverable VAT on cars with private use and business entertaining is known as .... VAT.
- There are two tests for determining when a business must register for VAT: the .... test and the .... test.

TRY QUESTIONS 88, 89, 90, 91, 92, 93, 94, 95, 96, 97, 98, 99, 100, 101 AND 102

Now consolidate your knowledge of Part F of the syllabus by attempting all the MULTIPLE CHOICE QUESTIONS in QUESTION 103.

Did you know? – Part F: Value added tax

Could you fill in the blanks? The answers are in bold. Use this page for revision purposes as you approach the exam.

- VAT payable is the total of **output** VAT less **input** VAT.
- The VAT fraction which we use to calculate standard rate VAT on a VAT inclusive figure is **1/6**.
- VAT may be reclaimed on amounts unpaid and written off after **six** months.
- The date goods are made available or delivered to the customer is known as the basic **tax point**.
- VAT may be reclaimed on fuel for private use so long as output VAT is provided for using **the fuel scale charge**.
- Irrecoverable VAT on cars with private use and business entertaining is known as **blocked** VAT.
- There are two tests for determining when a business must register for VAT: the **historic** test and the **future** test.

TRY QUESTIONS 88, 89, 90, 91, 92, 93, 94, 95, 96, 97, 98, 99, 100, 101 AND 102

Now consolidate your knowledge of Part F of the syllabus by attempting all the MULTIPLE CHOICE QUESTIONS in QUESTION 103.

88 Question with help: Value added tax payable

David has been trading successfully as a carpenter for many years. He is registered for value added tax (VAT), and has quarterly VAT accounting periods based on calendar quarters. He has produced the following statement for his business for the 12 months to 31 December 2020 (all figures exclude VAT):

	£	£
Services performed (Note 1)		88,000
Less expenses:		
bank overdraft interest, accrues evenly during year	280	
new tools (bought July 2020)	2,000	
telephone (Note 2)	440	
motor expenses (Note 3)	17,960	
		(20,680)
Profit		67,320

Notes

1   During the year to 31 December 2020, David's work has been invoiced as follows.

	£
February	14,000
March	6,000
June	12,000
September	18,000
October	24,000
December	14,000
	88,000

2   The telephone bills were due and paid in equal amounts each quarter.

3   Motor expenses (all from VAT registered suppliers) comprise the following.

	£
Fuel (£80 per month and no private mileage)	960
Servicing (March 2020)	200
Repairs (April 2020)	800
New car (invoiced 1 December 2020; private use 25%)	16,000
	17,960

Required

Calculate the VAT payable for each VAT accounting period, and state the due dates for payment of the tax.

Approaching the answer

Step 1	Work out the VAT quarters.
Step 2	Allocate the invoices to each quarter.
Step 3	Work out the output tax for each quarter.
Step 4	Allocate the expenses to each quarter. Is there any irrecoverable tax?
Step 5	Work out the input tax for each quarter.
Step 6	Deduct input tax from output tax for each quarter.
Step 7	Don't forget to state the due dates for payment of the VAT due.

89 Emma — 12 mins

Emma is a sole trader and is registered for value added tax (VAT). In the quarter ended 31 December 2020 Emma had the following transactions.

Sales (exclusive of VAT where applicable)

Standard rated	£450,000
Zero rated	£20,000

Purchases and expenses (inclusive of VAT at standard rate unless stated otherwise)

Purchases of inventory (all standard rated and exclusive of VAT)	£180,000
Wages	£120,000
Electricity	£40,000
Motoring expenses (all business)	£15,000

A discount of 4% on all sales is offered to customers if invoices are settled within 30 days and this is stated on each invoice. Only 50% of all invoices are paid within this time.

Debts of £1,200 and £900 (exclusive of VAT), which were due on 1 February 2020 and 13 September 2020 respectively, were written off by Emma in December 2020.

Required

Calculate the value added tax (VAT) payable or reclaimable by Emma for the quarter ended 31 December 2020. (10 marks)

90 Legg Ltd — 12 mins

Legg Ltd is registered for VAT and only makes standard rated supplies. In the quarter ended 30 September 2020, it had the following transactions.

	£
Purchases	
Inventory for resale	130,000
Office furniture	2,000
Fuel for cars	1,800
Business entertaining for UK customers	350
Sales	
Inventory	250,000

All amounts are VAT inclusive.

The fuel for cars includes private fuel for one car (CO_2 emissions 165g/km) provided to an employee. The VAT inclusive fuel scale charge for this car is £334 per quarter.

Required

Calculate the VAT payable by Legg Ltd for the quarter. (10 marks)

91 AccountsRUs — 12 mins

You are a tax technician working for AccountsRUs, a small accountancy firm. Your line manager has asked you to reply to a letter received on 6 December 2020 from a new client.

The letter is from John Starr, the managing director of Help4U Ltd, a newly formed company situated in Leeds. He has asked for advice on the value added tax (VAT) registration rules.

Required

Draft paragraphs to be included in a letter to John Starr giving brief details of the compulsory registration rules for VAT.

You should include:

- **Details of when registration for VAT is compulsory**
- **The dates by which HMRC must be notified of registration**
- **The effective date of registration**

(Details of voluntary registration for VAT and the rules on deregistration from VAT are not required.)

(10 marks)

92 City Merchandise — 12 mins

City Merchandise Ltd prepares value added tax (VAT) returns on a quarterly basis. It does not operate the cash accounting scheme. During the company's quarter ended 31 December 2020 the following transactions occurred.

	£
Standard rated sales (before any discount)	110,000
Zero rated sales	30,000
Standard rated purchases	60,000

The above three amounts are stated exclusive of VAT where applicable.

The company offers a 5% discount to customers who pay within 30 days and this is stated on its invoices. This discount is offered on all sales but only 50% of customers settle within the discount period.

The company also paid the following expenses during the same VAT quarter.

	£
Electricity	4,000
Wages	28,000
Accountancy fees	1,000
Machine repairs	2,500

The above four amounts are stated inclusive of standard rate VAT where applicable.

Required

Calculate the VAT due for the quarter ended 31 December 2020 and state by when this amount must be paid.

(10 marks)

93 The Stuart Partnership — 6 mins

The Stuart Partnership is registered for value added tax (VAT).

During the quarter ended 31 December 2020 the partnership had the following transactions.

- Standard rated sales of £180,000 excluding VAT.
- Standard rated purchases and expenses amounting to £85,000 excluding VAT.
- A machine was purchased for £7,050 including VAT.
- A car was purchased for £24,000 including VAT and was used by one of the partners for both business and private purposes.

Required

Calculate the VAT that was payable to HM Revenue and Customs (HMRC) by the Stuart Partnership for the quarter ended 31 December 2020. **(5 marks)**

94 Ivor — 6 mins

Ivor is registered for value added tax (VAT) and has recently heard about the annual accounting scheme. He has written to you for advice on this matter.

Required

Prepare draft notes, for a meeting with Ivor, outlining the rules and qualifying conditions of the annual accounting scheme. You are not required to deal with the circumstances in which a trader leaves the scheme.

(5 marks)

95 Resolute plc — 6 mins

The directors of Resolute plc have recently registered for value added tax (VAT). They have discovered that an error has been made on the first VAT return which has been submitted.

Required

Prepare draft notes, for a meeting with the directors, outlining how the error may be corrected. You are not required to deal with any penalties which may arise as a result of the error. **(5 marks)**

96 Bob — 6 mins

Bob has recently registered for value added tax (VAT). He provides building services. He is rather confused about the tax point for the supply of his services, although he understands that it is the deemed date of supply.

Required

Draft paragraphs for an email to be sent to Bob explaining:
- **(a) Two reasons why the tax point is important** **(2 marks)**
- **(b) What is the basic tax point** **(1 mark)**
- **(c) The two circumstances in which the basic tax point may be replaced by an actual tax point** **(2 marks)**

(Total = 5 marks)

Helping hand. This question only requires you to deal with tax point for services – do not deal with the rules for goods.

97 Martha and Dominic — 6 mins

(a) Martha started her own business on 1 October 2020 and has a taxable turnover of £15,000 for each month.

Required

State by when Martha must notify HM Revenue and Customs (HMRC) that she is liable to be registered for value added tax (VAT) and from what date the registration would normally be effective. (3 marks)

(b) Dominic has been in business for many years and is registered for VAT. Due to a downturn in his trade, he believes that his taxable supplies will be substantially reduced in the next 12 months. He wishes to deregister for VAT.

Required

Explain the conditions for Dominic to deregister for VAT and state from what date deregistration would be effective. (2 marks)

(Total = 5 marks)

98 Narrow Ltd — 6 mins

Narrow Ltd is registered for value added tax (VAT).

Required

State five types of expenditure on which the input VAT payable by a registered trader such as Narrow Ltd is treated as 'blocked' and therefore irrecoverable. (5 marks)

99 Celeste — 6 mins

Celeste has been in business for five years and is shortly to register for value added tax (VAT). She understands that some amounts of VAT which she has paid on goods and services prior to registration can be reclaimed.

Required

Draft paragraphs for a letter to Celeste explaining the extent to which she will be able to recover pre-registration VAT. (5 marks)

100 Dana — 6 mins

Dana is employed by LMN Ltd. From 1 February 2021 she is provided with a car with CO_2 emissions of 176g/km.

LMN Ltd pays all the petrol costs in respect of the car. Dana is not required to make any reimbursement in respect of private fuel. Total petrol costs for the quarter ended 31 March 2021 amount to £288 (including VAT).

VAT Scale rate (VAT inclusive) for three-month periods:

CO_2 emissions	£
175	362

Required

(a) **Calculate the output tax and input tax for LMN Ltd for the quarter ended 31 March 2021 in relation to the provision of the car to Dana.** (3 marks)

(b) **Briefly explain the VAT position if Dana bought all the fuel for the car and LMN Ltd reimbursed her for her business use fuel only.** (2 marks)

(Total = 5 marks)

QUESTIONS

101 Blue Ltd — 6 mins

Blue Ltd has recently registered for value added tax (VAT). Below is a sample of the invoice that it intends to use.

SALES INVOICE

Blue Ltd
1 High Street
Birmingham B5 3NJ

Customer: Jolly plc
Address: 11 Broad Road
Cardiff CF2 3PT

Invoice Number 20987
Invoice Date 13 August 2021

	£
Total price (excluding VAT)	6,000.00
Total price (including VAT)	7,200.00

Required

State the FIVE additional pieces of information that Blue Ltd will have to show on the sales invoice in order for it to be valid for VAT purposes. **(5 marks)**

102 Merrill — 6 mins

Merrill is registered for value added tax (VAT). In the quarter ended 31 December 2020, he had the following transactions.

	£
Standard rate sales	36,000
Zero rate sales	9,000
Standard rate purchases	22,000
Zero rate purchases	3,000

All the above figures are VAT-exclusive.

Required

(a) Calculate Merrill's VAT liability for the quarter ended 31 December 2020. **(1 mark)**

(b) State the figures that would be entered in Boxes 1, 3, 4, 5, 6 and 7 on the VAT 100 for the quarter ended 31 December 2020. Assume that Boxes 2, 8 and 9 have already been completed as shown. **(4 marks)**

(Total = 5 marks)

VAT 100

	Box	£
VAT due in this period on sales and other outputs	1	
VAT due in this period on acquisitions from other EC Member States	2	0.00
Total VAT due (the sum of Boxes 1 and 2)	3	
VAT reclaimed in the period on purchases and other inputs, including acquisitions from the EC	4	
Net VAT to be paid to HM Revenue & Customs or reclaimed by you (Difference between Boxes 3 and 4)	5	
Total value of sales and all other outputs excluding any VAT. Include your Box 8 figure	6	
Total value of purchases and all other inputs excluding any VAT. Include your Box 9 figure	7	
Total value of all supplies of goods and related costs, excluding any VAT, to other EC Member States	8	0
Total value of all acquisitions of goods and related costs, excluding any VAT, from other EC Member States	9	0

103 Multiple choice questions: Value added tax

Allow 2 minutes for each question.

103.1 Jason runs a printing business. He completed a contract for a customer on 20 March 2021. The customer paid the full contract price on 26 March 2021 and Jason issued a VAT invoice for the contract on 1 April 2021.

When is the tax point for this supply?

- ○ 20 March 2021
- ○ 26 March 2021
- ○ 1 April 2021
- ○ 30 April 2021 (2 marks)

103.2 For the quarter ended 31 March 2021 Addison Ltd had standard rated sales of £34,000 and standard rated expenses of £5,000. Both figures are inclusive of VAT. Addison Ltd calculates its VAT using the flat rate scheme, with the relevant flat rate scheme percentage being 14%.

How much VAT will Addison Ltd pay for the quarter ended 31 March 2021?

- ○ £4,060
- ○ £4,760
- ○ £3,383
- ○ £3,967 (2 marks)

103.3 During the quarter ended 31 December 2020, Leah makes purchases of office items for her business of £5,700. Her sales for the period are £35,250. All figures are inclusive of VAT and standard rated.

What is her total VAT liability?

- ○ £4,925
- ○ £5,875
- ○ £5,910
- ○ £7,050 (2 marks)

103.4 Y Ltd is registered for value added tax (VAT) and uses the flat rate scheme. In its VAT quarter ended 30 June 2021 it had a tax inclusive turnover of £110,000. This comprises of standard rated sales of £80,000, zero rated sales of £20,000 and exempt sales of £10,000. The flat rate scheme percentage for the company's trading sector is 9%.

The VAT payable by Y Ltd for the quarter ended 30 June 2021 is:

- ○ £9,900
- ○ £7,200
- ○ £9,000
- ○ £8,100 (2 marks)

103.5 Prospect Ltd gives its customers a discount of 5% of the amount payable if they pay within one month of the date of the sales invoice. Details of this discount are **not** stated on invoices.

How will Prospect Ltd calculate its output VAT?

- ○ On the selling price ignoring the discount
- ○ On the selling price less the discount with a further VAT invoice being issued if the discount is not taken
- ○ On the selling price ignoring the discount with a credit note being issued if the discount is taken
- ○ On the actual amount received from the customers (2 marks)

103.6 Joraver completed a contract for a customer on 27 September 2020, the customer having paid the full contract price on 20 September 2020. Joraver issued a VAT invoice for the contract on 3 October 2020.

When is the tax point for this supply?

- ○ 27 September 2020
- ○ 20 September 2020
- ○ 31 October 2020
- ○ 3 October 2020 (2 marks)

103.7 Banana plc is registered for value added tax (VAT). In the quarter ended 31 October 2020 it made taxable supplies (before any discounts) of £120,000, exclusive of VAT. All supplies are standard rated.

Banana plc offers a discount of 4% to all of its customers who settle their invoices within 30 days. Only 50% of all customers (representing half of the £120,000 above) are expected to pay within this time. Details of the discount are included on each VAT invoice.

How much output VAT should Banana plc show on its VAT return for the quarter ended 31 October 2020 in respect of the above supplies?

- ○ £23,040
- ○ £19,200
- ○ £23,520
- ○ £24,000 (2 marks)

103.8 J Ltd received an order for 18,000 widgets on 14 December 2020. J Ltd dispatched these to the customer on 18 December 2020. An invoice was sent on 31 December 2020 and full payment was received on 15 January 2021. J Ltd has value added tax (VAT) quarters coinciding with calendar quarters.

What is the tax point (ie the deemed date of sale for VAT purposes) for the sale of the widgets?

- ○ 18 December 2020
- ○ 31 December 2020
- ○ 15 January 2021
- ○ 31 March 2021 (2 marks)

103.9 **Which of the following is a requirement for a business to be allowed to join the value added tax (VAT) flat rate scheme?**

- ○ A tax exclusive annual taxable turnover of up to £150,000
- ○ A tax exclusive annual total turnover above £85,000
- ○ A tax exclusive annual turnover of up to £85,000
- ○ A tax exclusive standard rated turnover of up to £150,000

(2 marks)

103.10 Kevin has been in business since 1 June 2020 making plastic toys. His total taxable turnover for the seven months ended 31 December 2020 amounted to £45,000. He will prepare his first set of accounts for the 12 months ending 31 May 2021. On 1 January 2021 Kevin received an order for plastic ducks amounting to £88,000 to be delivered later that month.

On what date will HM Revenue and Customs (HMRC) register Kevin for value added tax (VAT) purposes?

- ○ 1 February 2021
- ○ 1 January 2021
- ○ 1 June 2021
- ○ 1 March 2021

(2 marks)

103.11 Minnie makes quarterly value added tax (VAT) returns using the normal calendar quarters. Accounts are made up annually to 30 September. Minnie sold goods amounting to £8,000 on 22 September 2020 with a due date of payment of 10 October 2020. The customer has defaulted on the payment and Minnie has written the debt off in her accounts. Minnie does not use the cash accounting scheme.

In which quarterly VAT return may relief for the impaired debt be claimed?

- ○ VAT quarter ended 31 December 2020
- ○ VAT quarter ended 31 March 2021
- ○ VAT quarter ended 30 June 2021
- ○ VAT quarter ended 30 September 2021

(2 marks)

103.12 Wilson sells inventory for £1,000 (exclusive of value added tax (VAT)) in March 2021. He offers a 10% discount if the invoice is settled within 14 days of the invoice date and details of this discount are included on the invoice. The invoice is actually paid three weeks after the invoice date.

How much VAT must Wilson charge on the sale?

- ○ £167
- ○ £150
- ○ £180
- ○ £200

(2 marks)

103.13 Gundeep is registered for value added tax (VAT). During his accounting period ended 31 March 2021, Gundeep paid £420 (inclusive of VAT) each month for the lease of a motor car for both business and personal use.

What is the input tax recoverable by Gundeep for the month of March 2021 in respect of the leasing cost of the motor car?

- ○ £70
- ○ £35
- ○ £84
- ○ £42

(2 marks)

103.14 VCA plc is registered for value added tax (VAT) and prepares accounts annually to 31 March.

In May 2020 VCA plc purchased a motor car with a CO_2 emission rate of 140 grams per kilometre for £12,000 plus VAT. The motor car is used for both business and private purposes by one of the company's directors.

What is the maximum amount of capital allowances VCA plc can claim, in respect of the motor car, for the year ended 31 March 2021?

- ○ £720
- ○ £2,592
- ○ £2,160
- ○ £864

(2 marks)

103.15 Horace is a sole trader registered for value added tax (VAT). On 29 May 2020 Horace received an order for goods. The goods were collected by the customer on 8 June 2020. An invoice was sent on 19 June 2020 and payment was received on 16 July 2020.

What is the tax point for the sale of the goods?

- ○ 29 May 2020
- ○ 8 June 2020
- ○ 19 June 2020
- ○ 16 June 2020

(2 marks)

Answers

ANSWERS

1 Multiple choice questions: Introduction to the UK tax system

1.1 It is responsible for raising revenue for the government through the tax system.

1.2 (ii) and (iii)

Statutory Instrument 2008/2682 and Taxation of Chargeable Gains Act 1992.

1.3 First Tier Tax Tribunal

Cases which are not complex and do not involve large amounts of tax are heard by the First Tier Tax Tribunal.

1.4 Capital gains tax

Income tax, corporation tax and national insurance are revenue taxes.

1.5 Value added tax

The others are direct taxes.

2 Answer to question with help: Adjustment of profit

George – adjusted trading profit for the year ended 31 January 2021

		£	£
Net profit			10,179
Deduct: bank interest received			(2,000)
			8,179
Add:	wages	0	
	rent, rates, light and heat	0	
	repairs	0	
	professional charges: debt collection	0	
	professional charges: accountancy	0	
	professional charges: advice regarding trading agreement	0	
	other expenses: Chamber of Commerce subscription (trade)	0	
	other expenses: other allowable	0	
	travelling and entertainment: general travelling	0	
	travelling and entertainment: George's car expenses (25% × £640)	160	
	travelling and entertainment: entertaining customers	874	
	impairment debts: trade debtors written off	0	
	impairment debts: non-trade debtors written off	795	
	depreciation	2,874	
			4,703
Adjusted trading profit			12,882

3 Leon

Leon – adjusted trading profit for the year ended 31 October 2020

	£	£
Net profit		40,120
Less: interest received		(240)
rent received		(4,400)
		35,480
Add: wages – staff	0	
wages – national insurance contributions	0	
wages – drawings (Leon)	26,500	
wages – Emily (W)	832	
lighting and heating (£720 × 60%)	432	
depreciation	400	
bank overdraft interest	0	
donations – Oxfam	200	
donations – local nature reserve (small donation to local charity)	0	
legal fees – trade debt collection	0	
legal fees – outstanding rent collection	300	
car expenses – running costs (£2,400 × 70%)	1,680	
car expenses – parking fines (Leon)	120	
car expenses – parking fines (staff)	0	
miscellaneous – internet services	0	
miscellaneous – gifts (drink not allowable)	230	
loss on sale of machinery	200	30,894
		66,374
goods for personal use (£1,400 × 100/80)		1,750
Adjusted trading profit		**68,124**

Working

	£
Paid	6,592
Equivalent amount due:	
(16 × 40) × £9 per hour	(5,760)
Adjustment required ie amount in excess of that paid to staff on similar contracts	832

Helping hand. The legal fees regarding the collection of the outstanding rent are not allowable in computing trading profits as they are not for the purposes of the trade. They would, however, be an allowable deduction from property income (not calculated in this question).

Marking scheme

	Marks
Net profit	½
Interest received	½
Rent received	1
Wages – staff	½
Wages – employer's NIC	½
Wages – Leon	½
Wages – Emily	2
Light and heating	1
Depreciation	½
Bank overdraft interest	½
Donation – Oxfam	½
Donation – small charitable donation	½
Legal fees – debt collecting legal fees	½
Legal fees – rent collection	½
Car expenses – motor running costs (70%)	1
Car expenses – parking fines (Leon)	½
Car expenses – parking fines (Staff)	½
Miscellaneous expenses – internet	½
Miscellaneous expenses – gifts	½
Loss on sale of machinery	½
Goods for personal use	2
	15

4 Sarah

Sarah – lease deduction

Amount taxable on landlord	£
Premium	18,000
Less 2% × £18,000 × (10 – 1)	(3,240)
Property business income	14,760

Sarah's annual deduction

$$\frac{£14,760}{10} = 1,476$$

Marking scheme

	Marks
Amount taxable on landlord	4
Deduction for Sarah	1
	5

5 Answer to question with help: Capital allowances

Capital allowances computation for the year ended 5 April 2021

	AIA	Main Pool	Private use car (1)	Private use car (2)		Allowances
	£	£	£	£		£
Balances b/f		31,200	600			
Additions qualifying for AIA						
01.05.20 Plant	25,000					
AIA	(25,000)					25,000
Additions not qualifying for AIA						
18.08.20 Car				19,000		
Disposals						
20.04.20 Plant (cost)		(10,000)				
21.05.20 Car			(920)			
Balancing charge			(320)	× 75%		(240)
09.09.20 Plant		(800)				
		20,400				
WDA @ 18%		(3,672)				3,672
WDA @ 18%				(3,420)	× 75%	2,565
Balances c/f		16,728		15,580		
Allowances						30,997

6 Jim

(a) **Jim – calculation of adjusted profits**

Period ending 31 May 2022

	£
Profit per accounts	1,415,602
Less capital allowances (W)	(1,335,602)
Adjusted profit	80,000

Year ending 31 May 2023

	£	£
Profit per accounts		1,660,000
Add: depreciation	12,000	
warehouse (capital, qualifying for SBAs)	123,649	
goods for own use (£2,850 × 100/75)	3,800	
		139,449
		1,799,449
Less: interest received	3,200	
capital allowances (W1)	1,293	
SBAs (W2)	3,400	
		(7,893)
Adjusted profit		1,791,556

Workings

W1 Capital allowances

	AIA £	Main pool £	Allowances £
P/e 31.05.22			
Addition qualifying for AIA			
18.05.22 Plant and machinery	1,342,876		
AIA £1,000,000 × 16/12	(1,333,333)		1,333,333
Transfer balance to pool	9,453	9,453	
WDA @ 18% × 16/12		(2,269)	2,269
Balances c/f		7,184	
Allowances			1,335,602
Y/e 31.5.22			
WDA @ 18%		(1,293)	1,293
Balances c/f		5,891	
Allowances			1,293

W2 Structures and buildings allowances (SBAs)

£123,649 × 3% × 11/12 = £3,400

(b) **Jim – trading income for first four years of trading**

16 months to 31.05.22	£80,000
Y/e 31.05.23	£1,794,956
1st tax year – 2020/21 – actual	
01.02.21 to 05.04.21 2/16 × £80,000	£10,000
2nd tax year – 2021/22 – actual	
06.04.21 to 05.04.22 12/16 × £80,000	£60,000
3rd tax year – 2022/23	
12 months to 31.05.23 12/16 × £80,000	£60,000
4th year – 2023/24 CYB	
Y/e 31.05.23	£1,791,556

Marking scheme

				Marks
(a)	(i)	*Period ending 31 May 2022*		
		Capital allowances	2	
		Adjusted profit	1	
				3
	(ii)	*Year ending 31 May 2023*		
		Depreciation	1	
		Warehouse	1	
		Goods for own use	1	
		Bank interest deduction	1	
		Capital allowances	1	
		SBAs	1	
		Adjusted profit	1	
				7
(b)		First tax year	1½	
		Second tax year	1½	
		Third tax year	1	
		Fourth tax year	1	
				5
				15

7 Amanda

(a) **Trading profits y/e 31.5.23**

	£	£
Net profit		7,760
Less bank interest		(450)
		7,310
Add		
Private use electricity		
£810 × 40%	324	
Accountant's fees	0	
Depreciation	120	
Drawings	640	
Private use car expenses		
£1,840 × 40%	736	1,820
		9,130
Less capital allowances		(3,442)
Trading profit		5,688

(b) **Trading profits 2020/21 to 2023/24**

2020/21

1st year – actual

	£	£
01.12.20 to 05.04.21		
4/6 × £4,260		2,840

2021/22

2nd year – first 12 months

01.12.20 to 31.05.21	4,260	
01.06.21 to 30.11.21		
6/12 × £8,190	4,095	8,355

2022/23

3rd year – period of account ending in tax year

Y/e 31.05.22	8,190

2023/24

Y/e 31.05.23	5,688

(c) **Overlap profits**

	£
01.12.20 to 05.04.21	2,840
01.06.21 to 30.11.21	4,095
Total overlap profits	6,935

ANSWERS

Marking scheme

			Marks
(a)	Adjustments – bank interest	1	
	– electricity	1	
	– accountant's fees	1	
	– depreciation	1	
	– drawings	1	
	– car	1	
	– CAs	1	
			7
(b)	2020/21	2	
	2021/22	2	
	2022/23	1	
	2023/24	1	
			6
(c)	01.12.20 to 05.04.21	1	
	01.06.21 to 30.11.21	1	
			2
			15

8 Ian

(a) **Ian – opening year assessable profits**

				£
Year 1	2018/19	Actual basis		
		1 February 2019 to 5 April 2019		
		2/5 × £18,000		7,200
Year 2	2019/20	First 12 months of trading		
		1 February 2019 to 30 June 2019		18,000
		1 July 2019 to 31 January 2020		
		7/12 × £30,000		17,500
				35,500
Year 3	2020/21	Current year basis		
		Y/e 30 June 2020		30,000

Helping hand. You must state the actual tax years to which the profits relate, not just Year 1, Year 2 etc.

(b) **Ian – overlap profits**

	£
1 February 2019 to 5 April 2019	7,200
1 July 2019 to 31 January 2020	17,500
Total overlap profits	24,700

Marking scheme

		Marks
(a)	2018/19	3
	2019/20	3
	2020/21	2
		8
(b)	Overlap: first period	1
	Overlap: second period	1
		2
		10

9 Jackie

	£	£
2016/17		
1st year – 01.05.16 to 05.04.17		
11/15 × £18,000		13,200
2017/18		
2nd year 12 months to 31.07.17 (01.08.16 to 31.07.17)		
12/15 × £18,000		14,400
Overlap period is 01.08.16 to 05.04.17		
ie 8/15 × £18,000 = £9,600		
2018/19		
3rd year y/e 31.07.18		11,700
2019/20		
Y/e 31.07.19		8,640
2020/21		
Y/e 31.07.20	6,800	
P/e 28.02.21	4,100	
	10,900	
Less overlap relief	(9,600)	1,300

Marking scheme

	Marks
2016/17	2
2017/18	2
Overlap profits	1
2018/19	1
2019/20	1
2020/21	3
	10

10 Owen

Owen – opening year tax assessments

2019/20	Actual 1 October 2019 to 5 April 2020 6/7 × £21,000	£18,000
2020/21	First 12 months of trading 1 October 2019 to 30 September 2020 £21,000 + (£72,000 × 5/12)	£51,000
Following tax years	Current year basis	

Helping hand. You must state the actual tax years, not just Year 1, Year 2.

Marking scheme

	Marks
2019/20	
Actual basis	½
Basis period	½
Assessment	1
2020/21	
First 12 months of trading	½
Basis period	½
Assessment	1½
Following tax years	
CYB	½
	5

11 Donna

(a) Factors that will influence an individual's choice of loss relief claim are:

(i) The rate of income tax at which relief will be obtained, with preference being given to income charged at the additional rate of 45%, then the higher rate of 40%.

(ii) The timing of the relief obtained, with a claim against general income of the current year or preceding year resulting in earlier relief than a carry forward claim against future trading profits.

(iii) The extent to which the personal allowance will be wasted by using a claim against general income.

(b) **Donna – taxable income**

	2019/20 £	2020/21 £	2021/22 £
Trading income	75,900	0	18,600
Less trading loss relief carried forward	(0)	(0)	(7,000)
	75,900	0	11,600
Property business income	2,100	3,800	2,000
	78,000	3,800	13,600
Less trading loss relief against general income (N)	(78,000)	(0)	(0)
Net income	0	3,800	13,600
Less personal allowance	(0)	(3,800)	(12,500)
Taxable income	0	0	1,100

Note. Loss relief has been claimed against general income for 2019/20 since this gives relief at the earliest date and at the highest rate of tax. No claim should be made to set the loss against general income in 2020/21 since this is already covered by the personal allowance for that year.

Trading loss memorandum

	£
Loss 2020/21	85,000
Less used 2019/20	(78,000)
Available for c/f	7,000
Less used 2021/22	(7,000)
Loss unused	0

Marking scheme

			Marks
(a)	Rate of tax	1	
	Timing of relief	1	
	Waste of personal allowance	1	
			3
(b)	Trading income	1	
	Trading loss relief carried forward	1	
	Property income	1	
	No relief claimed against general income in year of loss	1	
	Trading loss relief against general income in preceding year	2	
	Personal allowances	1	
			7
			10

12 Answer to question with help: Partnerships

Partners share of profits

	Total £	Clare £	Justin £	Malcolm £
Y/e 31.01.21				
01.02.20 to 30.04.20				
(3/12 × £117,000) 29,250		9,750	19,500	0
01.05.20 to 31.01.21				
(9/12 × £117,000) 87,750		29,250	29,250	29,250
	117,000	39,000	48,750	29,250
Y/e 31.01.22	72,000	24,000	24,000	24,000

Taxable amounts 2020/21

	Clare £	Justin £	Malcolm £
Clare and Justin: y/e 31.01.21	39,000	48,750	
Malcolm: 01.05.20 – 05.04.21 (first year actual basis)			
01.05.20 to 31.01.21			29,250
01.02.21 to 05.04.21 (2/12 × £24,000)			4,000
			33,250

13 Carol, Wendy and Bob

Carol, Wendy and Bob – taxable income y/e 31.1.21

	Total £	Carol £	Wendy £	Bob £
Salary – Carol	10,000	10,000		
Interest on capital	2,800			2,800
Bal. in PSR (3:1:1)	67,200	40,320	13,440	13,440
	80,000	50,320	13,440	16,240

Marking scheme

	Marks
Salary	1
Interest	1
Balance	3
	5

14 Peter, Sam and Martha

(a) **Peter, Sam and Martha – partnership profits y/e 31 December 2019 and y/e 31 December 2020**

Year to 31 December 2019

	Peter £	Sam £	Martha £	Total £
Salary	10,000	10,000	10,000	30,000
Balance 40:40:20	12,000	12,000	6,000	30,000
	22,000	22,000	16,000	60,000

Year to 31 December 2020

	Peter £	Sam £	Martha £	Total £
First 9 months				
Salary × 9/12	7,500	7,500	7,500	22,500
Balance 40:40:20	4,500	4,500	2,250	11,250
	12,000	12,000	9,750	33,750
Last 3 months				
Salary × 3/12	2,500	2,500	–	5,000
Balance 50:50	3,125	3,125	–	6,250
	5,625	5,625	–	11,250
Totals	17,625	17,625	9,750	45,000

(b) **Martha – taxable profits 2019/20 and 2020/21**

2019/20	CYB – year ended 31 December 2019		£16,000
2020/21	CYB – period end 30 September 2020	£9,750	
	Overlap profits	£(4,000)	£5,750

> **Helping hand.** Don't forget to deduct overlap profits in the last tax year where there is a cessation.

Marking scheme

			Marks
(a)	Salary	1	
	Balance 40:40:20	1	
	Salary × 9/12	1½	
	Balance 40:40:20	1½	
	Salary × 3/12	1	
	Balance 50:50	1	
			7
(b)	Martha: year ended 31 December 2019	1	
	Martha: period ended 30 September 2020	1	
	Martha: overlap profits	1	
			3
			10

ANSWERS

15 Norman

Norman – full self-employed supplementary pages

Box 15	90000
Box 17	20000
Box 20	4200
Box 24	1000
Box 31	25200
Box 35	840
Box 46	840
Box 47	65640

Marking scheme

	Marks
Boxes 15, 17, 20, 24, 35, 46 (½ mark each)	3
Boxes 31, 47 (1 mark each)	2
	5

16 Danny

(a) **Danny – taxable profit 2020/21**

Actual basis 6 October 2020 to 5 April 2021	£
06.10.20 to 31.12.20	
£126,000 × 3/12 × 1/3	10,500
01.01.21 to 05.04.21	
£90,000 × 3/12 × 1/3	7,500
	18,000

(b) **Danny – short partnership supplementary page**

Box 3	06 10 2020
Box 6	06 10 2020
Box 7	05 04 2021
Box 8	10500
Box 9	7500
Box 16	18000

> **Helping hand.** The figure in Box 8 is Danny's share of the partnership profit which will be shown on the partnership's return for 2020/21 which is based on the year ended 31 December 2020. However, Danny is also taxable in 2020/21 on his share of the partnership profit from 1 January 2021 to 5 April 2021 and so this amount must be shown in Box 9 to give the full taxable trading profit for the tax year. Overlap profits will be shown on the 2021/22 return.

Marking scheme

		Marks
(a)	06.10.20 to 31.12.20	1
	01.01.21 to 05.04.21	1
		2
(b)	½ mark for each entry	3
		5

17 Multiple choice questions: Adjusted profit/loss computations for trades and professions

17.1 £3,220

All three items are disallowed and must be added back.

17.2 1 January 2020 to 5 April 2020 and 1 November 2020 to 31 December 2020

First tax year (2019/20)
Actual basis
Basis period 01.01.20 to 05.04.20

Second tax year (2020/21)
Period of account in 2nd year less than 12 months
Basis period 01.01.20 to 31.12.20

Third tax year (2021/22)
Current year basis
Basis period 01.11.20 to 31.10.21

Overlap profits
Period of overlap 01.01.20 to 05.04.20 and 01.11.20 to 31.12.20

17.3 £7,800

Last tax year (2020/21)

Basis period 01.01.20 to 31.03.21

	£
Y/e 31.12.20	5,600
P/e 31.03.21	4,500
	10,100
Less overlap profits	(2,300)
	7,800

17.4 £3,745

Y/e 31.3.21

	£
(£50,000 − £9,500) = £40,500 × 9%	3,645
(£55,000 − £50,000) = £5,000 × 2%	100
	3,745

17.5 £750

	Private use asset £	Allowances £
TWDVs b/f	7,000	
Disposal	(6,000)	
Balancing allowance	1,000 × 75%	750

17.6 £5,000

£60,000/3 = £20,000 × 3/12 (01.01.21 to 05.04.21) = £5,000

17.7 The cost of redecorating his showroom

The other expenditure is capital expenditure and so is not allowable.

17.8 £17,000

The business ceases in 2020/21 and therefore the basis period is the entire period from the end of the basis period for 2019/20 (ie 1 August 2019 to 31 December 2020). This amount can then be reduced by the unused overlap profit.

(£14,000 + £7,000) − £4,000 = £17,000

17.9 6 April 2020 to 5 April 2021

If there is no period of account ending in 2020/21, the assessment is on an actual basis.

17.10 £18,000

2020/21 is the second tax year of Cherry's business. The basis period for this year is the 12 months ending on the accounting date. Therefore 12/14 × £21,000 = £18,000.

17.11 £7,300

Depreciation is not an allowable expense (usually being replaced by capital allowances), legal fees for acquiring (not renewing) short leases and entertainment of customers are also not allowable expenses for tax purposes.

17.12 £900

Motor cars are not entitled to the annual investment allowance so the writing down allowance (WDA) applies. The car is special rate expenditure so the WDA is 6%. The WDA is restricted because of Louella's private use. The WDA is therefore £20,000 × 6% × 75% = £900.

17.13 £2,553

> **Examining team's comments.** This question was set in the June 2019 examination and is a question that caused problems.
>
> Class 4 NIC is payable by the self-employed and is calculated only by reference to taxable profits. The majority of candidates wrongly included the property income figure in their calculation and incorrectly selected the third option.
>
> Well prepared candidates ignored property income, reduced the tax adjusted profit by the 'nil band' of £9,500 and the remainder was multiplied by 9% to give the correct answer of £2,475.
>
> Future candidates are encouraged to improve their chances of passing by practising multiple choice questions, available through approved learning providers, as much as possible.

17.14 £7,000

The qualifying cost excludes legal fees, so is £400,000. The WDA is time-apportioned in the accounting period that the building is brought into qualifying use.

18 Answer to question with help: Income tax liability

	Non-savings £	Savings £	Dividends £	Total £
Employment income	53,320			
Building society interest		4,915		
Lotto winnings		0		
Dividend income			1,500	
Total income	53,320	4,915	1,500	59,735
Less eligible interest	(800)			(800)
Net income	52,520	4,915	1,500	58,935
Less personal allowance	(12,500)	0	0	(12,500)
Taxable income	40,020	4,915	1,500	46,435

Income tax

	£
Non-savings income	
37,500 × 20%	7,500
2,520 (40,020 – 37,500) × 40%	1,008
Savings income	
500 × 0% (savings income nil rate band)	0
4,415 (4,915 – 500) × 40%	1,766
Dividend income	
1,500 × 0% (dividend nil rate band)	0
Income tax liability	10,274
Less tax deducted under PAYE	(7,500)
Balance of tax still to pay	2,774

19 Fred

Fred – taxable benefits 2020/21

		£	£
House	Annual value	3,150	
	Additional benefit: £(305,000 – 75,000) @ 2.25%	5,175	8,325
Furniture	£8,000 × 20% × 3/12		400
Total benefits			8,725

Helping hand. The market value when Fred starts to occupy the house is not relevant because the house had been acquired less than six years before his first use.

Marking scheme

	Marks
House: annual value	1
House: additional charge	2
Furniture	2
	5

20 Linda

Linda – income tax payable 2020/21

	Non-savings income £	Savings income £	Dividend income £	Total £
Employment income (W)	56,000			
Property income	3,000			
Bank interest		2,000		
Dividend			3,000	
National savings certificate interest		0		
National savings investment account interest		400		
Net income	59,000	2,400	3,000	64,400
Less personal allowance	(12,500)			(12,500)
Taxable income	46,500	2,400	3,000	51,900

> **Helping hand.** Don't forget to use a zero to show that the national savings certificates interest is not taxable – if you just leave the item out you will not get credit for this point.

Tax payable	£
Non-savings income	
£37,500 × 20%	7,500
£9,000 (46,500 – 37,500) × 40%	3,600
Savings income	
£500 × 0%	0
£1,900 (2,400 – 500) × 40%	760
Dividend income	
£2,000 × 0%	0
£1,000 (3,000 – 2,000) × 32.5%	325
Tax liability	12,185
Less PAYE	(10,600)
Tax payable	1,585

Working

Employment income	£
Salary	50,000
Bonus received February 2021	8,000
Bonus received May 2021 (taxable 2021/22)	0
Employer pension contributions (exempt benefit)	0
	58,000
Less: professional subscription	(200)
employee pension contribution	(1,800)
Employment income	56,000

Marking scheme

	Marks
Employment income:	
Salary	½
Bonuses – amount taxable in 2020/21	2
Professional subscription	1
Employee pension contribution	1
Employer pension contribution	1
Property income	1
Bank interest	1
Dividend	1
National savings certificates interest	1
National savings investment account	1
Personal allowance	1
Tax liability	3
Tax deducted	½
	15

21 Mary

Mary – taxable benefits 2020/21

Car

		£
CO_2 emission (rounded down)	120	
Base figure	(55)	
	65	
Divided by 5	13	
Starting percentage	14	
Diesel addition	4	
Final percentage	31	
List price	£15,000	
Benefit £15,000 × 31% × 7/12		2,712
Fuel		
£24,500 × 31% × 7/12		4,430
(partial contributions are not deductible)		
Total benefits for 2020/21		7,142

ANSWERS

Marking scheme

	Marks
Car	
CO_2 emissions rounded down less base figure	1
Divide by 5	½
Starting percentage	½
Diesel addition	½
List price	½
Benefit	1
Fuel	
Calculation and no deduction for contribution	1
	5

22 Valero

(a) **Valero – taxable benefits 2020/21**

	£	£	£
Loan			
Average method			
$\frac{£40,000 + £32,000}{2} =$	36,000		
£36,000 × 2.25%	810		
Strict method			
£40,000 × 2.25% × 3/12	225		
£32,000 × 2.25% × 9/12 =	540		
	765		
Valero should choose to use the strict method as it gives a lower benefit figure			
Benefit using strict method	765		
Less interest paid			
£40,000 × 0.5% × 3/12	(50)		
£32,000 × 0.5% × 9/12	(120)		595
Cinema system			
Use for 2020/21 £4,000 × 20%		800	
Gift: current market value;	900		
or			
original cost	4,000		
less 20% for:			
2017/18	(800)		
2018/19	(800)		
2019/20	(800)		
2020/21	(800)		
	800		
The higher amount is taken		900	1,700
Pension contributions			0
Total benefits for 2020/21			2,295

(b) PQT plc must submit form P11D to HM Revenue and Customs (HMRC) in respect of Valero by 6 July 2021.

Marking scheme

		Marks
(a)	*Loan*	
	Average method	1
	Strict method	1
	Valero would choose strict method	½
	Deduct interest paid	1
	Cinema system	
	Use benefit for year	1
	Gift: market value	½
	Gift: original cost less benefits taxed	2
	Take higher amount	1
	Pension contributions	1
		9
(b)	P11D form by 6 July 2021	1
		10

23 Patrick

Patrick – income tax payable 2020/21

	£	Total £	Non-savings income £	Savings income £	Dividend income £
Salary	158,850				
Pension contributions (£400 × 12)	(4,800)				
Employment income		154,050	154,050		
Trading income		20,000	20,000		
Dividends		4,000			4,000
Bank interest		3,000		3,000	
NSC interest		0		0	
Premium bond winnings		0		0	
Net income		181,050	174,050	3,000	4,000

No PA as net income exceeds £125,000

Basic rate limit increased: £37,500 + (£800 × 100/80) = £38,500
Higher rate limit increased: £150,000 + (£800 × 100/80) = £151,000

	£		£
Non-savings basic rate	38,500	× 20%	7,700
Non-savings higher rate	112,500	× 40%	45,000
	151,000		
Non-savings additional rate	23,050	× 45%	10,373
	174,050		
Savings additional rate	3,000	× 45%	1,350
Dividend nil rate	2,000	× 0%	0
Dividend additional rate	2,000	× 38.1%	762
	4,000		
Tax liability			65,185
PAYE			(53,400)
Tax payable			11,785

No savings income nil rate band as additional rate taxpayer

> **Helping hand.** Remember that the higher rate band is always £112,500. This is because it starts at the basic rate limit and ends at the higher rate limit, both of which are increased by the gift aid donation.

Marking scheme

	Marks
Salary	1
Pension contributions	1
Trading income	1
Dividend	1
Bank interest	1
National savings certificates – exempt	½
Premium bond winnings – exempt	½
Personal allowance not available	1
Basic rate limit increased for gift aid	2
Higher rate limit increased for gift aid	2
Basic rate band tax	½
Higher rate tax on non-savings income	½
Additional rate tax on non-savings income	½
Additional rate tax on savings income (no nil rate band)	1
Nil rate tax on dividend income	½
Additional rate tax on dividend income	½
PAYE	½
	15

24 Peppy

Peppy – taxable benefits 2020/21

	£	£
Car		
(125-55)/5 = 14 + 14 = 28%		
List cost	28,000	
Less capital contribution (max)	(5,000)	
	23,000	
£23,000 × 28% × 9/12 (01.07.20 to 05.04.21)	4,830	
Less private use payment £40 × 9	(360)	4,470

Marking scheme

	Marks
Base figure	½
CO_2 calculation	1
Starting percentage	½
List price as reduced	1
Benefit	1
Contribution for private use	1
	5

25 Beryl

Beryl – taxable benefits 2020/21

	£	£
Medical treatment		
Up to £500		0
Staff suggestion scheme		
Less than £5,000		0
Mileage		
10,000 × (0.55 – 0.45)		1,000
Relocation expenses		
Expenses paid	10,000	
Less exempt	(8,000)	2,000
Workplace nursery		
Wholly exempt		0
Flowers		
Trivial benefit up to £50		0
Loan		
£15,000 × 2.25% × 8/12		
(average and strict method give the same result)		225
Total benefits		3,225

Helping hand. Medical treatment up to £500 per tax year is an exempt benefit if it is recommended in writing by a health professional (eg doctor, nurse) and the purpose of the treatment is to assist the employee to return to work after a period of injury or ill-health of at least 28 days.

Marking scheme

	Marks
Medical treatment	½
Staff suggestion scheme award	½
Mileage	1
Relocation expenses	1
Workplace nursery	½
Trivial benefit	½
Loan	1
	5

26 Coral

Coral – income tax payable 2020/21

	Non-savings income £	Savings income £	Dividend income £	Total £
Employment income (W1)	108,200			
Property income				
£4,800 ÷ 2	2,400			
BI		1,100		
BSI (in ISA)		0		
Lotto prize		0		
Dividends			3,000	
Net income	110,600	1,100	3,000	114,700
Less personal allowance (W2)	(7,650)			(7,650)
Taxable income	102,950	1,100	3,000	107,050

Income tax	£
Non-savings income	
£42,500 × 20% (W3)	8,500
£60,450 (102,950 – 42,500) × 40%	24,180
Savings income	
£500 × 0%	0
£600 (1,100 – 500) × 40%	240
Dividend income	
£2,000 × 0%	0
£1,000 (3,000 – 2,000) × 32.5%	325
Tax liability	33,245
Less PAYE	(28,640)
Tax payable	4,605

Workings

1   *Employment income*

	£
Salary	99,000
Bonus	7,000
Benefits	2,500
	108,500
Less: payroll deduction scheme	(120)
professional subscription	(180)
Employment income	108,200

2   *Personal allowance*

	£
Net income	114,700
Less pension contribution £4,000 × 100/80	(5,000)
Adjusted net income	109,700
Less income limit	(100,000)
Excess	9,700
Personal allowance	12,500
Less ½ × £9,700	(4,850)
Adjusted personal allowance	7,650

3   *Pension contributions*

Increase basic rate limit by £4,000 × 100/80 = £5,000 + £37,500   £42,500

> **Helping hand.** Personal pension contributions are given basic rate tax relief at source by the taxpayer making a contribution net of 20% tax. Higher rate relief is given by increasing the basic rate limit by the gross contribution.

Marking scheme

	Marks
Employment income (½ for each item)	2½
Property income	1½
Bank interest	1
BSI – exempt	½
Lotto prize – exempt	½
Dividends	1
Personal allowance	2½
Increase in basic rate limit	2
Tax on non-savings income	1
Tax on savings income	1
Tax on dividend income	1
PAYE	½
	15

27 Stephen

Stephen – income tax 2020/21

	Non-savings income £	Savings income £	Dividend income £	Total £
Employment income (W)	54,960			54,960
Building society interest		1,375		1,375
National Savings certificate interest		0		0
Dividend			1,200	1,200
Net income	54,960	1,375	1,200	57,535
Less personal allowance	(12,500)			(12,500)
Taxable income	42,460	1,375	1,200	45,035

	£
Tax payable	
Non-savings income	
£37,500 × 20%	7,500
£4,960 (42,460 – 37,500) × 40%	1,984
Savings income	
£500 × 0%	0
£875 (1,375 – 500) × 40%	350
Dividend income	
£1,200 × 0%	0
Tax liability	9,834
Less: PAYE	(7,900)
Tax payable	1,934

ANSWERS

Working: Employment income

		£	£
Salary			50,730
Car:	List price:	£22,000	
	CO_2 emissions (rounded down)	105	
	Base figure	(55)	
		50	
	Divide by 5	10	
	Basic %	14	
		24	
	Diesel addition	4	
	Final percentage	28	
	28% × £22,000	6,160	
	Less £250 × 12 months	(3,000)	3,160

Note. There is no fuel benefit because Stephen pays for all his private fuel.

Medical insurance:	Cost to employer	750
Computer:	£1,600 × 20%	320
Birthday cake:	Trivial benefit not exceeding £50	0
Employment income		54,960

Marking scheme

	Marks
Employment income:	
Salary	1
Car benefit	3
No fuel benefit	1
Medical insurance	1
Computer	1
Birthday cake	1
Building society interest	1
NS&I certificate interest – exempt	1
Dividend	1
Personal allowance	1
Tax liability	2½
Tax deducted at source	½
	15

28 Alison

Alison – income tax 2020/21

	Non-savings income £	Savings income £	Dividend income £	Total £
Trading profit (W)	12,000			12,000
Employment income	14,500			14,500
Building society interest		1,375		1,375
Premium bond prize		0		0
Dividends			3,400	3,400
Net income	26,500	1,375	3,400	31,275
Less personal allowance	(12,500)			(12,500)
Taxable income	14,000	1,375	3,400	18,775

Premium bond prize is tax free.

Tax payable   £

Non-savings income
£14,000 × 20%   2,800

Savings income
£1,000 × 0%   0
£375 (1,375 – 1,000) × 20%   75

Dividend income
£2,000 × 0%   0
£1,400 (3,400 – 2,000) × 7.5%   105
Tax liability   2,980
Less PAYE   (400)
Tax payable   2,580

Working

2020/21 first year of trading. Actual basis 1.7.20 to 5.4.21

	£
6 months to 31 December 2020	7,500
3 months from y/e 31 December 2021 3/12 × £18,000	4,500
	12,000

> **Helping hand.** Basic rate taxpayers are entitled to a savings income nil rate band of £1,000. All taxpayers are entitled to a dividend nil rate band of £2,000.

Marking scheme

	Marks
Trading profit	2
Employment income	1
Building society interest	1
Premium bond prize	1
Dividends	1
Personal allowance	1
Tax payable	3
	10

29 Liam and Jordan

Liam
Class 1 employee contributions
Calculated on salary only – £4,300 per month
Employee threshold £9,500 ÷ 12 = £792
Upper earnings limit £50,000 ÷ 12 = £4,167

	£
£(4,167 – 792) = £3,375 × 12% × 12	4,860
£(4,300 – 4,167) = £133 × 2% × 12	32
	4,892

Jordan

Class 2	£	£
52 weeks × £3.05		159
Class 4		
£(50,000 – 9,500) = £40,500 × 9%	3,645	
£(56,000 – 50,000) = £6,000 × 2%	120	3,765
		3,924

Marking scheme

	Marks
Class 1	2
Class 2	1
Class 4	2
	5

30 Declan

Declan – taxable benefits for 2020/21

			£
Car:	List price:	80,000	
	Less contribution (limited to £5,000)	(5,000)	
		75,000	
	Benefit percentage (from tax tables)	6%	
	6% × £72,000	4,320	
	Less contribution to private use (£100 × 12 months)	(1,200)	
			3,120
	Fuel benefit (£24,500 × 6%)		1,470
Computer:			
	£800 × 20%		160

Marking scheme

	Marks
Car benefit:	
List price	½
Capital contribution	1
Percentage	½
Taxable benefit	1½
Fuel benefit	½
Computer	1
	5

31 Nancy

Nancy – taxable benefits for 2020/21

	£	£
Loan:		
Average method		
$\dfrac{£(20,000 + 14,000)}{2} \times 2.25\%$	383	
Less: interest paid		
£20,000 × 1% × 9/12	(150)	
£14,000 × 1% × 3/12	(35)	
	198	
Strict method		
£20,000 × 2.25% × 9/12	338	
£14,000 × 2.25% × 3/12	79	
	417	
Less: interest paid		
£20,000 × 1% × 9/12	(150)	
£14,000 × 1% × 3/12	(35)	
	232	
HMRC will usually only choose strict method if it appears that the average method is being exploited by the taxpayer which does not appear to be the case here.		198
Expenses:		
Overseas trips – daily amount in excess of £10 therefore full amount is taxable £12 × 60 days		720
UK trips – daily amount below £5 therefore exempt		0

Marking scheme

	Marks
Loan:	
Average method	1
Strict method	1½
HMRC choice	½
Expenses:	
Overseas	1
UK	1
	5

32 Stuart

Stuart – income tax payable 2020/21

	Non-savings income £	Savings income £	Dividend income £	Total £
Partnership profit (W)	69,150			69,150
National savings certificate		0		0
NS investment a/c		1,665		1,665
Premium bond prize		0		0
Dividends			5,000	5,000
Total income	69,150	1,665	5,000	75,815
Less: eligible interest £10,000 × 8%	(800)			(800)
Net income	68,350	1,665	5,000	75,015
Less personal allowance	(12,500)			(12,500)
Taxable income	55,850	1,665	5,000	62,515

Working

£115,250 × 60% = £69,150

Tax payable

	£
Non-savings income	
£39,500 × 20% (W)	7,900
£16,350 (55,850 – 39,500) × 40%	6,540
Savings income	
£500 × 0%	0
£1,165 (1,665 – 500) × 40%	466
Dividend income	
£2,000 × 0%	0
£3,000 (5,000 – 2,000) × 32.5%	975
Tax liability/tax payable	15,881
Less payments on account	(12,000)
Tax to be paid by 31 January 2022	3,881

Working

Increase in basic rate limit £37,500 + (£1,600 × 100/80) = £39,500

Helping hand. Eligible interest is deducted from total income to arrive at net income. Interest on a loan to buy partnership plant qualifies as eligible interest. This means, in the case of Stuart, who is a higher rate taxpayer, that tax relief is given on the interest at the rate of 40%.

Marking scheme

	Marks
Partnership profit	2
National savings certificate interest – exempt	1
National savings interest	1
Premium bond prize – exempt	1
Dividend	1
Eligible interest payment	2
Personal allowance	1
Increase in basic rate limit	2
Non-savings basic rate	½
Non-savings higher rate	½
Savings nil rate	½
Savings higher rate	½
Dividend nil rate	½
Dividend higher rate	½
Payments on account	1
	15

33 Doreen

Doreen – property income 2020/21

	£	£
Rent received £1,200 × 11 months		13,200
Security deposit retained		300
Expenses paid:		
Cleaning	300	
Replacement furniture (cost of replacement only)	1,280	
		(1,580)
Property income		11,920

Marking scheme

	Marks
Rent received	1
Security deposit retained	1
Cleaning	1
Replacement furniture	2
	5

34 Sonia

Sonia – Property income for the tax year 2020/21

	£
Rent: accrued amount	12,000
Less: expenses	
insurance April to December 2020 £300 × 9/12	(225)
insurance January to March 2021 £360 × 3/12	(90)
agent's fees	(600)
table £(750 – 50)	(700)
Property income	10,385

> **Helping hand.** Under the accruals basis, rent is taxable in the tax year in which it accrues, whether or not it is received in that tax year and expenses are deducted for the period for which they accrue.

Marking scheme

	Marks
Rent	1½
Insurance	2
Agent's fees	½
Replacement furniture	1
	5

35 David

Your friend is probably taking advantage of the rent a room scheme. This is a scheme to encourage people to let out spare rooms in their houses. It is part of UK tax law, so it is not in any sense a 'dodge'. It works as follows.

(a) If an individual lets rooms, furnished, in their main residence, and gross rents (before deducting any expenses) in a tax year do not exceed £7,500, the rents are not taxable and any expenses are ignored.

(b) The £7,500 limit is halved to £3,750 if anyone else (including the taxpayer's spouse or civil partner) also receives income from letting accommodation in the property.

(c) If gross rents exceed the limit (£7,500 or £3,750), the taxpayer can choose between the following alternatives.

   (i) Ignore the scheme and be taxed on rents minus expenses.
   (ii) Be taxed on gross rents minus £7,500 (or £3,750), and ignore expenses.

(d) Even if gross rents do not exceed £7,500 (or £3,750), the taxpayer may still choose to ignore the scheme. This can be useful when expenses exceed rents. A loss can then be generated and set against other rental income.

Marking scheme

	Marks
Identify rent a room scheme	1
Furnished rooms	1
Not a tax dodge	1
Main residence	1
Exemption	1
Any one else receiving income	1
Alternative basis if limit exceeded	2
Alternative basis if limit not exceeded	2
	10

36 Jules

Furnished holiday letting advantages

Capital expenditure on furniture allowable when incurred (or capital allowances if accruals basis used) instead of replacement furniture relief.

Income qualifies as relevant earnings for personal pension contributions.

Capital gains tax business reliefs (eg replacement of business assets relief, business asset disposal relief) may be available.

> **Helping hand.** Note that FHLs are treated as a trade but that trade loss relief against general income is not available.

Marking scheme

	Marks
Capital expenditure	2
Pension contributions	1
CGT reliefs	2
	5

37 Jenny

Jenny – income tax payable 2020/21

	Non-savings income £	Savings income £	Dividend income £	Total income £
Salary (W1)	30,302			30,302
Bonus – receipts basis	12,090			11,292
Car benefit				
£12,450 × 12% × 11/12	1,370			2,168
Dividends			10,000	10,000
BI		1,100		1,100
Premium bond prizes		0		
Property income	1,658			1,658
Net income	45,420	1,100	10,000	56,520
Less personal allowance	(12,500)			(12,500)
Taxable income	32,920	1,100	10,000	44,020

	£
Non-savings income	
£32,920 × 20%	6,584
Savings income	
£500 × 0%	0
£600 (1,100 – 500) × 20%	120
Dividend income	
£2,000 × 0%	0
£1,680 (37,700 – 32,920 – 1,100 – 2,000) × 7.5%	126
£6,320 (10,000 – 2,000 – 1,680) × 32.5%	2,054
Tax liability	8,884
Less PAYE	(5,565)
Tax payable	3,319

Workings

1 *Salary*

	£
01.05.20 to 31.12.20	
£32,700 × 8/12	21,800
01.01.21 to 31.03.21	
£32,700 × 104% × 3/12	8,502
	30,302

2 *Gift Aid donation*

	£
£160 × 100/80	200
Increase the basic rate limit by this amount to £(37,500 + 200) =	£37,700

Marking scheme

	Marks
Salary	2
Bonus	1
Car benefit	1½
Dividends	1
Bank interest	1
Premium bond prizes	1
Property income	½
Personal allowance	1
Non savings income – basic rate	1
Savings income – nil rate	½
Savings income – basic rate	½
Dividend income – nil rate	½
Dividend income – basic rate	½
Dividend income – basic rate limit increase	2
Dividend income – higher rate	½
PAYE	½
	15

38 Laslo

Laslo – property income 2020/21 (cash basis)

		£	£
Rent:	£400 × 8		3,200
Less:	insurance paid	360	
	furniture (replacement only)	342	(702)
Property income			2,498

Notes

1. The rent paid due on 6 March 2021 paid on 6 April 2021 will be taxed in 2021/22.
2. The cost of building the garden wall is a capital expense and so not deductible.

Marking scheme

	Marks
Rent received	1½
Insurance paid	1
Furniture	1½
Garden wall (capital)	1
	5

39 Simon

Simon – income tax payable 2020/21

	Total £	Non-savings Income £	Savings £	Dividend £
Salary	70,000			
Bonus	26,760			
	96,760			
Occupational pension (5% × £70,000)	(3,500)			
Professional fees	(390)			
Employment income	92,870	92,870		
Property income £(750 × 12) – 7,500	1,500	1,500		
Bank interest	4,500		4,500	
Dividends	1,000			1,000
ISA dividend	0			0
Net income	99,870	94,370	4,500	1,000
Personal allowance	(12,500)	(12,500)		
	87,370	81,870	4,500	1,000

Tax payable:

	£	£
Non-savings	37,900 × 20% (W)	7,580
	43,970 × 40%	17,588
Savings	500 × 0%	0
	4,000 (4,500 – 500) × 40%	1,600
Dividend	1,000 × 0%	0
		26,768
Less tax deducted at source:		
PAYE		(25,300)
Tax payable		1,468

Working
Increase in basic rate limit: £37,500 + (£320 × 100/80)   £37,900

Marking scheme

	Marks
Salary	1
Bonus	1
Occupational pension	1½
Fees	1
Property business income	1½
Bank interest	1
Dividends	1
ISA dividend – exempt	1
Personal allowance	1
Increase of basic rate limit	2
Non-savings basic rate	½
Non-savings higher rate	½
Savings nil rate	½
Savings higher rate	½
Dividend nil rate	½
Tax deducted at source	½
	15

40 Amber

Amber – taxable benefits 2020/21

House The house was acquired for more than £75,000 and therefore an additional benefit applies. It was purchased more than six years before Amber first occupies it, therefore the market value at occupation is used.

	£	£
Annual value	8,000	
Additional: (£215,000 – £75,000) × 2.25%	3,150	
	11,150	
6 months only – 6/12 × £11,150	5,575	
Less contribution (£600 × 6)	(3,600)	
	1,975	1,975

Parking Exempt — 0
Expenses UK trips – exempt level is £5 per night. Full amount taxable £6 × 80 — 480
Overseas trips – exempt level is £10 per night – full amount exempt — 0
Total benefits — 2,630

Marking scheme

	Marks
House	2
Parking – exempt	1
Expenses	2
	5

41 Hamish

Hamish – income tax payable for the tax year 2020/21

	Non-savings income £	Savings income £	Dividend income £	Total £
Salary	180,000			
Employer pension contributions (exempt)	0			
Less employee pension contributions	(14,000)			
Employment income	166,000			
Building society interest (BSI)		2,000		
Premium bond prize		0		
Dividends			3,000	
Net income	166,000	2,000	3,000	171,000
Less personal allowance (N)	(0)			
Taxable income	166,000	2,000	3,000	171,000

Note. Net income is above £125,000 so no personal allowance is available.

Increase in basic rate limit: £37,500 + (£1,200 × 100/80) = £39,000
Increase in higher rate limit: £150,000 + (£1,200 × 100/80) = £151,500

			£	£
Tax payable:				
Non-savings income:	basic rate		39,000 × 20%	7,800
	higher rate		112,500 × 40%	45,000
			151,500	
	additional rate		14,500 × 45%	6,525
			166,000	
Savings income				
(no nil rate band for additional rate taxpayer)			2,000 × 45%	900
Dividend income:	nil rate		2,000 × 0%	0
Dividend income:	additional rate		1,000 × 38.1%	381
Tax liability				60,606
Less tax deducted at source: PAYE				(59,000)
Tax payable				1,606

Helping hand. There is no savings income nil rate band for an additional taxpayer but all taxpayers are entitled to the dividend nil rate band.

Marking scheme

	Marks
Salary	½
Pension contributions by company	½
Pension contributions by taxpayer	1
Building society interest	½
Dividend	½
Premium bond prize	½
Personal allowance	1½
Increase in basic rate limit	2
Increase in higher rate limit	1
Non-savings income basic rate	1
Non-savings income higher rate	1
Non-savings income additional rate	1
Savings income additional rate (no nil rate band applied)	1½
Dividend nil rate band	1
Dividend income additional rate	1
PAYE	½
	15

42 Paul

Meeting notes

1. The maximum employee contribution on which tax relief is available is the higher of £3,600 or 100% of earned income, subject to an annual allowance of £40,000.

2. Method of relief: if an occupational scheme – the actual payments are deducted from employment income before tax is deducted under PAYE. This gives tax relief at all rates.

    Method of relief: if a personal pension scheme – the amount is paid net of tax at 20% and higher rate relief is given by increasing the basic rate limit by the amount paid grossed up by 100/80.
    This increases the basic rate band for the taxpayer and so the amount of tax payable at the basic rate rather than at the higher rate. If the individual is an additional rate taxpayer, the higher rate limit must also be increased by this gross amount to preserve the amount of the higher rate band and so give additional rate relief.

3   Company contributions are exempt benefits. They are, however, deductible for the purposes of corporation tax.

There is no limit to the amount the employer may contribute, but they always count towards the annual allowance and will also affect the value of the pension fund for the lifetime allowance (£1,073,100).

> **Helping hand.** Make sure that you cover the three issues raised in the question, but do not waste time dealing with other aspects of pensions as such points will not receive any marks.

Marking scheme

	Marks
£3,600 or 100% of earnings	1
Annual allowance	1
Relief for occupational scheme	2
Personal scheme paid net of basic rate tax	1
Basic rate limit increased for higher rate tax relief	1
Higher rate limit increased for additional rate taxpayer	1
Company contributions – exempt benefits	1
Deductible for company	1
No limit, but contribute towards AA and LA	1
	10

43 Lin

Lin – payment dates for the tax year 2020/21

Payments on account are required for income tax and Class 4 national insurance contributions on 31 January in the tax year and 31 July next following the end of the tax year with a balancing payment or repayment on 31 January next following the end of the tax year.

First payment on account – 31 January 2021
50% of 2019/20 income tax and Class 4 contributions
£(16,000 + 3,000) × 50%   £9,500
Second payment on account – 31 July 2021
Calculated as above   £9,500
Balancing payment – 31 January 2022
Balancing payment £(19,300 + 3,500) – (£9,500 × 2)   £3,800

Marking scheme

	Marks
Payment on 31 January 2021	½
Amount of payment	1½
Payment on 31 July 2021	½
Amount of payment	½
Payment on 31 January 2022	½
Balancing payment	1½
	5

ANSWERS

44 Richard

(a) The form required is the P45.

There are four parts.

One part is retained by Richard and the other three parts are given by Richard to Tape Ltd.

(b) The P45 form shows Richard's PAYE code, and details of his income and tax paid to date.

Tape Ltd will use these details to calculate income tax due under PAYE on a cumulative basis when the payroll is next run.

Marking scheme

		Marks	
(a)	P45	½	
	Four parts	½	
	What Richard does with the parts	1	
			2
(b)	Information on P45	1½	
	Used by Tape Ltd to compute IT cumulatively	1½	
			3
			5

45 Alisha

Alisha – tax forms

(a) Form giving details of taxable earnings and tax deducted for 2020/21 – P60, receivable by 31 May 2021.

(b) Form giving details of benefits for 2020/21 – P11D, receivable by 6 July 2021.

(c) Latest date for submission of electronic tax return for 2020/21 – 31 January 2022.

Marking scheme

		Marks	
(a)	Form	1	
	Date	1	
			2
(b)	Form	1	
	Date	1	
			2
(c)	Date		1
			5

46 Barry

(a) Barry should have given notice to HM Revenue and Customs (HMRC) of his chargeability to income tax for 2019/20 by 5 October 2020.

The maximum penalty for careless late notification is 30% of the Potential Lost Revenue (PLR) to HMRC which will be Barry's tax payable on the return for 2019/20.

(b) HMRC must start a compliance check by the first anniversary of the actual filing date of the return.

Some returns are selected for a compliance check enquiry at random.

Other returns are selected for a particular reason, for example, if HMRC believes that there has been an underpayment of tax due to the taxpayer's failure to comply with tax legislation.

Marking scheme

		Marks	
(a)	Notification date	1	
	Maximum penalty	1	
			2
(b)	Date to start check	1	
	Random check	1	
	Failure to comply with legislation	1	
			3
			5

47 Multiple choice questions: Income tax liability

47.1 Dividends from a UK company

The other types of income are all exempt income.

47.2 £3,000

The personal allowance is restricted by half of the excess of net income over £100,000.

£(106,000 − 100,000) = £6,000/2 = £3,000

47.3 £9,000

	£
Salary	6,000
Bonus received 30 June 2020	3,000
Employment income	9,000

47.4 30%

CO_2 emissions are 118g/km, round down to 115g/km

Appropriate percentage: (115 − 55) = 60g/km in excess of threshold

60/5 = 12%

14% + 12% + 4% (diesel addition) = 30%

47.5 Chris

Harry has a permanent workplace in Cardiff and is not entitled to deduct travelling expenses from home to his workplace. Robin has two permanent workplaces so he is not entitled to deduct travelling expenses to either of them. Chris is employed in a temporary workplace for less than 24 months, so travel from home to his temporary workplace is allowable.

47.6 £(800) allowable deduction

	£
Amount reimbursed 8,000 × 35p	2,800
Less: statutory allowance	
8,000 miles @ 45p	(3,600)
Allowable deduction	(800)

47.7 Class 1 employee's contributions on £13,000, Class 1 employer's contributions on £13,000, Class 1A contributions on £400

Class 1 employee's and employer's contributions are generally payable on cash earnings. Class 1A contributions are payable on non-cash benefits by the employer only.

47.8 P11D – 6 July 2021

Taxable benefits are reported on Form P11D which must be provided to HMRC by 6 July following the end of the tax year.

47.9 £300

MV when first provided to any employee for private use × 20% × 5/12

£3,600 × 20% × 5/12 = £300

47.10 £2,100

(£27,000 – £9,500) × 12% = £2,100

47.11 32%

14% + 18% (145 – 55 = 90/5) = 32%

47.12 £1,260

Accommodation provided for private use by an employer is taxed on the annual value plus an additional amount if the accommodation cost the company more than £75,000. The correct calculation of the additional benefit is:

(£131,000 – £75,000) × 2.25% (official rate of interest) = £1,260.

47.13 £168

The £12 per night exceeds the statutory figure of £10 and therefore the whole amount is a taxable benefit. The taxable benefit is £168 (£12 × 14).

47.14 £1,420

Non-savings income is taxed at 20%. Savings income is taxed at 0% where such income falls within the first £5,000 of taxable income and within the savings income nil rate band which is £1,000 for a basic rate taxpayer. The remainder, as in this case, is then taxed at 20%. The tax is therefore:

	£
Non-savings income	
£4,800 × 20%	960
Savings income	
£200 (5,000 – 4,800) × 0% (starting rate band)	0
£1,000 × 0% (savings income nil rate band)	0
£2,300 (3,500 – 200 – 1,000) × 20%	460
Tax liability	1,420

47.15 £3,067

Class 1 employers' national insurance contributions (NIC) are calculated on cash earnings. The first £8,788 is exempt and the remainder is charged at 13.8%. The employment allowance of £4,000 is deducted since Sally is the only employee.

The NIC is therefore £(60,000 − 8,788) × 13.8% = £(7,067− 4,000) = £3,067.

47.16 Travel to and from a permanent place of work

47.17 £542

Total earnings received in December 2020 are £11,000 (£3,000 (£36,000/12) + £8,000).

NIC payable is therefore:

	£
(£4,167 − £792) × 12%	405
(£11,000 − £4,167) × 2%	137
	542

47.18 £5,600

House

	£
Rent received (cash basis)	6,300
Less: expenses paid (cash basis)	(700)
Property income	5,600

Room in own house

Exempt under rent a room (gross rent less than £7,500)

47.19 £16,400

	£
Premium received	20,000
Less £20,000 × 2% × (10 − 1)	(3,600)
	16,400

47.20 £3,600

The maximum amount of contributions attracting tax relief made by an individual in a tax year is the higher of the individual's relevant earnings chargeable to income tax in the year and the basic amount (£3,600 for 2020/21).

47.21 31 January 2023

As an employee with no supplementary income other than interest she need only retain her records for one year after the 31 January following the end of the tax year, otherwise the period would be five years from that date.

47.22 Payments on account 31 January 2021 and 31 July 2021, balancing payment 31 January 2022

Payments on account are due on 31 January in the tax year and 31 July following the end of the tax year. Balancing payment is due on 31 January following the end of the tax year.

47.23 £750

Only the cost of a replacement cooker is allowable. The chairs are not allowable as they are new, not replacement, furniture.

47.24 Payments on account of £6,000 will be made on 31 January and 31 July 2021, with the balance of £3,000 being paid on 31 January 2022.

Payments on account are payable based on 50% of the relevant amount (income tax plus Class 4 NICs) for 2019/20.

47.25 £24,000

	£
Premium received	30,000
Less £30,000 × 2% × (11 – 1)	(6,000)
	24,000

47.26 Five years after the 31 January following the tax year

47.27 £960

The maximum penalty for a careless error is 30% of the potentially lost revenue (PLR). The PLR in this instance is 40% × £8,000 = £3,200. The penalty is therefore 30% × £3,200 = £960.

47.28 £2,724

	£
Van £3,490 × 8/12	2,327
Van fuel £666 × 8/12	444
Total taxable benefits	2,771

The van benefit scale charge and the van fuel benefit are show in the Tax Rates and Allowances available in the exam.

The CO_2 emissions and list price are not relevant for vans, only for cars.

47.29 £680

6% (from tax tables) × £34,000 × 4/12 = £680

Car benefit is always calculated using the list price of the vehicle rather than the cost to the employer.

47.30 £2,800

	£
Electricity	400
Gas	600
Redecoration	3,000
Total expenses	4,000
Restricted to 10% of earnings £28,000 × 10%	2,800

Examining team's comments. This question was set in the December 2014 examination and was not well answered.

Living expenses (not capital costs) paid by an employer for the benefit of an employee is normally assessable in full as a taxable benefit. However if the accommodation provided is job related then the benefit is limited to a maximum of 10% of the employee's net earnings. The cost of the new roof tiles is not an 'expense' and should therefore have been disregarded, decoration is not capital and is regarded as a cost of living expense and therefore is included with the gas and electric to give total expenses of £4,000. The normal choice should therefore have been £4,000 but the job related rule mentioned above means the correct answer was £2,800 (10% of £28,000).

47.31 £9,000

Rent received £8,250 × 2 = £16,500 – less rent a room relief of £7,500 = £9,000.

Examining team's comments. This question was set in the December 2015 examination.

When an individual lets out a room or rooms in their residence they are entitled to £[7,500] of tax free income if rent a room relief is claimed. The exemption is applied to gross rents (without the deduction of any expenses) and is not per room.

> Answer £12,900 is simply the £[16,500] rent less the normal expenses of £[3,600] – ie the method of assessment if rent a room relief was not claimed. Answer £1,500 is the £[16,500] rent less £[7,500] per room. Answer £5,400 is the £[16,500] rent less the normal expenses of £[3,600] and the rent a room relief of £[7,500]. Therefore, all of the incorrect answer options are indicative of the mistakes that candidates commonly make and candidates must carefully consider before selecting the correct answer.

47.32 £160

£1,600 x 20% x 6/12

> **Examining team's comments.** This question was set in the December 2019 examination.
>
> The first issue was to choose between the two values given; the original cost and the current market value. It would be unfair for the employee to bear the cost of something he did not benefit from, therefore the market value at the time it was given to him would apply. The second issue is the percentage – this is a figure that must be learnt – it is always 20%. Finally, candidates should have checked the time the asset was used, in this case only for six months. This final point is often overlooked. The correct answer would then be £1,600 x 20% x 6/12, ie £160. The correct answer was therefore C.

48 Answer to question with help: Capital gains tax liability

(a) **The cottage**

		£	£
Proceeds £(100,600 – 800)			99,800
Less: cost		22,000	
enhancement expenditure		8,000	
			(30,000)
Gain			69,800

(b) **The disposal of shares in JVD Products plc**

(i) Match disposal first with acquisition in next 30 days

	£
Proceeds $\frac{500}{4,000}$ × £40,000	5,000
Less cost	(4,500)
Gain	500

(ii) Then match with share pool

	No. of shares	Cost £
06.06.91 Acquisition	5,000	10,000
12.05.08 Acquisition	2,800	12,000
	7,800	22,000
14.09.20 Disposal	(3,500)	(9,872)
c/f	4,300	12,128

	£
Proceeds $\frac{3,500}{4,000}$ × £40,000	35,000
Less cost	(9,872)
Gain	25,128

(c) **The oil painting**

	£
Proceeds (loss restricted)	6,000
Less cost	(6,800)
Loss	(800)

Capital gains tax

	Residential property £	Other gains £
Cottage (a)	69,800	
Shares (b)(i)		500
Shares (b)(ii)		25,128
Gains		25,628
Less loss (c) (best use)	(800)	(0)
Net gains	69,000	25,628
Less AEA (best use)	(12,300)	(0)
Taxable gains	56,700	25,628

Tax

	£
£(37,500 – 23,900) = 13,600 × 18% (residential property)	2,448
£(56,700 – 13,600) = 43,100 × 28% (residential property)	12,068
£25,628 × 20% (other gains)	5,126
Total capital gains tax	19,642

49 Silas

(a) **Silas – capital gains for the tax year 2020/21**

	£
Land	
Net proceeds (£30,000 – £1,700)	28,300
Cost	
£80,000 × $\frac{30,000}{30,000+190,000}$	(10,909)
	17,391
Painting	
Insurance proceeds	18,000
Less cost	(10,000)
Gain	8,000
Amount not reinvested and chargeable now	(3,000)
Amount deducted from the base cost of the new asset	5,000

(b) **Silas – capital gains tax payable for the tax year 2020/21**

	£
Total gains from part (a) – £17,391 + £3,000	20,391
Less annual exempt amount	(12,300)
	8,091
Less capital loss brought forward	(100)
Taxable gains	7,991
Tax payable:	
£7,991 × 20% (higher rate taxpayer)	£1,598

Payment due: 31 January 2022

Helping hand. Make sure you get the easy marks for calculating capital gains tax and stating the due date for payment of tax.

Marking scheme

		Marks	
(a)	Land – net proceeds	1	
	Land – cost	2	
	Painting – gain	1	
	Amount not reinvested and chargeable now	1	
	Amount deducted from the base cost of the new asset	1	
			6
(b)	Total gains from part (a)	½	
	Annual exempt amount	½	
	Capital loss brought forward	1	
	Tax payable	1	
	Payment due date	1	
			4
			10

50 Jack

(a) **Jack – taxable gain 2020/21**

	£
Proceeds	190,000
Less cost	(80,000)
	110,000
Amount not reinvested – gain now chargeable £(190,000 – 175,000)	(15,000)
Amount rolled over	95,000
Gain now chargeable	15,000
Less annual exempt amount	(12,300)
Taxable gain	2,700

(b) **Base cost of replacement asset**

	£
Cost	175,000
Less rolled over	(95,000)
Base cost	80,000

Marking scheme

			Marks
(a)	Proceeds – cost	1	
	Amount not reinvested – chargeable now	1	
	Amount rolled over	1	
	Annual exempt amount	1	
			4
(b)	Base cost of replacement asset		1
			5

51 Ravi

Ravi – chargeable gains for the tax year 2020/21

	£	£
Shares		
Proceeds	28,000	
Less cost (W)	(23,600)	
Gain		4,400
Painting		
Proceeds	7,500	
Less cost	(3,500)	
Gain	4,000	
Cannot exceed 5/3 × £(7,500 – 6,000)	2,500	
		2,500
Car		
Exempt		0
Chargeable gains		6,900

Working

	No. of shares	Cost £
May 2006 acquisition	4,000	8,180
August 2008 acquisition	3,000	9,600
	7,000	17,780
June 2012 rights 1 for 2 @ £2	3,500	7,000
	10,500	24,780
July 2020 disposal	(10,000)	(23,600)
c/f	500	1,180

> **Helping hand.** Watch out for the relief on chattels sold for more than £6,000. The gain cannot exceed 5/3rds of the difference between the gross proceeds and £6,000.

Marking scheme

	Marks
Shares	
May 2006 acquisition	1
August 2008 acquisition	1
June 2012 rights issue	1
Disposal cost	1
Gain	1
Painting	
Actual gain	1
Marginal relief	2
Gain chargeable	1
Car	1
	10

52 Trudy

(a) **Trudy – taxable gain 2020/21**

Share value:

$£1.90 + ½ (£2.00 – £1.90)$ = £1.95

Taxable gain

	£
Proceeds 14,000 × £1.95	27,300
Less cost	(8,000)
Chargeable gain	19,300
Less: annual exempt amount	(12,300)
	7,000
Less: loss brought forward	(2,400)
Taxable gain	4,600

> **Helping hand.** When a gift is made, there is a disposal at market value. In the case of listed shares, this is computed as the lower of the two prices shown in the Stock Exchange Daily Official List plus one-half of the difference between those two figures.

(b) **SA108**

Box 23	1
Box 24	27300
Box 25	8000
Box 26	19300
Box 45 (note that box 27 is nil)	2400

Marking scheme

			Marks
(a)	Value		2
	Proceeds		1
	Cost		1
	Capital loss brought forward		1
	Annual exempt amount		1
			6
(b)	½ each for first two entries, others 1 each entry to a maximum of		4
			10

53 Ivan

Ivan – capital gains tax payable for the tax year 2020/21

	£
Current year net gains £(31,300 – 8,000)	23,300
Less annual exempt amount	(12,300)
	11,000
Less capital loss brought forward	(7,000)
Taxable gains	4,000
Tax	
£(37,500 – 36,500) = 1,000 × 10%	100
£(4,000 – 1,000) = 3,000 × 20%	600
Total capital gains tax	700

Marking scheme

	Marks
Current year net gains	1
Annual exempt amount	1
Capital loss b/f	1
Basic rate tax	1
Higher rate tax	1
	5

54 Tony

Tony – capital gains tax payable for the tax year 2020/21

	£	£
Disposal not qualifying for business asset disposal relief:		
Shares		
Gain		12,300
Less annual exempt amount		(12,300)
Taxable gain		Nil
Disposal qualifying for business asset disposal relief: sale of business		
Factory		
Proceeds	800,000	
Less cost	(200,000)	
Gain		600,000
Land		
Proceeds	180,000	
Less cost	(213,000)	
Loss		(33,000)
Taxable gain		567,000
Tax payable		
£567,000 × 10%		£56,700

Helping hand. The annual exempt amount is set against the gain not qualifying for business asset disposal relief first. This maximises the tax saving as the gain on the shares is taxed at 20% whereas the net gain on the disposal of the business is only taxed at 10%. Note that the loss on the asset qualifying for business asset disposal relief can only be set against the gain on the asset qualifying for business asset disposal relief to give the net gain on sale of the business.

Marking scheme

	Marks
Use of annual exempt amount against gain not qualifying for relief	1
Gain on factory	1
Loss on land	1
Net gains	1
Tax @ 10%	1
	5

… FTX FOUNDATIONS IN TAXATION

55 Carla

(a) **Carla – chargeable gain 2020/21**

	£
Proceeds (market value)	100,000
Less cost	(70,000)
	30,000
Excess proceeds over cost £(80,000 – 70,000) gain now chargeable	(10,000)
Gift relief	20,000
Gain now chargeable	10,000

(b) **Becky – base cost of asset**

	£
Market value	100,000
Less gift relief	(20,000)
Base cost	80,000

Marking scheme

		Marks	
(a)	Gain before relief	1	
	Proceeds over cost	1	
	Gift relief	1	
	Chargeable gain	1	
			4
(b)	Base cost for Becky		1
			5

56 Alberto

(a) **Alberto – capital gains for the tax year 2020/21**

Painting

	£
Deemed proceeds	6,000
Less cost	(9,000)
Loss	(3,000)

Shares
Share pool

	No. of shares	Cost £
Purchase	4,000	5,600
Bonus issue – 1 for 1	4,000	
	8,000	5,600
Disposal	(6,000)	(4,200)
	2,000	1,400

Gain

	£
Proceeds	38,500
Less cost	(4,200)
Gain	34,300

(b) **Alberto – taxable gains for the tax year 2020/21**

	£
Gain	34,300
Less current year loss	(3,000)
Net chargeable gains	31,300
Less: annual exempt amount	(12,300)
	19,000
Less: b/f loss	(19,000)
Taxable gains	Nil

Marking scheme

			Marks
(a)	Painting	2	
	Shares	4	
			6
(b)	Gain	1	
	Current year loss	1	
	Annual exempt amount	1	
	Brought forward loss	1	
			4
			10

57 Sandra

(a) **Sandra – chargeable gain**

	£
Gain	80,000
Less proceeds not re-invested	(10,000)
Gain deferred	70,000
Chargeable gain	10,000

(b) **Sandra – deferred gain**

The gain will be held over until the earliest of:

- The sale of the plant and machinery
- The plant and machinery ceasing to be used as a business asset
- The tenth anniversary of the purchase date of the plant and machinery

Marking scheme

		Marks	
Gain before relief			
(a)	Proceeds not reinvested	1	
	Deferral claim	1	
			2
(b)	Sale	1	
	Ceasing to be used	1	
	Ten years	1	
			3
			5

58 Jessie

Jessie – capital gains tax payable 2020/21

	£	£
Car		
Exempt asset		0
Field		
Proceeds	210,000	
Less cost	(105,000)	
Gain		105,000
Painting		
Proceeds (net)	8,200	
Less cost £(3,100 + 300)	(3,400)	
Gain	4,800	
Cannot exceed £([8,200 + 200] – 6,000) × 5/3		4,000
Building		
Proceeds	140,000	
Less cost	(160,000)	
Loss		(20,000)
Net chargeable gains		89,000
Less annual exempt amount		(12,300)
Taxable gains		76,700
CGT @ 20% (higher rate taxpayer)		15,340

Marking scheme

		Marks
Car	– exempt	1
Field	– gain	1
Painting	– gain	1
	– restriction	2
Building	– loss	1
Net gains		½
Annual exempt amount		1
Taxable gains		½
CGT payable	– rate	1
	– amount	1
		10

59 Eddie

Eddie – capital gains tax for 2020/21

Antique table

	£
Proceeds (deemed)	6,000
Less expenses of sale	(300)
Net proceeds of sale	5,700
Less cost	(8,000)
Allowable loss	(2,300)

Painting

	£
Proceeds	28,000
Less expenses of sale	(500)
Net proceeds of sale	27,500
Less cost	
$\dfrac{28,000}{28,000 + 140,000} \times £60,000$	(10,000)
Chargeable gain	17,500

Tax payable

	£
Net current year gains £(17,500 – 2,300)	15,200
Less annual exempt amount	(12,300)
	2,900
Less losses brought forward	(2,300)
Taxable gains	600
CGT @ 20% (higher rate taxpayer)	120

Due date: 31 January 2022

Marking scheme

	Marks
Antique table	
Deemed proceeds	1
Expenses of sale	½
Cost	½
Painting	
Net proceeds	1
Cost	2
Tax	
Current year net gains	1
Annual exempt amount	1
Loss brought forward	1
CGT @ 20%	1
Payment due date	1
	10

60 Tanya

(a) **Tanya – private residence relief (PRR)**

Event	Exempt years	Chargeable years	Reason
1	8.5		Actual residence
2	4		Employed elsewhere in UK (up to four years)
3	3		Actual residence
4	3	3	Any reason (up to three years)
5	0.25		Actual residence
6	0.75	5.5	Last nine months of ownership exempt
	19.5	8.5	

> **Helping hand.** Periods of absence must normally be preceded and followed by periods of actual occupation in order to be treated as exempt. This condition is satisfied for Events 2 and 4; there is no minimum reoccupation period. The last nine months are always treated as exempt if the property has been the taxpayer's private residence at any time.

(b) Capital gains tax on residential property is due within 30 days of disposal. The due date for any CGT payable by Tanya is therefore 30 March 2021.

Marking scheme

	Marks
Actual occupation	½
Employed UK 4 years	1
Actual occupation	½
3 years any reason / 3 years non-qualifying	1
Actual occupation	½
Last 9 months of ownership	½
Due date	1
	5

61 Marion

Marion – capital gains tax for the tax year 2020/21

			£
15 May 2020	Proceeds		7,500
	Less expenses of sale		(1,300)
	Net proceeds		6,200
	Less: cost		(2,800)
	purchase expenses		(400)
	Gain		3,000
	Cannot exceed 5/3 × £(7,500 – 6,000)		2,500
	Lower gain taken		2,500
19 August 2020	Proceeds		32,200
	Less cost		(6,400)
	Gain		25,800

	£
Total gains £(2,500 + 25,800)	28,300
Less annual exempt amount	(12,300)
Taxable gains	16,000

Basic rate band remaining £(37,500 – 30,900) = £6,600

	£
£6,600 × 10%	660
£(16,000 – 6,600) = 9,400 × 20%	1,880
CGT payable	2,540

> **Helping hand.** Remember there are special rules for calculating gains on chattels (tangible moveable property) such as paintings. Look out for assets with relatively low values and then consider if you need to apply the special chattels rules. Don't forget to deduct the annual exempt amount to calculate taxable gains.

Marking scheme

	Marks
15 May 2020	
Proceeds	½
Sale expenses	½
Cost	½
Purchase expenses	½
Restriction	2
Lower gain taken	½
19 August 2020	
Proceeds	½
Cost	½
Total gains	½
Annual exempt amount	1
Unused basic rate band	1
Tax at basic rate	1
Tax at higher rate	1
	10

62 Multiple choice questions: Capital gains tax

62.1 A vintage Bentley motor car worth £70,000

Cars are always exempt assets for CGT even if they are vintage cars of considerable value.

62.2 £3,612

	£
Chargeable gain	25,200
Less annual exempt amount	(12,300)
Taxable gain	12,900
CGT @ 28% (residential property)	3,612

62.3 £15,000

	£
Gain	25,000
Amount not invested (£80,000 – £70,000)	(10,000)
Eligible for rollover relief	15,000

62.4 £1,667

	£
Proceeds	7,000
Less cost	(1,500)
Gain	5,500

The maximum gain is 5/3 × £(7,000 – 6,000) = £1,667

The chargeable gain is the lower of £5,500 and £1,667, so it is = £1,667.

62.5 £16,470

	£
Gains	177,000
Less annual exempt amount	(12,300)
Taxable gains	164,700
CGT @ 10%	16,470

62.6 £81,897

Actual occupation is nine years and the last nine months is exempt. The total period of ownership is 14.5 years. The exempt gain is therefore (9 + 0.75)/14.5 × £250,000 = £168,103 and so the chargeable gain is £81,897.

62.7 Against the 8,000 shares purchased in the 30 days following the disposal ie on 10 February 2021. Then against the share pool ie 2,000 of the shares purchased on 2 May 2006.

62.8 £200,000

	£
CGT @ 10% on first £1m of gains	100,000
(AEA used up against investment asset gain)	
CGT @ 20% on remaining £500,000	100,000
Total CGT payable	200,000

62.9 (i), (ii) and (iii)

Only the compensation for destroyed or lost assets and goodwill are subject to capital gains tax.

62.10 12 August 2030

When a depreciating asset is purchased to replace a non-depreciating asset the gain on the sale is deferred until the earliest of:

- The sale of the depreciating asset – 14 October 2030
- Ceasing to use the depreciating asset in a business – not applicable here
- The ten-year anniversary of the purchase of the depreciating asset – 12 August 2030

62.11 £17,200 – £3,000 (current year loss) – £12,300 (annual exempt amount) – £1,900 (brought forward loss)

Current year capital losses must always be used in full against the current year capital gains. Then the annual exempt amount is deducted. Finally, any remaining gains are reduced to nil by using brought forward losses. Therefore in this case only £1,900 of the brought forward figure needs to be used.

62.12 £16,770

The rate of tax to be applied to gains qualifying for business asset disposal relief is 10%. This is applied after the deduction of the annual exempt amount. Therefore the tax payable in this instance is £16,770 ((£180,000 – £12,300) × 10%).

62.13 31 January 2022, no penalty

Capital gains tax (CGT) is always due by 31 January following the relevant tax year (except on residential property which is due within 30 days of disposal). Therefore the CGT for the tax year 2020/21 is due on 31 January 2022. A penalty is chargeable where tax is paid after the penalty date. The penalty date is 30 days after the due date for the tax so no penalty arises if the tax is paid within 30 days of the due date.

62.14 £1,342

Gains subject to business asset disposal relief are taxed at 10%. The residential property gain will be reduced by the annual exempt amount and then taxed in this case, at 18%, because Alyson has total gains and income less than the basic rate limit of £37,500. The capital gains tax (CGT) payable is therefore £1,342 [(£10,000 × 10%) + ((£14,200 – £12,300) × 18%)].

62.15 £41,356 payable on 30 January 2021.

The residential property gain will be reduced by the annual exempt amount and then taxed at 28% as Anil is a higher rate taxpayer. The capital gains tax (CGT) payable is therefore (£160,000 – £12,300) × 28% = £41,356. Capital gains tax on residential properties is payable 30 days from the date of disposal.

62.16 £56,769

82,000 × £90,000/£130,000

> **Examining team's comments.** This question was set in the December 2019 examination.
>
> This was a common part disposal question which has been examined on many previous occasions. Candidates must learn the formula for calculating the cost in these circumstances. If the formula is known, then a simple calculation would get the correct answer. The formula is: the original full cost (including any purchase costs) multiplied by the disposal proceeds divided by the disposal proceeds plus the market value of the retained part. The costs of disposal are not used in the formula. It would appear that many candidates were unsure what to do with the costs of purchase and disposal. The correct answer is therefore A − £82,000 × £90,000/£130,000, ie £56,769.

63 Answer to question with help: Corporation tax

Corporation tax computation year ended 31 March 2021

	£	£
Trading income		244,000
Property business income		15,000
Interest income		5,000
Chargeable gains £(35,000 + 7,000)	42,000	
Less losses brought forward	(8,000)	
		34,000
Profits		298,000
Less qualifying charitable donation		(7,000)
Taxable total profits		291,000
FY20		
Corporation tax £291,000 × 19%		55,290

64 Taps Ltd

(a) **Capital allowances y/e 31 March 2021**

	AIA £	Main pool £	Special rate pool £	Allowances £
Balances b/f		197,000		
Additions qualifying for AIA				
01.05.20 Plant	1,018,000			
AIA	(1,000,000)			1,000,000
	18,000			
Balance transferred to pool	(18,000)	18,000		
Additions not qualifying for AIA				
01.12.20 Car			40,000	
Disposals				
02.02.21 Plant		(60,000)		
		155,000		
WDA @ 18%		(27,900)		27,900
WDA @ 6%			(2,400)	2,400
Balances c/f		127,100	37,600	
Allowances				1,030,300

> **Helping hand.** Remember that private use of an asset is not relevant when computing the capital allowances for a company. Instead, the director will be assessed on a taxable benefit as part of his employment income for his private use of the car.

(b) **Corporation tax y/e 31 March 2021**

	£	£
Trading profit	1,960,000	
Less capital allowances (from part (a))	(1,030,300)	929,700
Interest income		
Received	20,000	
Accrued at 31.03.21	2,000	
	22,000	
Less: loan interest paid	(1,800)	
loan interest accrued at 31.03.21	(300)	19,900
Property business income (accruals basis)		15,000
Gain (W)		118,880
Total profits		1,083,400
Less carry forward trading loss relief		(258,700)
Less qualifying charitable donation		(4,000)
Taxable total profits		820,780
FY20		
£820,780 × 19%		155,948

Working

Gain	£
Net proceeds £(211,040 – 3,200)	207,840
Cost £(78,000 + 2,000)	(80,000)
	127,840
Indexation allowance £80,000 × 0.112 (frozen at 12.17)	(8,960)
Gain	118,880

Marking scheme

			Marks
(a)	Plant – acquisition	½	
	AIA	1	
	Transfer balance to pool	½	
	Car – acquisition	½	
	Plant – disposal	½	
	WDAs	2	
			5
(b)	Trading profit after capital allowances	1	
	Interest receivable	1	
	Interest payable	1	
	Property business income	1	
	Gain – net proceeds	1	
	Gain – total cost	1	
	Gain – indexation allowance	1	
	Loss	1	
	Qualifying charitable donation	1	
	Tax on taxable total profits	1	
			10
			15

65 XYZ Ltd

(a) **XYZ Ltd – adjusted trading profit for the eight-month period ended 31 December 2020**

	£	£
Net profit per accounts		1,327,300
Deduct:		
Loan interest – non-trading income		(20,000)
		1,307,300
Add back:		
Legal expenses: breach of contract claim	0	
Legal expenses: health and safety fine	10,000	
Legal expenses: staff contracts	0	
Administration costs: food hampers to customers	11,500	
Administration costs: staff entertainment	0	
Loan interest payable	0	
Depreciation	32,000	
Motor expenses: employee parking fines	0	
Motor expenses: director's private use	0	
Motor expenses: lease payments (W)	900	
Wages	0	
Donations and subscriptions: national charity	2,000	
Donations and subscriptions: Chamber of Commerce	0	
Staff pension contributions	0	56,400
		1,363,700
Capital allowances		(115,000)
Adjusted trading profit		1,248,700

Working

Car lease:	£
Payments	6,000
Restriction: £6,000 × 15% (CO_2 emissions exceed 110g/km)	(900)
Allowable	5,100

(b) **XYZ Ltd – corporation tax liability for the eight-month period ended 31 December 2020**

	£
Adjusting trading profit (part (a))	1,248,700
Interest	20,000
Taxable total profits	1,268,700

FY20

£1,268,700 × 19% (Due date 1 October 2021)	241,053

(c) The due date for the return for the eight-month period ended 31 December 2020 is 31 December 2021.

If the return is two months late, the penalty chargeable is £100.

Marking scheme

		Marks	
(a)	Car lease add-back	1½	
	Other adjustments – each ½	3	
	Deduction of capital allowances	1	
	Items unadjusted – each ½	4½	
			10
(b)	Adjusted trading profit	½	
	Interest	½	
	Tax payable	1	
	Due date	1	
			3
(c)	Due date	1	
	Penalty payable if two months late	1	
			2
			15

66 Bush Ltd

Bush Ltd – adjusted trading income for the year ended 31 March 2021

	£	£
Net profit before taxation		149,600
Deduct:		
Loan stock interest	(21,000)	
Property business income	(9,000)	
Dividends	(18,000)	
Compensation for damaged stock	0	(48,000)
		101,600
Add back:		
Directors' remuneration	0	
Wages and salaries	0	
Depreciation	12,000	
Entertainment – staff	0	
– clients	14,800	
Legal fees – renewal of 60-year lease	4,500	
– debt collecting	0	
Qualifying charitable donation	2,600	
Patent royalties	0	
Loss on sale of van	1,200	35,100
Adjusted trading income		136,700

Helping hand. The legal fees are related to the renewal of a lease which is not a short lease. Therefore they are a capital expense and are disallowed in the computation of trading income.

Marking scheme

	Marks
Loan stock interest	½
Property business income	1
Dividends	½
Compensation for damaged stock	½
Directors' remuneration	½
Wages and salary	½
Depreciation	1
Staff entertaining	1
Client entertaining	1
Renewal of long lease	1
Debt collecting	½
Qualifying charitable donation	1
Patent royalties	½
Loss on sale of van	½
	10

67 Fires Ltd

Fires Ltd – capital allowances for the year ended 31 March 2021

	AIA £	Main pool £	Special rate pool £	Short life asset £	Allowances £
TWDV b/f		120,000			
Acquisitions eligible for AIA					
02.05.20 Machine £1,226,400 × 100/120 (N1)	1,022,000				
AIA (N2)	(1,000,000)				1,000,000
	22,000				
Transfer balance to main pool	(22,000)	22,000			
06.08.20 Computer £7,200 × 100/120 (N1)				6,000	
Acquisition not eligible for AIA					
14.10.20 Car (N3)			16,000		
Disposal					
16.09.20 Machine £24,000 × 100/120 (N4)		(20,000)			
		122,000			
WDA @ 18%		(21,960)		(1,080)	23,040
WDA @ 6%			(960)		960
TWDV c/f		100,040	15,040	4,920	
Allowances					1,024,000

Notes

1. Capital allowances on the machine and the computer are calculated on the cost net of VAT because the input tax can be recovered on these items.
2. The Annual Investment Allowance is used against the main pool acquisition in priority to the short life asset because this is more tax efficient.
3. The full cost of the car is used because the input VAT cannot be recovered due to private use. The car is a special rate pool asset because it has CO_2 emissions in excess of 110g/km.
4. The disposal proceeds of the machine are restricted to its original cost net of VAT.

Marking scheme

	Marks
Machine	
Cost	1½
AIA	1
Computer	
Cost	1½
Car	
Cost	1½
Machine	
Disposal proceeds	1½
WDA @ 18%	2
WDA @ 6%	1
	10

68 Radiators Ltd

Radiators Ltd – corporation tax for the year ended 31 March 2021

	£	£
Adjusted trading profit		1,164,840
Less capital allowances (W1)		(1,024,840)
Tax adjusted trading profit		140,000
Interest received	8,000	
Less interest payable	(3,000)	
		5,000
Property business income rental accrued £2,500 × 8		20,000
Property business income premium (W2)		10,560
Chargeable gain		24,000
Total profits		199,560
Less qualifying charitable donation		(4,560)
Taxable total profits		195,000

FY20:
£195,000 × 19% (due date 1 January 2022) £37,050

Workings

1

	AIA £	Main pool £	Allowances £
1 April 2020 to 31 March 2021			
TWDV b/f		150,000	
Addition qualifying for AIA			
Machinery	1,010,000		
AIA	(1,000,000)		1,000,000
	10,000		
Transfer balance to pool	(10,000)	10,000	
Disposal			
Machinery (restricted to cost)		(22,000)	
		138,000	
WDA £138,000 × 18%		(24,840)	24,840
TWDV c/f		113,160	
Allowances			1,024,840

2

	£
Premium received	12,000
Less: 2% × (7 – 1) × 12,000	(1,440)
Taxable as rent received	10,560

Marking scheme

	Marks
Calculation of taxable total profits	
Trade profit	1
Interest received	1
Interest paid	1
Property business income: rental income accrued	1
Chargeable gain	1
Qualifying charitable donation	1
Calculation of corporation tax	
Tax on taxable total profits	1
Due date	1
Working 1	
TWDV b/f	1
Addition	1
AIA	1
Disposal	1
WDA	1
Working 2	
Premium taxable as property business income	2
	15

69 Broad Ltd

(a) **Broad Ltd – adjusted trade profit for the year ended 31 March 2021**

	£	£
Net profit per accounts		1,640,000
interest	4,300	
non-current asset profit	102,000	(106,300)
		1,533,700
Add back: loan stock interest (trading purposes)	0	
qualifying charitable donation	10,000	
legal fees (long lease – capital)	8,000	
legal fees (staff employment contracts)	0	
payments for loss of office	0	18,000
		1,551,700
Less capital allowances (£455,556 × 18% WDA)		(82,000)
Adjusted trade profit		1,469,700

(b) **Broad Ltd – corporation tax for the year ended 31 March 2021**

	£	£
Adjusted trade profit (part (a))		1,469,700
Interest income		4,300
Chargeable gain	63,568	
Less loss brought forward	(16,600)	46,968
Total profits		1,520,968
Less qualifying charitable donation		(10,000)
Taxable total profits		1,510,968
Tax payable: £1,510,968 × 19%		287,084

(c) Broad Ltd must pay its corporation tax liability in instalments because its taxable total profits exceed the profits threshold of £1,500,000 and it is not the first year that it is a large company because it paid its corporation tax by instalments in the year ended 31 March 2020.

Each instalment is £287,084/4 = £71,771.

The instalments are due on 14 October 2020, 14 January 2021, 14 April 2021 and 14 July 2021.

Marking scheme

			Marks
(a)	Net profit per accounts	½	
	– interest	½	
	– capital profit	½	
	Add – qualifying charitable donation	1	
	– legal fees on lease	1	
	Capital allowances	2	
	Items not adjusted (3 items)	1½	
			7
(b)	Adjusted trade profit	½	
	Interest income	½	
	Chargeable gain	1	
	Deduct loss	1	
	Qualifying charitable donation	1	
	Tax	1	
			5
(c)	Why needs to pay by instalments	1½	
	Each instalment	½	
	Instalment dates	1	
			3
			15

70 Rose Ltd

Rose Ltd – corporation tax for the two accounting periods ended 31 May 2021

	1 April 2020 – 31 March 2021 £	1 April 2021 – 31 May 2021 £
Profit: £420,000 (12:2)	360,000	60,000
Capital allowances (W)	(41,380)	(2,239)
Adjusted trading profit	318,620	57,761
Chargeable gain (loss c/f)	102,380	
Profits	421,000	57,761
Less: qualifying charitable donation		(22,000)
Taxable total profits	421,000	35,761

Tax payable

Year ended 31 March 2021   £
£421,000 × 19%   79,990

2 months ended 31 May 2021
£35,761 × 19%   6,795

Working

Capital allowances

	AIA £	Main pool £	Allowances £
Year ended 31 March 2021			
TWDV b/f		91,000	
Purchase qualifying for AIA	25,000		
AIA	(25,000)		25,000
WDA @ 18%		(16,380)	16,380
TWDV c/f		74,620	
Allowances			41,380
Period ended 31 May 2021			
WDA @ 18% × 2/12		(2,239)	2,239
TWDV c/f		72,381	
Allowances			2,239

Marking scheme

	Marks
Profit	1
Capital allowances:	
Purchase	1
AIA	1
WDA	1
WDA × 2/12	1
Chargeable gain	1
Capital loss c/f	1
Qualifying charitable donation	1
CT for y/e 31 March 2021	1
CT for p/e 31 May 2021	1
	10

71 BDD Ltd

BDD Ltd – capital allowances for the eight-month period ended 31 December 2020

	AIA £	Main pool £	Special rate pool £	Short-life asset £	Allowances £
Balances brought forward		290,000	16,000		
Addition qualifying for AIA					
Machine – 31 May 2020	668,000				
AIA: £1,000,000 × 8/12	(666,667)				666,667
	1,333				
Transfer balance to pool	(1,333)	1,333			
Plant – 25 August 2020				15,000	
Addition not qualifying for AIA					
Car – 31 December 2020			35,000		
Disposals					
Machine – 12 June 2020		(12,000)			
Car – 31 December 2020			(8,000)		
		279,333	43,000	15,000	
WDA – 18% × 8/12		(33,520)		(1,800)	35,320
WDA – 6% × 8/12			(1,720)		1,720
Balances carried forward		245,813	41,280	13,200	
Total allowances					703,707

Notes

1. The AIA and WDA are prorated for the short accounting period.
2. The AIA is used against the main pool expenditure in preference to the SLA expenditure.
3. The expenditure on the car consists of the trade-in value of the old car plus the amount paid by the company in cash.
4. The disposal proceeds of the machine are limited to original cost.

Marking scheme

	Marks
Balances b/f	1
AIA prorated	2
Transfer to main pool	1
Plant into SLA pool	1
Car into special rate pool	1
Machine 12 June	½
Car disposal	½
WDAs pro-rated	3
	10

72 Cargo Ltd

Cargo Ltd – capital allowances for the year ended 31 March 2021

Y/e 31 March 2021	AIA £	Main pool £	Special rate pool £	Allowances £
TWDV b/f		248,000	8,000	
Additions qualifying for AIA				
16.05.20 Plant	15,000			
14.06.20 Machinery	7,000			
	22,000			
AIA	(22,000)			22,000
Additions not qualifying for AIA				
18.08.20 Car			26,000	
02.11.20 Car £(3,000 + 6,000)		9,000		
Disposals				
17.07.20 Plant		(18,000)		
20.08.20 Car			(7,000)	
02.11.20 Car		(3,000)		
		236,000	27,000	
WDA @ 18%		(42,480)		42,480
WDA @ 6%			(1,620)	1,620
TWDVs c/f		193,520	25,380	
Allowances				66,100

157

Marking scheme

	Marks
Additions – AIA	1
AIA	1
Additions – not AIA	2
Disposals	3
Total pools	1
WDA @ 18%	1
WDA @ 6%	1
	10

73 Stem Ltd

(a) **Stem Ltd – capital allowances for the nine-month period ending 31 December 2020**

	AIA £	Main pool £	Special rate pool £	Allowances £
TWDV b/f		220,000		
Acquisitions qualifying for AIA				
25 June Machine	365,500			
4 August Machine	367,650			
7 October Machine	30,350			
	763,500			
AIA £1,000,000 × 9/12	(750,000)			750,000
	13,500			
Transfer balance to pool	(13,500)	13,500		
Acquisition not qualifying for AIA				
2 December Car			20,000	
Disposal				
14 October (restrict to cost)		(4,000)		
Balancing allowance		229,500		
WDA @ 18% × 9/12		(30,983)		30,983
WDA @ 6% × 9/12			(900)	900
TWDV c/f		198,517	19,100	
Allowances				781,883

Helping hand. Remember that the annual investment allowance and writing down allowance must be pro-rated in a short accounting period. An asset bought on hire purchase is treated as if purchased outright and capital allowances are available on the purchase price at the date the agreement begins.

(b) **Tax relief of construction of factory**

Land and legal and professional fees - no relief is available as this is capital expenditure and does not qualify for any form of capital allowances.

Building construction costs - these qualify for structures and buildings allowances (SBAs) at 3% per year. The SBA would be pro-rated in the year ended 31 December 2021, for the number of months of qualifying use.

Integral features - these qualify for plant and machinery capital allowances in the special rate pool at 6% pa. The AIA should be allocated to such expenditure in priority to main pool items, giving 100% relief on the first £1 million per year (covering the full amount of the projected expenditure).

ANSWERS

Marking scheme

		Marks	
(a)	Acquisitions qualifying for AIA	1½	
	AIA	1½	
	Balance to pool	1	
	Acquisition not qualifying for AIA	1	
	Disposal	2	
	WDA @ 18% × 9/12	1½	
	WDA @ 6% × 9/12	1½	
			10
(b)	Land	½	
	Legal and professional fees	½	
	Building	2	
	Integral features	2	
			5
			15

74 Petal Ltd

Petal Ltd – sale of shares

	No. of shares	Cost £	Indexed cost £
14 June 2007 acquisition	1,000	3,000	3,000
Indexed cost to July 2011			
0.132 × £3,000			396
			3,396
17 July 2011 acquisition	3,000	10,000	10,000
	4,000	13,000	13,396
Indexed cost to December 2017			
0.185 × £13,396			2,478
			15,874
19 October 2020 disposal (cost × 3,000/4,000)	(3,000)	(9,750)	(11,906)
c/f	1,000	3,250	3,968

Gain

	£
Proceeds	21,000
Less indexed cost	(11,906)
Gain	9,094

Marking scheme

	Marks
Acquisition 14 June 2007	½
Indexed to July 2011	1
Acquisition 17 July 2011	½
Indexed to December 2017	1
Disposal	1
Gain	1
	5

75 Roof Ltd

Capital gain on disposal of the office block

	£
Net proceeds	477,000
Less: cost	(192,000)
enhancement expenditure	(71,000)
Unindexed gain	214,000
Less: indexation on cost	
£192,000 × 0.478 (frozen at 12.17)	(91,776)
indexation on enhancement	
£71,000 × 0.293 (frozen at 12.17)	(20,803)
Indexed gain	101,421

Marking scheme

	Marks
Cost	1
Extension	1
Indexation – cost	1½
– extension	1½
	5

76 Box plc

Box plc – chargeable gains y/e 31.3.2021

Summary of gains and losses

	£
Shares: last nine days (W1)	400
Shares: FA 1985 pool (W2)	34,322
	34,722
Less painting (W3)	(2,000)
Net chargeable gains	32,722

Workings

1 *Crate plc shares – acquisition in previous nine days*

	£
Proceeds 2,000/20,000 × £124,000	12,400
Less cost	(12,000)
Gain	400

Acquisitions matched with disposals under the 9-day rule never enter the FA 1985 pool.

2 *Crate plc shares – FA 1985 pool*

	No. of shares	Cost £	Indexed cost £
26.05.00 Acquisition	13,000	24,000	24,000
24.10.06			
IA 0.174 × £24,000			4,176
			28,176
Acquisition	5,000	27,500	27,500
c/f	18,000	51,500	55,676

	No. of shares	Cost £	Indexed cost £
26.05.20			
IA £55,676 × 0.388 (frozen to 12.17)			21,602
			77,278
Disposal	(18,000)	(51,500)	(77,278)
c/f	Nil	Nil	Nil

> **Helping hand.** Remember to add the indexation allowance to the pool, not take it away!

Gain	£
Proceeds 18,000/20,000 × £124,000	111,600
Less cost	(51,500)
Unindexed gain	60,100
Less indexation allowance	
£(77,278 – 51,500)	(25,778)
Indexed gain	34,322

3   *Painting*

	£
Proceeds (deemed)	6,000
Less cost	(8,000)
Loss	(2,000)

Marking scheme

	Marks
Shares: matching	1
Previous nine days	2
FA 1985 pool	4
Total gain	1
Painting	2
	10

77 Andsnes Ltd

Chargeable gains computation

	£
Warehouse (W1)	35,305
Plot of land (W2)	40,824
Vase – exempt (proceeds and cost £6,000 or less)	0
Chargeable gains	76,129

Workings

1   *Warehouse*

	£
Proceeds	120,000
Less cost	(65,000)
	55,000
Less indexation allowance £65,000 × 0.303 (frozen at 12.17)	(19,695)
	35,305

Rollover relief is not available as the replacement asset was acquired outside the qualifying period.

2   The plot of land

	£
Proceeds	69,000
Less: cost	(20,000)
expenditure in July 2013	(4,000)
	45,000
Less indexation allowance	
£20,000 × 0.186 (frozen at 12.17)	(3,720)
£4,000 × 0.114 (frozen at 12.17)	(456)
	40,824

Marking scheme

	Marks
Total gains	1
Warehouse: unindexed gain	1
indexation allowance	1
indexed gain	1
no rollover relief	1
Plot of land: unindexed gain	2
indexation allowances	1
indexed gain	1
Vase: exempt	1
	10

78 Jasmine plc

Jasmine plc – chargeable gain for the year ended 31 December 2020

		£
Gain:	Proceeds	560,000
	Less cost	(275,000)
		285,000
	Less indexation allowance	
	£275,000 × 0.234 (frozen at 12.17)	(64,350)
		220,650
	Amount rolled over	(180,650)
	Gain chargeable now £(560,000 – 520,000)	40,000

Helping hand. The gains chargeable now is the amount of proceeds not 'reinvested' in the replacement asset, even though the replacement asset was acquired before the disposal of the original asset.

Marking scheme

	Marks
Gain	1
Indexation allowance	1
Amount rolled over	1
Gain chargeable now	2
	5

79 Answer to question with help: Loss reliefs

(a)

	Year ended 31 March		
	2021	2022	2023
	£	£	£
Trading income	125,000	0	80,000
Interest income	263,000	185,000	24,000
Chargeable gains	60,360	0	3,000
Total profits	448,360	185,000	107,000
Less current period loss relief	0	(185,000)	0
	448,360	0	107,000
Less carry back loss relief	(448,360)	0	0
	0	0	107,000
Less carry forward loss relief	0	0	(63,640)
	0	0	43,360
Less qualifying charitable donation	0	0	(30,000)
Taxable total profits	0	0	13,360
Unrelieved qualifying charitable donations	£40,000	£57,000	

Loss memorandum

Trading loss

	£
Loss in y/e 31.03.22	697,000
Less used y/e 31.03.22	(185,000)
Less used y/e 31.03.21	(448,360)
Less used y/e 31.03.23	(63,640)
Loss remaining unrelieved	0

There is no corporation tax liability for either of the first two years.

For the third year, the position is as follows.

	£
Corporation tax	
£13,360 × 19% (assumed rate)	2,538

(b) The due date for payment of the corporation tax for the year to 31 March 2023 is 1 January 2024. Galbraith Ltd is not required to pay its anticipated corporation tax liability in quarterly instalments because its taxable total profits do not exceed the profits threshold of £1,500,000.

The filing date is 31 March 2024.

80 Laurel Ltd

(a) The two factors that will influence a company's choice of loss relief claims are:

  (i) Timing: loss relief against total profits is quicker than carry forward loss relief.

  (ii) The extent to which relief for qualifying charitable donations might be lost as current period and carry back relief are before deducting these but carry forward relief can be restricted to keep an amount equal to donations in charge.

(b) **Laurel Ltd – taxable total profits y/ends 31 December 2019, 2020 and 2021**

	Y/e 31.12.19 £	Y/e 31.12.20 £	Y/e 31.12.21 £
Trading income	44,000	0	95,200
Property business income	9,400	6,600	6,500
Chargeable gains	5,100	0	0
Total profits	58,500	6,600	101,700
Less current period loss relief	(0)	(6,600)	(0)
Less carry back loss relief	(58,500)		(0)
Less carry forward loss relief	(0)	(0)	(8,700)
	0	0	93,000
Less qualifying charitable donations	(0)	(0)	(1,200)
Taxable total profits	0	0	91,800
Unrelieved qualifying charitable donations	800	1,000	

Loss memorandum
Trading loss £
Loss in y/e 31.12.20 73,800
Less used y/e 31.12.20 (6,600)
Less used y/e 31.12.19 (58,500)
Less used y/e 31.12.21 (8,700)
Loss remaining unrelieved 0

Capital loss £
Loss in y/e 31.12.20 7,500
Less used y/e 31.12.21 (6,000)
Loss remaining unrelieved 1,500

Marking scheme

			Marks
(a)	Timing of relief	1	
	Qualifying charitable donations not relieved	1	
			2
(b)	Trading income	1	
	Carry forward loss relief	1	
	Property business income	1	
	Chargeable gains/losses	1	
	Current year loss relief	1	
	Carry back loss relief	1	
	Qualifying charitable donations	1	
	Unrelieved losses	1	
			8
			10

ANSWERS

81 Caution Ltd

Caution Ltd – taxable total profits y/ends 31 March 2018, 2019, 2020 and 2021

	Y/e 31.03.18 £	Y/e 31.03.19 £	Y/e 31.03.20 £	Y/e 31.03.21 £
Total profits	105,000	60,000	27,000	16,000
Less: current period loss relief				(16,000)
carry back loss relief	(17,000)	(60,000)	(27,000)	
Taxable total profits	88,000	0	0	0

Loss memorandum

	£
Loss in y/e 31.03.21	120,000
Less used y/e 31.03.21	(16,000)
Loss of y/e 31.03.21 available for 3-year carry back	104,000
Less used y/e 31.03.20	(27,000)
	77,000
Less used y/e 31.03.19	(60,000)
	17,000
Less used y/e 31.03.18	(17,000)
Loss remaining unrelieved	Nil

Marking scheme

	Marks
Total profits	1
Current period loss relief	1
Carry back loss relief	3
	5

82 Waddle Ltd

(a) **Waddle Ltd – taxable total profits y/e 31 March 2020 and 31 March 2021**

	Y/e 31.03.20 £	Y/e 31.03.21 £
Trading profit	0	5,300
Property business profit	3,950	4,500
Chargeable gain £(3,200 – 1,000)	0	2,200
Total profits	3,950	12,000
Less: current period relief	(3,950)	0
Less: carried forward relief	0	(10,950)
Less: qualifying charitable donation (wasted in y/e 31.03.20)	(200)	(1,050)
Taxable total profits	0	0

(b) **Loss memorandum**

	£
Loss in y/e 31.3.20	18,000
Less used y/e 31.3.20	(3,950)
Less used y/e 31.3.21 £(12,000 – 1,050) restricted to relieve QCD	(10,950)
Loss remaining unrelieved at 31.03.21	3,100

165

Marking scheme

		Marks
(a)	Y/e 31.03.20	
	Trading income	½
	Property business income	½
	Chargeable gain	½
	Current period relief	1
	Qualifying charitable donations not relieved	1
	Y/e 31.03.21	
	Trading income	½
	Property business income	½
	Chargeable gain	2
	Carry forward period relief	2
	Qualifying charitable donation	½
		9
(b)	Unrelieved loss	1
		10

83 Alphabetic Ltd

> **Helping hand.** There are automatic tax geared penalties as well as fixed penalties if a CT return is more than six months late. Both tax geared penalties are based on the tax unpaid six months after the return is due.

(a) The underpayments for the year to 30 September 2020:

Due date	Amount Due £	Underpaid £
14.04.20	200,000	44,000
14.07.20	200,000	44,000
14.10.20	200,000	44,000
14.01.21	200,000	44,000

Interest will run on each of the amounts of £44,000 underpaid from the day after the due date until the date of payment, 1 July 2021.

(b) (i) *Fixed rate penalties*

   (1) Where the return is up to three months late – £100

   (2) Where the return is more than three months late – £200

   (3) Where the return is the third consecutive one to be filed late the above penalties are increased to £500 and £1,000 respectively.

(ii) *Tax geared rate penalties*

A tax geared penalty is triggered in addition to the fixed rate penalties if a return is more than six months late.

The penalty is 10% of any tax unpaid 6 months after the return was due if the total delay is up to 12 months.

The penalty is 20% of that tax if the return is over 12 months late.

Marking scheme

	Marks
(a) 1 for each instalment	4
(b) (i) 1 mark for each point	3
(ii) 1 mark for each point	3
	10

84 Peter Collins

Five differences between sole trader/company

Difference	Sole trader	Company
Tax on profits/gains	Income tax/capital gains tax	Corporation tax on both
Due date for tax on profits	31 January following end of tax year; payments on account will probably be required	Nine months after end of accounting period; no payments on account for company which is not large
Extraction of profits from the business	Taxed on profits as they arise – no further implications when extracted	Profits only taxed on individual when taken out of the company: Dividends – dividend income, first £2,000 of dividends taxable at 0% Salary – employment income
National insurance	Classes 2 and 4 payable by individual	None on company itself If salary paid, company pays employer's contributions and individual has employee's contributions deducted No NICs on dividends
Use of business assets privately	No further charge; may restrict capital allowances	Charge to income tax may arise as taxable benefits. No restrictions on company's CAs for private use

Marking scheme

	Marks
Type of tax	1
Due date for tax on profits	2
Extraction of profits	2
National insurances	2½
Use of business assets privately	2½
	10

167

85 Heaters Ltd

Heaters Ltd – corporation tax payment dates for y/e 31 March 2021

Instalment amount £380,000 × 1/4 = £95,000

	Amount £	Due
First instalment	95,000	14 October 2020
Second instalment	95,000	14 January 2021
Third instalment	95,000	14 April 2021
Fourth instalment	95,000	14 July 2021
	380,000	

Marking scheme

	Marks
Instalment amount	1
Amount and due dates (1 mark each)	4
	5

86 Flower plc

Flower plc – corporation tax payments

Corporation tax for the year ended 31 March 2021:

	£
Instalment amount: $\dfrac{£342,000}{4}$	85,500

Payment dates:

	£
14 October 2020	85,500
14 January 2021	85,500
14 April 2021	85,500
14 July 2021	85,500

> **Helping hand.** The information in the question showed that Flowers plc was a large company in the previous accounting period, as well as the current period, and so was required to pay corporation tax in instalments in the current accounting period.

Marking scheme

	Marks
Instalment amount	1
1st instalment	1
2nd instalment	1
3rd instalment	1
4th instalment	1
	5

ANSWERS

87 Multiple choice questions: Corporation tax liabilities

87.1 1 January 2020 to 30 June 2020

> **Examining team's comments.** This question was set in the June 2019 examination and is an example of one that candidates found difficult.
>
> The basic rule to remember here is that companies can never have a chargeable period of more than 12 months. If there is a period of account in excess of this then the period has to be split into two separate chargeable periods. The first period is always the first 12 months and the second is the balancing period – six months in this instance.
>
> Therefore the correct answer was the third option – the first period being the 12 months to 31 December 2018 and the balancing period of six months forming the second chargeable period. Most candidates incorrectly split the period by taking the first six months and then the last 12.

87.2 £1,500

£(12,500 – 14,000 (lower of cost and proceeds)) = £1,500

> **Examining team's comments.** This question was set in the December 2018 examination and is one that some candidates found difficult.
>
> To answer this question correctly candidates needed to know two facts – firstly, on disposal the amount included in the pool is always the lower of the original cost and the sales proceeds, and secondly, that private usage by an employee or director has no effect on the capital allowance calculation.
>
> £14,000 is therefore deducted from the pool balance leaving a negative figure of £1,500 which represents the balancing charge on the pool. It is not reduced by the private usage.
>
> Future candidates should note that the private percentage never reduces the cost or proceeds figure.

87.3 £57,500

	£
Indexed gain	70,000
Less rollover relief (balancing figure)	(57,500)
Chargeable gain: amount not reinvested £(200,000 – 187,500)	12,500

87.4 £35,000

	£
Trading income	175,000
Interest income	28,000
Chargeable gains	12,000
Total profits	215,000
Less carry forward trading loss relief	(180,000)
Taxable total profits	35,000

87.5 £100

The return was due on 31 December 2021 and is therefore less than three months late. The fixed penalty is therefore £100 since this was the first late return.

87.6 £36,000

	£
Premium	60,000
2% (21 – 1) × £60,000	(24,000)
	36,000

87.7 £2,720

	£
Leasing cost	3,200
£3,200 × 15% disallowance as CO_2 emissions exceed 110g/km	(480)
Allowable deduction	2,720

87.8 £11,010

	£
Rental income (accruals basis)	13,200
Less general letting expenses	(1,750)
Less replacement furniture	(440)
Property business income	11,010

87.9 Return date 31 December 2021, Tax payable date 1 October 2021

The return must be submitted within 12 months of the end of the accounting period and the tax paid nine months and one day after the end of the accounting period.

87.10 £484,496

	£
Net proceeds £(640,000 – 6,000)	634,000
Less cost £(120,000 + 8,000)	(128,000)
	506,000
Less indexation £128,000 × 0.168 (frozen at 12.17)	(21,504)
Chargeable gain	484,496

87.11 £800

Only the legal fees for the purchase of a new building are not allowable as they are a capital expense. Staff entertainment is fully allowable, although any amount over £150 (inc VAT) per staff member should be included as a benefit on an employee's P11D.

87.12 £26,000

A company must first make a current year loss claim against total profits if it wishes to make a claim to carry a loss back. A company is permitted to carry back to 12 months only, against total profits (ie before qualifying charitable donations). Therefore the maximum carry back is the total profits in the year to 31 December 2019 ie £26,000. This is less than the loss remaining, of £30,000, following the current year claim.

87.13 On cessation, trade losses can be carried back against total profits for 36 months

Property losses can be used against total income of the same period and carry forward relief is against total profits of future accounting periods. Capital losses cannot be carried back to previous years. Trade losses can be carried forward and usually used against total profits. Therefore all of the first three statements are untrue. On cessation, trade losses can be carried back against total profits for 36 months. Therefore the final statement is true.

87.14 £120,000

	£
Proceeds	600,000
SBAs y/e 31.12.20 (7/12 × 3% × £500,000)	8,750
SBAs y/e 31.12.21 (9/12 × 3% × £500,000)	11,250
Net proceeds	620,000
Cost	(500,000)
Chargeable gain	120,000

SBA are given as deductions from trading profits up until the date of disposal. Any SBAs claimed by the company are added onto proceeds in the chargeable gain calculation.

Remember there is no indexation on the disposal as the factory was purchased after December 2017.

87.15 10 January 2031

> **Examining team's comments.** This question was set in the December 2014 examination. It was not well attempted by the majority of candidates.
>
> Candidates should have dismissed the third option, given that the company is trying to delay paying tax this date would be too close and possibly in the same chargeable period. As the reinvestment of the proceeds was in a depreciating asset (the fixed plant and machinery) the gain can be deferred until the earliest of (i) the date the replacement asset is sold; (ii) the date the replacement asset ceases to be used in the business; and (iii) ten years from the date the replacement asset was purchased. If candidates had simply remembered the ten-year rule then the first option could also have been quickly dismissed leaving just the remaining two options to choose from. The way to remember this is to measure the ten-year period from the date that the proceeds are reinvested as this is the event which triggers the possible claim for deferment of the gain.

87.16 £82,000

> **Examining team's comments.** This question was set in the December 2016 examination. It was not well attempted by the majority of candidates.
>
> The question required the use of two types of losses by a company, the correct answer being dependent on knowing which type of income each of the losses could be used against.
>
> To answer this question the candidate needed to know which income the losses could be set against. The easiest decision was the capital loss. Capital losses brought forward (for individuals and companies) MUST be used against capital gains only – therefore the capital loss of £8,000 could reduce the gain of £7,000 only – ruling out the first option immediately which uses all the losses and the second option which doesn't use any of the capital losses. Brought forward property losses are used against the total profits (not restricted to other property income) therefore **all** of the property loss will be claimed (since the question states that loss relief is always claimed as early as possible) leaving the correct answer of £82,000 (all of the income less all of the £22,000 property loss). [BPP note. These comments have been updated for the change in use of carry forward losses from 1 April 2017.]

88 Answer to question with help: Value added tax payable

	Quarter ended			
	31.03.20 £	30.06.20 £	30.09.20 £	31.12.20 £
Outputs				
Invoice work	20,000	12,000	18,000	38,000
Output VAT @ 20%	4,000	2,400	3,600	7,600
Inputs				
Telephone	110	110	110	110
New tools			2,000	
Fuel	240	240	240	240
Servicing	200			
Repairs		800		
	550	1,150	2,350	350
Input VAT thereon	110	230	470	70
Net VAT payable	3,890	2,170	3,130	7,530
Due date	07.05.20	07.08.20	07.11.20	07.02.21

VAT on the new car is not recoverable and financial services (overdraft interest) are exempt.

89 Emma

Emma – VAT for quarter ended 31 December 2020

	£	£
Output tax		
Standard rated sales		
(£450,000 × 96% × 20% × 50%) + (£450,000 × 20% × 50%)		88,200
Zero rated sales		–
Input tax		
Inventory £180,000 × 20%	36,000	
Wages – outside scope of VAT	0	
Electricity £40,000 × 1/6	6,667	
Motoring expenses £15,000 × 1/6	2,500	
Impairment debt – £1,200 × 20%	240	
Impairment debt – £900 but less than six months old	0	(45,407)
VAT payable		42,793

Marking scheme

	Marks
Output tax	
Standard rated	2½
Zero rated	1
Input tax	
Inventory	1
Wages	½
Electricity	1½
Motoring expenses	1½
Impairment debt £1,200	1
Impairment debt £900	1
	10

90 Legg Ltd

	£	£
Output VAT		
Inventory sold £250,000 × 1/6		41,667
Private fuel £334 × 1/6		56
		41,723
Input VAT		
Inventory purchased £130,000 × 1/6	21,667	
Office furniture £2,000 × 1/6	333	
Business entertaining – irrecoverable	0	
Fuel £1,800 × 1/6	300	(22,300)
VAT payable		19,423

ANSWERS

Marking scheme

	Marks
Output VAT	
Inventory	1½
Fuel	2
Input VAT	
Inventory	1½
Office furniture	1½
Business entertaining – irrecoverable	1
Fuel	1½
VAT payable	1
	10

91 AccountsRUs

Compulsory registration

Compulsory registration is required if either of the following two tests is met.

(1) *Historic test*

At the end of any month, the cumulative turnover (excluding VAT) of taxable supplies in the previous 12 months exceeded the £85,000 threshold.

(2) *Future test*

If at any time it is forecast that turnover (excluding VAT) of taxable supplies in the next 30 days alone will exceed £85,000.

Notification

In both cases, HM Revenue and Customs (HMRC) must be notified within 30 days. For the **historic test** notification is due within 30 days of the month end. For the **future test**, the deadline for HMRC to receive notification of registration coincides with the end of the 30-day period.

Effective date

Registration will be effective from the end of the month following the month in which the threshold was exceeded for the **historic test**. For the **future test**, registration is effective from the start of the 30-day period.

Marking scheme

	Marks
12-month historic test	2
30-day future test	2
Notification to HMRC	3
Effective registration date	3
	10

92 City Merchandise

VAT due quarter to 31 December 2020

	£	£
Standard rated sales		
(£110,000 × 20% × 95% × 50%) + (£110,000 × 20% × 50%)(N1)		21,450
Less: standard rated purchases £60,000 × 20%	12,000	
electricity £4,000 × 1/6	667	
accounting £1,000 × 1/6	167	
machine repairs £2,500 × 1/6	417	(13,251)
VAT due 7 February 2021		8,199

Notes

1. Where a discount is offered for prompt payment, VAT is charged on the actual amount received.
2. Wages are outside the scope of VAT.

Marking scheme

	Marks
Standard rate sales	2½
Standard rate purchases	1
Electricity	1½
Accounting	1½
Repairs	1½
Due date	1
Wages outside scope	1
	10

93 The Stuart Partnership

Value added tax (VAT) for the quarter ended 31 December 2020

		£	£
Output tax:			
Standard rated sales	£180,000 × 20%		36,000
Input tax:			
Purchases and expenses	£85,000 × 20%	17,000	
Machine	£7,050 × 1/6	1,175	
Car	VAT not recoverable	0	(18,175)
VAT payable			17,825

Marking scheme

	Marks
Output tax	
Standard rated sales	1
Input tax	
Purchases and expenses	1
Machine	2
Car	1
	5

ANSWERS

94 Ivor

Ivor – notes for meeting on annual accounting scheme

- Open to traders who regularly pay VAT to HM Revenue and Customs (HMRC).
- Allows traders to prepare only one VAT return per year.
- Taxable turnover (excluding VAT) is not expected to exceed £1,350,000 in the next 12 months.
- All VAT returns must be up to date.
- The annual return must be submitted within two months of the VAT year end.
- Nine payments on account are required during months 4 to 12 of the annual VAT period.
- Payments are made by direct debt.
- Each payment equals 10% of the net VAT payable for the previous year.
- Any balance due must be paid with the return.
- There is an option to pay three larger interim instalments.

Marking scheme

	Marks
½ mark for each point	5

95 Resolute plc

If the net error does not exceed the greater of £10,000 or 1% × turnover (subject to an overall £50,000 limit), an adjustment can be made on the next VAT return.

In addition, the relevant HMRC VAT Error Correction Team may be informed, in writing and preferably using Form VAT 652. The box on the form should be ticked to show that the error has been adjusted for on the return.

If the net error is more than the above limits, it cannot be adjusted for on the next VAT return. Instead the relevant HMRC VAT Error Correction Team must be informed in writing as a voluntary disclosure using Form VAT 652.

Marking scheme

	Marks
Error may be corrected on next return	½
Limits	2
May inform Error Correction Team	½
Tick box on form	½
Larger errors cannot be corrected on next return	½
Must inform Error Correction Team	1
	5

96 Bob

(a) The tax point determines the VAT period in which output tax must be accounted for and credit for input tax will be allowed.

The tax point also determines which rate applies if the rate of VAT or a VAT category changes (for example when a supply ceases to be zero-rated and becomes standard-rated).

(b) The basic tax point is the date on which services are completed.

(c) If a VAT invoice is issued or payment is received before the basic tax point, the earlier of these dates automatically becomes the tax point instead of the basic tax point.

If the earlier date rule does not apply and if the VAT invoice is issued within 14 days after the basic tax point, the invoice date becomes the tax point instead of the basic tax point.

Marking scheme

		Marks	
(a)	VAT period	1	
	Rate of VAT	1	
			2
(b)	Date services completed		1
(c)	Invoice/payment before basic tax point	1	
	Invoice within 14 days after basic tax point	1	
			2
			5

97 Martha and Dominic

(a) The VAT registration limit is £85,000. Martha's taxable turnover will exceed this at the end of March 2021 (£15,000 × 6 months).

Martha must therefore notify HMRC within 30 days of 31 March 2021, ie by 30 April 2021.

Martha will be registered from the end of the month following the month in which the £85,000 was exceeded, ie 1 May 2021 (or an earlier date, if requested).

(b) Dominic is eligible for voluntary deregistration if HMRC are satisfied that the value of his taxable supplies (net of VAT) in the following one-year period will not exceed £83,000.

HMRC will cancel Dominic's registration from the date the request is made or from an agreed later date.

Marking scheme

		Marks	
(a)	Registration limit exceeded	1	
	Notification date	1	
	Registration date	1	
			3
(b)	Deregistration limit	1	
	Deregistration date	1	
			2
			5

98 Narrow Ltd

VAT is blocked and therefore can not be recovered on the following items:

- Motor cars not used entirely for business purposes (private use by a proprietor or an employee is non-business use)

- Business entertainment (other than for overseas customers)

ANSWERS

- Expenses incurred on domestic accommodation for directors
- Non-business items passed through the accounts
- VAT which does not relate to the making of supplies by the buyer in the course of a business

Marking scheme

	Marks
1 mark for each point	5

99 Celeste

Value added tax (VAT) input tax paid on the supply of goods to you before registration can be reclaimed if:

- The goods were acquired for the purpose of your business which was being carried on at the time of supply.
- The goods have not been supplied to your customers or consumed before registration (although they can have been used to make other goods which are still held).
- The VAT must have been incurred in the four years before registration.

Value added tax (VAT) input tax paid on the supply of goods to you before registration can be reclaimed if:

- The services were supplied for the purpose of your business which was being carried on at the time of supply.
- The services were supplied within the six months before registration.

Marking scheme

	Marks
Goods	
Acquired for purpose of business	1
Not supplied/consumed	1
Four years	1
Services	
Supplied for purpose of business	1
Six months	1
	5

100 Dana

(a)

	£
£362 × 2/3 =	241
Output tax:	
1/6 × £241	£40
Input tax:	
1/6 × £288	£48

(b) If the fuel is bought by Dana who is reimbursed for the actual cost of business fuel then LMN Ltd can deduct the input tax relating to business use and there is no fuel scale charge.

LMN Ltd must hold a VAT invoice (or invoices) showing sufficient VAT to cover the input tax claim being made.

Marking scheme

			Marks
(a)	Scale charge	1	
	Output tax	1	
	Input tax	1	
			3
(b)	Input tax on business use	1	
	Invoice required	1	
			2
			5

101 Blue Ltd

Tax invoice – additional information

- The supplier's registration number
- The tax point
- A description of the goods or services supplied, giving for each description the quantity, the unit price, the rate of VAT, and the VAT exclusive amount
- The VAT rate(s) applicable
- The total amount of VAT

Marking scheme

	Marks
1 mark for each additional piece of information	5

102 Merrill

	£
Output VAT on standard rate sales £36,000 × 20%	7,200
Less input VAT on standard rate purchases £22,000 × 20%	(4,400)
Net output VAT due to HMRC	2,800

VAT 100

Box 1	7,200.00
Box 3	7,200.00
Box 4	4,400.00
Box 5	2,800.00
Box 6	45,000
Box 7	25,000

Note. The total in Box 6 is standard rate sales (£36,000) plus zero rate sales (£9,000). All are excluding VAT, as specified on the form. Similarly, the total in Box 7 is standard rated purchased (£22,000) plus zero rate purchases (£3,000).

Marking scheme

		Marks	
(a)	Standard rate sales	½	
	Standard rate purchases	½	
			1
(b)	Boxes 1, 3, 4, 5 (½ mark each)	2	
	Boxes 6 and 7 (1 mark each)	2	
			4
			5

103 Multiple choice questions: Value added tax

103.1 1 April 2021

The basic tax point is the date on which the services are completed (20 March 2021), but the actual tax point is the date of the invoice as this is issued within 14 days. The date of payment is only relevant if it is before the basic tax point.

103.2 £4,760

£34,000 × 14% = £4,760. The flat rate percentage is applied to tax inclusive turnover.

103.3 £4,925

	£
Output VAT: £35,250 × 1/6	5,875
Less input VAT: £5,700 × 1/6	(950)
VAT due	4,925

Look carefully at the information given in the question. You were told that the figures were inclusive of VAT and therefore you needed to use the VAT fraction to work out the VAT.

103.4 £9,900

£110,000 × 9% = £9,900. The flat rate percentage is applied to the full tax inclusive turnover including all standard, zero and exempt supplies.

103.5 On the selling price ignoring the discount with a credit note being issued if the discount is taken

Since details of the discount are not included on the invoice, output VAT should be calculated on the selling price ignoring the discount with a credit note being issued if the discount is taken.

103.6 20 September 2020

The tax point is 20 September 2020, the date when the customer made the payment. The basic tax point (27 September 2020) is overridden as payment is received before that date.

103.7 £23,520

Discounts for prompt payment are only taken into account when the discount is taken up. Therefore the VAT due is (£120,000 × 96% × 20% × 50%) + (£120,000 × 20% × 50%) = £23,520.

103.8 31 December 2020

The tax point is generally the earliest of: the date of delivery, the invoice date and the cash receipt date. However, if as in this case, the invoice is issued within 14 days of delivery, then the invoice date becomes the tax point.

103.9   A tax exclusive annual taxable turnover of up to £150,000

The taxable turnover of £150,000 is exclusive of value added tax and should include both zero rated supplies and standard rated supplies. The £85,000 limit relates to normal registration.

103.10   1 January 2021

Kevin will be liable to register for value added tax (VAT) when he is aware that his taxable turnover during the next 30 days will exceed the VAT registration limit of £85,000 (the future test). HM Revenue and Customs (HMRC) will then register Kevin from the first day of that 30-day period. In this instance – 1 January 2021.

103.11   VAT quarter ended 30 June 2021

The value added tax (VAT) on an impaired debt may only be reclaimed once the debt has been outstanding for six months from the due date. The due date in this instance is 10 October 2020; therefore the VAT can be reclaimed in the quarter ended 30 June 2021.

103.12   £200

Value added tax (VAT) is calculated on the amount actually received where details of the discount are included on the invoice. Since the discount does not apply in this case, the VAT due is therefore £200 (£1,000 × 20%).

103.13   £35

> **Examining team's comments.** This question was set in the June 2017 examination. It was not well answered by the majority of candidates.
>
> To answer this question the candidate firstly needed to realise that the cost given was inclusive of VAT and therefore the total amount of VAT paid was £70 (ie £420 × 1/6) not £84 (ie £420 × 20%). The distinction between inclusive and exclusive is a point that many candidates have trouble understanding. The second piece of knowledge to be applied was that only 50% of the VAT can be reclaimed if the car is being used for any amount of private use. Therefore the correct answer was £35 (ie £70 × 50% = £35).

103.14   £864

> **Examining team's comments.** This question was set in the December 2017 examination. It was not well answered by the majority of candidates.
>
> Candidates should have known that Value Added Tax (VAT), in relation to the purchase of motor cars, can never be reclaimed if there is any private use at all. Therefore the starting point for calculating writing down allowance (WDA) is the VAT inclusive cost of £14,400. Candidates should then have checked the percentage WDA that this particular motor car is entitled to. To do this, candidates should have checked the tax rates and allowances tables at the start of the exam – for a motor car with a CO_2 emission rate of 140 grams per kilometre the percentage is 6%. If this is then used to multiply the VAT inclusive cost of £14,400 the correct allowance of £864 results.

103.15　　19 June 2020

Examining team's comments. This question was set in the December 2019 examination.

The deemed date of sale, the tax point, is important for several reasons including which rate of value added tax (VAT) is to be used and in which VAT quarter the sale should be accounted for. The supply date is usually the tax point, however this can be amended when either payment is received or an invoice is issued before this date. Note that the order date is never relevant because the seller may never actually supply the goods. In addition, if the invoice is issued within 14 days of the supply then this date would become the tax point. Therefore, the offer date, 29 May, can be ignored and because the payment date, 16 July, was after the date of supply that can also be ignored. The invoice date was within 14 days of supply therefore the correct answer in this case is the invoice date, ie 19 June 2020. The correct answer was therefore C.

Mock Exam 1
(Specimen exam updated for FA 2020)

Foundations in Accountancy

Foundations in Taxation (UK)
Mock Examination 1

Specimen Exam updated for FA 2020

Questions	
Time allowed	2 hours
All questions are compulsory and MUST be attempted	

DO NOT OPEN THIS EXAM UNTIL YOU ARE READY TO START UNDER EXAMINATION CONDITIONS

Section A – ALL 15 questions are compulsory and MUST be attempted

1. **Which form shows an employee's end of year pay summary, and by which date should he or she receive it?**

   - ○ P11D by 6 July following the relevant tax year
   - ○ P11D by 31 May following the relevant tax year
   - ○ P60 by 6 July following the relevant tax year
   - ○ P60 by 31 May following the relevant tax year

   (2 marks)

2. James is a sole trader preparing accounts annual to 31 March. James uses his motor car for both business and private purposes throughout the whole of the year ended 31 March 2021. The motor car has a CO_2 emission rate of 120 grams per kilometre and had cost £18,000. The private mileage for James' accounting period ended 31 March 2021 represented 20% of the total mileage for that year.

   What is the maximum amount of capital allowances that James can claim in respect of the motor car for the accounting year ended 31 March 2021?

   - ○ £864
   - ○ £3,240
   - ○ £1,080
   - ○ £2,592

   (2 marks)

3. Bernie is an employee. His employer provided him with the use of free accommodation for the whole of the tax year 2020/21. It was not deemed to be job related.

   The accommodation cost Bernie's employer £100,000 in February 2017 and has an annual value of £8,000. The market value of the property on 6 April 2020 was £190,000.

   In addition to the basic charge of £8,000, what is Bernie's taxable benefit in respect of the accommodation provided in the tax year 2020/21?

   - ○ £2,588
   - ○ £4,275
   - ○ £563
   - ○ £2,250

   (2 marks)

4. Rosie is a sole trader and had £40,000 tax adjusted trading profits for her accounting year ended 31 August 2020.

   What is Rosie's class 4 national insurance contributions (NIC) liability for the tax year 2020/21?

   - ○ £3,660
   - ○ £2,745
   - ○ £4,800
   - ○ £3,600

   (2 marks)

5. Ted, Pearl and Aide are in partnership sharing profits and losses equally. In their accounting year ended 31 March 2021 they made a trading loss of £39,000. Aide left the partnership on 31 December 2020.

   Which of the following statements is true?

   - ○ Aide's share of the trading loss is £13,000
   - ○ Aide can carry his share of the trading loss back to 2019/20 against total income
   - ○ Ted can give Pearl his share of the trading loss
   - ○ Ted and Pearl can carry their own share of the trading loss forward against total income

   (2 marks)

6   Nigel has use of an asset provided by his employer from 6 November 2020. The asset had cost the employer £4,000 but the market value of the asset in November 2020 was £3,000. Nigel pays £20 a month for the use of the asset. The asset has not been used by any other employee.

What is Nigel's taxable benefit in respect of the asset provided for his use in the tax year 2020/21?

- ○ £233
- ○ £700
- ○ £150
- ○ £500

(2 marks)

7   A company prepared financial statements for the 15-month period of account ended 31 December 2020. The company is regarded as small for corporation tax purposes.

By which date(s) should the company pay its corporation tax liability for the period of account ended 31 December 2020 to avoid incurring interest and penalties?

- ○ One payment by 1 October 2021
- ○ Two separate payments by 1 July 2021 and 1 October 2021
- ○ Two separate payments by 1 October 2020 and 1 October 2021
- ○ One payment by 31 January 2022

(2 marks)

8   **With regards to a company, which of the following statements is true?**

- ○ Property business losses can only be used against property business income
- ○ Allowable capital losses can be used against chargeable gains of the previous year
- ○ Trading losses can be carried forward and used against taxable total profits in future years
- ○ Trading losses can be carried forward against future trade income only

(2 marks)

9   A company had the following expenses in its period of account ended 31 March 2021:

Legal expenses in respect of trade debt collecting	£800
Depreciation of plant and machinery	£1,200
Staff entertainment	£900
Gifts of food to clients	£600

How much should the company add back to its accounting profit to arrive at its tax adjusted profit?

- ○ £2,700
- ○ £2,600
- ○ £1,800
- ○ £2,100

(2 marks)

10   A UK taxpayer sold two assets in the tax year 2020/21. One resulted in a chargeable gain and the other in an allowable loss.

In which circumstances is there no need to report full details of these disposals to HM Revenue and Customs (HMRC)?

- ○ Where the net gains (after losses) are less than £12,300
- ○ Where the proceeds of sale are less than £49,200
- ○ Where the net gains (after losses) are less than £12,300 and the proceeds of sale are less then £49,200
- ○ Where the total gains (before losses) are less than £12,300 and the proceeds of sale are less than £49,200

(2 marks)

11   Mary has two taxable gains (after deduction of the annual exempt amount) in the tax year 2020/21:

£10,000 – qualifying for business asset disposal relief
£12,000 – not qualifying for business asset disposal relief or liable to residential property rates of capital gains tax

Mary has taxable income of £30,000 in the tax year 2020/21.

What is Mary's capital gains tax liability for the tax year 2020/21?

- ○ £2,200
- ○ £2,950
- ○ £3,400
- ○ £4,400 (2 marks)

12   Chi gives his daughter some shares in the family business. The shares had cost Chi £80,000 and have a current market value of £120,000. The company's total assets are worth £800,000 of which 10% are held for investment and 20% is in cash.

What is the maximum gift relief which Chi and his daughter may claim in respect of the gift of shares?

- ○ £40,000
- ○ £32,000
- ○ £28,000
- ○ £35,000 (2 marks)

13   In the tax year 2020/21 Silvia pays £8,000 to her employer's HM Revenue and Customs approved occupational pension scheme. Silvia's employer contributes £4,000.

Which of the following statements is true?

- ○ Silvia's taxable employment income is reduced by £12,000
- ○ The basic rate band is extended by the gross contribution of £10,000
- ○ Silvia has a taxable benefit of £4,000 and her taxable employment income is reduced by £8,000
- ○ Silvia has a tax-exempt benefit of £4,000 and her taxable employment income is reduced by £8,000 (2 marks)

14   A sole trader, who is registered for value added tax (VAT), sells standard rated inventory valued at £1,000 (exclusive of VAT) in March 2020. A trade discount of 10% is applied to the value of £1,000.

How much VAT must the sole trader charge on the sale?

- ○ £200
- ○ £167
- ○ £180
- ○ £150 (2 marks)

15   **In regard to value added tax (VAT) which of the following is true?**

- ○ When traders cease to make taxable supplies they must notify HM Revenue and Customs within 30 days and the company will be deregistered from the day of notification
- ○ Traders making taxable supplies, with a turnover below the VAT registration threshold, can voluntarily register for VAT at any time
- ○ Traders can voluntarily deregister if any time their turnover was below the VAT deregistration threshold in the last 12 months
- ○ Traders do not pay VAT on purchases if they are not registered for VAT (2 marks)

(Total = 30 marks)

Section B – ALL EIGHT questions are compulsory and MUST be attempted

16 Stella

Stella is an employee of a large company. Stella received a salary of £188,412 for the tax year 2020/21.

In May 2020 Stella received a bonus of £12,000 based on the company profits for the year ended 31 December 2019.

Stella's company provided Stella with the use of a company van on 6 October 2020. Stella uses the van 40% for private purposes and 60% for business purposes. The company pays for all of the petrol for both private and business mileage.

Stella's employer has deducted £75,223 income tax (under PAYE) from Stella's income for the tax year 2020/21.

During the tax year 2020/21 Stella also received the following amounts of other income:

Dividend income	£4,000
National savings bank (NSB) interest	£600
Bank deposit interest	£2,000

During the tax year 2020/21 Stella contributed £8,000 net contributions to her personal pension fund.

Required

Calculate the income tax payable by, or refundable to, Stella for the tax year 2020/21. (15 marks)

17 Lace Ltd

Lace Ltd is registered for value added tax (VAT). Lace Ltd prepared financial statements annually to 31 March. During October 2020, the company decided to change its accounting date to 31 December.

As a consequence, Lace Ltd prepared its most recent set of financial statements for the nine months ended 31 December 2020.

Lace Ltd had the following results for the nine-month period of account ended 31 December 2020:

	£
Adjusted trading profit (before capital allowances)	1,801,800
Non-trade investment income	45,000
Chargeable gain	195,000
Dividend received	9,000
Qualifying charitable donation	14,000

The investment income was the full amount receivable for the nine-month period ended 31 December 2020.

Lace Ltd brought forward capital losses of £10,000 and trading losses of £28,000 on 1 April 2020, both of which arose in the year ended 31 March 2020.

For capital allowances purposes Lace Ltd brought forward the following tax written down values as at 1 April 2020:

Main pool	£210,000
Special rate pool	£40,000

Lace Ltd purchased a new machine for £960,000 on 14 June 2020 and sold an old machine, which had cost £24,000, for £28,800 on 4 December 2020. All figures relating to machinery additions and disposals are inclusive of VAT.

Required

Calculate the corporation tax payable by Lace Ltd for the nine-month period of account ended 31 December 2020. Your answer should identify any item which is not taxable and state why it is not included in your calculation.

(15 marks)

18 Rebecca

Rebecca made the following disposals of capital assets in the tax year 2020/21:

15 August 2020	Part of a field was sold for £24,000. This was part of a ten-hectare field, which Rebecca had purchased in 2009 for £80,000. The remaining part of the field had a market value of £126,000 in August 2020. Expenses of sale amounted to £1,500.
14 November 2020	A military medal was sold for £8,000. Rebecca had inherited the medal from her father (who had been awarded the medal in 1946) in 2006 when it had a market value of £1,400.
2 January 2021	A building which was held as an investment was sold for £295,000. Expenses of sale amounted to £15,000. The building had cost £190,000 in August 2009 and was extended at a cost of £20,000 in May 2014. The building was not a residential property.

None of the assets were business assets.

Rebecca earns a salary of £120,000 per year.

Required

Calculate the capital gains tax payable by Rebecca for the tax year 2020/21. (10 marks)

19 Bud plc

Bud plc is registered for value added tax (VAT). During the three-month VAT period ended 31 March 2021, Bud plc made the following transactions.

	£
Sales:	
Standard rated sales	240,000
Zero rated sales	80,000
Purchases:	
Inventory (all standard rated)	110,000
A machine for use in the business	40,000
A car for both private and business use	25,000

Two debts were written off during the three-month period ended 31 March 2021:

	£
A debt which was due on 31 August 2020	3,000
A debt which was due on 30 November 2020	5,000

Both debts relate to standard rated sales.

All figures are exclusive of VAT.

Required

Calculate the valued added tax (VAT) that was payable to HM Revenue and Customs (HMRC) by Bud plc for the three-month period ended 31 March 2021.

Note. Your answer should clearly state why any VAT is not calculated on any of the figures listed in the scenario.

(10 marks)

20 Betty

Betty is a basic rate tax payer. Included in her total income for the tax year 2020/21 were the following amounts of investment income

	£
National Savings Bank (NSB) interest	400
Interest from an individual savings account (ISA) held in a UK bank	1,000
Interest from a UK bank deposit account	6,000
Interest from a UK bank current account	500
Proceeds from national savings and investment (NS&I) certificates	3,000
Dividends from UK companies	7,000
Dividends from UK ISA account	900
Premium bond winnings	250

Required

An extract from the self-assessment tax return is shown below. Using the information provided, complete the entries for boxes 1, 2, 4 and 5 only.

Interest and dividends from UK banks and building societies

1	Taxed UK interest	5	Other dividends
	£		£
2	Untaxed UK interest	6	Foreign dividends (up to £300)
	£		£
3	Untaxed foreign interest (up to £2,000)	7	Tax taken off foreign dividends
	£		£
4	Dividends from UK companies		
	£		

(Adapted from HMRC, 2020)

(5 marks)

MOCK EXAM 1 (SPECIMEN EXAM) // QUESTIONS

21 Jennifer

In the tax year 2020/21, Jennifer rented out a furnished residential property for an annual rent of £12,000. The full amount was received in the tax year, with the exception of £1,000 due for March 2021, which was received in May 2021.

Jennifer paid the following expenses in connection with the property:

	£
Water rates	400
Insurance	300
Kitchen extension	3,000
Redecoration	500
New bed	750

The old bed was sold for £50.

Required

Calculate Jennifer's property income for the tax year 2020/21. Your answer should clearly state why any item is not included in your calculation. **(5 marks)**

22 Plant plc

Plant plc prepares financial statements annually to 31 March. On 31 January 2021, Plant plc sold a factory, which it had used in its business, for £840,000. The factory had originally cost Plant plc £410,000 in May 2003.

In August 2021, Plant plc intends to purchase a plot of land, which will be used in its business, for £780,000.

Plant plc always claims any reliefs that it is entitled to.

Required

Calculate Plant plc's chargeable gain for the year ended 31 March 2021.

Note. The indexation factor for May 2003 to December 2017 is 0.532. **(5 marks)**

23 David

David commenced trading as a sole trader on 1 October 2018. David decided to prepare accounts to 31 January each year. David's results for his first three periods of account are as follows.

	£
Period to 31 January 2019	10,500
Year ended 31 January 2020	36,000
Year ended 31 January 2021	40,000

Required

Calculate David's assessable trading profits, and any overlap profit, for the three tax years affected by the above accounting results. Your answer should clearly state the tax years and the basis periods that apply.

(5 marks)

193

Mock Exam 1:

Answers

BPP Note. The following answers are based on the ACCA Examination team's answers to the Specimen Exam. They have been updated by BPP Learning Media to reflect the Finance Act 2020.

Section A

1 P60 by 31 May following the relevant tax year

Form P60 must be given to an employee by 31 May following the relevant tax year. A P11D is the form used to report the benefits given to an employee.

2 £864

Motor cars are not entitled to the annual investment allowance. The motor car will be treated as a special rate item and will therefore be entitled to a writing down allowance of 6%. The allowance will be restricted because of the private use. The maximum amount of capital allowances James can claim is therefore: £18,000 × 6% × 80% ie £864.

3 £625

Accommodation provided for private use by an employer is taxed on the annual value plus an additional amount if the accommodation cost the company more than £75,000. The market value at the beginning of the tax year has no relevance because Bernie moved into the property no more than six years after his employer purchased it. The correct calculation of the additional benefit is therefore £(100,000 − 75,000) × 2.25% ie £563.

4 £2,745

Class 4 national insurance contributions are calculated at 9% on the amount of tax adjusted trading profits between the thresholds of £9,500 and £50,000. Therefore the amount due for the tax year 2020/21 is £(40,000 − 9,500) × 9% ie £2,745.

5 Aide can carry his share of the trading loss back to the tax year 2019/20 against total income

Aide left the partnership on 31 December 2020. On that date his interest in the partnership is deemed to cease and therefore his share of the profit/loss will stop on that date so his share of the loss will be £39,000 × 1/3 × 9/12 = £9,750. Aide cannot carry his loss forward as he has ceased to trade however he can choose to carry back his share of the trading loss to the tax year 2019/20 against total income. Partners cannot surrender losses between themselves as each partner is treated as carrying on their own sole trade. Ted and Pearl can carry their own share of the trading loss forward against trading profits only.

6 £150

The benefit is calculated by multiplying the market value of the asset at the time when it is first used by an employee, by 20%. The benefit is time apportioned for the period it is available for use in the tax year. Any employee contribution towards the use of the asset is deducted from the benefit value. Therefore the benefit for the tax year 2020/21 is £((3,000 × 20% × 5/12) − (20 × 5)) ie £150.

7 Two separate payments by 1 July 2021 and 1 October 2021

A 15-month period of account is split into two chargeable periods, the first being the first 12 months and the second being the remaining three months. Each period has a separate tax calculation resulting in different payment dates of 9 months and 1 day after each relevant period. Note that the filing deadline for both returns will be 31 December 2021, ie 12 months after the end of the second accounting period.

8 Trading losses can be carried forward and used against taxable total profits in future years

Property business losses can be used against total income of the same period before qualifying charitable donations. Capital losses cannot be carried back to previous years. Trade losses can be carried forward against taxable total profits, not just against future trade income.

9 £1,800

Legal fees for debt collecting are trade expenses, staff entertainment is specifically allowable by statute (entertainment of customers would not be allowed), depreciation is disallowed and replaced by capital allowances and gifts of food are never allowable expenses. Therefore the amount to be added back to trading profits is £(1,200 + 600) ie £1,800.

10   Where the total gains (before losses) are less than £12,300 and the proceeds of sale are less than £49,200

There is no need to report details of capital disposals where the total chargeable gains **before** allowable losses are less than the annual exempt amount (£12,300) and proceeds are less than four times the annual exempt amount (£49,200).

11   £3,400

Chargeable gains subject to business asset disposal relief are taxed at 10%. These chargeable gains will use up, before non-qualifying gains, any remaining basic rate band not used by total income for income tax purposes. Therefore the chargeable gains not entitled to business asset disposal relief will be taxed at 20%. The correct answer is therefore £(10,000 ×10%) + £(12,000 × 20%) ie £3,400.

12   £35,000

The amount of the gift relief claim is restricted to the total gain multiplied by the ratio of chargeable business assets to total chargeable assets. Cash is not a chargeable asset and investments are not business assets. Therefore the claim is £40,000 × £(560,000/640,000) ie £35,000.

13   Silvia has a tax-exempt benefit of £4,000 and her taxable employment income is reduced by £8,000

Employee contributions to an occupational pension scheme reduce the employee's employment income. Employer contributions are an exempt benefit.

14   £180

Value added tax (VAT) is calculated on the discounted price. The amount is exclusive of VAT therefore the rate of 20% is used to calculate the amount to be added. The VAT due is therefore £(1,000 × 90% × 20%) ie £180.

15   Traders making taxable supplies, with a turnover below the VAT registration threshold, can voluntarily register for VAT at any time

Cessation would take effect on the day taxable supplies cease: a non-value added tax (VAT) registered trader would still have to pay VAT on its purchases; voluntary deregistration is allowed if the turnover in the next 12 months is expected to be below the VAT deregistration threshold and therefore the correct answer is voluntary registration is allowed at any time provided the trader is making taxable supplies.

Section B

16 Stella

Stella – income tax payable or repayable for the tax year 2020/21

	Non-savings income £	Savings income £	Dividend income £	Total £
Salary	188,412			
Bonus (receipts basis)	12,000			
Van benefit (W)	2,078			
Employment income	202,490			
Bank deposit interest		2,000		
National Savings Bank interest		600		
Dividend income			4,000	
Net income	202,490	2,600	4,000	209,090
Less personal allowance (N)	nil			
Taxable income	202,490	2,600	4,000	209,090

Working

	£
Use of van: £3,490 × 6/12	1,745
Petrol for van: £666 × 6/12	333
	2,078

Note. Net income is above £125,000 so no personal allowance is available.

Increase in basic rate limit: £37,500 + (£8,000 × 100/80) = £47,500
Increase in higher rate limit: £150,000 + (£8,000 × 100/80) = £160,000

			£	£
Tax payable:				
Non-savings income:	basic rate		47,500 × 20%	9,500
	higher rate		112,500 × 40%	45,000
			160,000	
	additional rate		42,490 × 45%	19,120
			202,490	
Savings income				
(no nil rate band for additional rate taxpayer)			2,600 × 45%	1,170
Dividend income:	nil rate		2,000 × 0%	0
Dividend income:	additional rate		2,000 × 38.1%	762
Tax liability				75,552
Less tax deducted at source: PAYE				(75,223)
Tax payable				329

Helping hand. Don't forget to increase both the basic rate limit and the higher rate limit by the grossed-up personal pension contribution. Remember that this does not increase the amount of the higher rate band (which is always £112,500 in 2020/21), it just preserves it.

Marking scheme

	Marks
Salary	½
Bonus	½
Van benefit	1½
Van fuel benefit	1½
Bank deposit interest	1
National Savings Bank interest	1
Dividends	1
Personal allowance not available	1
Increase in basic rate limit	1½
Increase in higher rate limit	1½
Non-savings income basic rate	½
Non-savings income higher rate	½
Non-savings income additional rate	½
Savings income additional rate (no nil rate band applied)	½
Dividend nil rate band	½
Dividend income additional rate	½
PAYE	½
Tax payable	½
	15

17 Lace Ltd

Lace Ltd – Corporation tax payable for the nine-month period ended 31 December 2020

	£	£
Adjusted trading profit (before capital allowances)	1,801,800	
Less capital allowances (W)	(784,200)	
Trading income		1,017,600
Investment income		45,000
Chargeable gain	195,000	
Less capital loss b/f	(10,000)	
Net chargeable gain		185,000
Total profits		1,247,600
Less trading loss b/f		(28,000)
Less qualifying charitable donation		(14,000)
Taxable total profits		1,205,600

Dividend income is not taxable.

Tax payable £1,205,600 × 19% 229,064

Working

	AIA £	Main pool £	Special rate pool £	Allowances £
TWDVs b/f		210,000	40,000	
Additions				
qualifying for AIA				
14 June 2020				
£960,000 × 100/120 (net of VAT)	800,000			
AIA £1,000,000 × 9/12	(750,000)			750,000
	50,000			
To pool	(50,000)	50,000		
Disposal				
4 December 2020				
£24,000 (limited to cost) × 100/120 (net of VAT)		(20,000)		
		240,000		
WDA × 18% × 9/12		(32,400)		32,400
WDA × 6% × 9/12			(1,800)	1,800
TWDVs c/f		207,600	38,200	
Allowances				784,200

Helping hand. Stating that the dividend is not taxable is an easy mark – make sure you get it!

Marking scheme

	Marks
Capital allowances:	
Addition	1½
Annual investment allowance	1½
Transfer to pool	½
Disposal	1½
WDA on main pool	1½
WDA on special rate pool	1½
Investment income	1
Chargeable gain	1
Capital loss b/f	1
Trading loss b/f	1
Qualifying charitable donation	1
Dividend income not taxable	1
Tax payable	1
	15

18 Rebecca

Rebecca – Capital gains tax for the tax year 2020/21

		£
15 August 2020	Proceeds	24,000
	Less expenses of sale	(1,500)
	Net proceeds	22,500
	Less cost: £80,000 × $\dfrac{24,000}{24,000 + 126,000}$	(12,800)
	Gain	9,700
14 November 2020	Medal (exempt)	0
2 January 2021	Proceeds	295,000
	Less expenses of sale	(15,000)
	Net disposal proceeds	280,000
	Less cost	(190,000)
	Less enhancement expenditure (extension)	(20,000)
	Gain	70,000
Total gains £(9,700 + 70,000)		79,700
Less annual exempt amount		(12,300)
Taxable gains		67,400
CGT payable £67,400 × 20%		13,480

Helping hand. Don't forget to deduct the annual exempt amount to calculate taxable gains.

Marking scheme

	Marks
Part disposal	
Proceeds	½
Sale expenses	½
Cost	2½
Medal	1
Building	
Proceeds	½
Expenses of sale	½
Cost	1
Extension	1
Total gains	½
Annual exempt amount	1
Tax	1
	10

19 Bud plc

Bud plc – Value added tax (VAT) return for the three months ended 31 March 2021

			£	£
Output tax:				
Sales	– Standard rated	£240,000 × 20%		48,000
	– Zero rated			0
				48,000
Input tax:				
	– Inventory	£110,000 × 20%	22,000	
	– Machine	£40,000 × 20%	8,000	
	– Motor car	VAT not recoverable	0	
Impaired debts	– 31 August 2020	£3,000 × 20%	600	
	– 30 November 2020	less than 6 months old	0	
				(30,600)
				17,400

> **Helping hand.** The rule concerning private use of cars is that no VAT is recoverable on car purchases if there is any element of private use, rather than the VAT being apportioned between business use and private use.

Marking scheme

	Marks
Standard rated sales	1½
Zero rated sales	1
Inventory	1½
Machine	1½
Motor car	1
Impaired debt allowed	1½
Impaired debt not allowed	1½
VAT payable	½
	10

20 Betty

Box 1	0
Box 2	6900
Box 4	7000
Box 5	0

> **Helping hand.** You don't need to include exempt income (ie the ISA interest and dividends, NS&I certificate proceeds and the premium bond winnings).

Marking scheme

	Marks
½ mark for each correct action (each of 8 sources of income)	4
Stating all correct amounts in full (ie not deducting savings income nil rate band and dividend nil rate band)	1
	5

21 Jennifer

Jennifer – Property income for the tax year 2020/21

	£
Rent: Amount received (cash basis)	11,000
Less: Expenses	
Water rates	(400)
Insurance	(300)
Redecoration	(500)
Bed £(750 – 50)	(700)
Property income	9,100

Kitchen extension not allowable expense as capital item

> **Helping hand.** You should assume the cash basis applies to property income computations for individuals unless you are told otherwise.

Marking scheme

	Marks
Rent	1
Water rates	½
Insurance	½
Redecoration	½
Replacement furniture	1½
Kitchen extension	1
	5

22 Plant plc

Plant Ltd – chargeable gain for the year ended 31 March 2021

		£
Gain:	Proceeds	840,000
	Less cost	(410,000)
		430,000
	Less indexation allowance	
	£410,000 × 0.532 (frozen at 12.17)	(218,120)
		211,880
	Amount rolled over	(151,880)
	Gain chargeable now £(840,000 – 780,000)	60,000

Helping hand. Remember that the only chargeable gains relief that applies to companies is rollover relief.

Marking scheme

	Marks
Gain	1
Indexation allowance	1
Amount rolled over	1
Gain chargeable now	2
	5

23 David

David – opening year tax assessments

2018/19	Actual 1 October 2018 to 5 April 2019 £10,500 + 2/12 × £36,000	£16,500
2019/20	Current year basis Year to 31 January 2020	£36,000
2020/21	Current year basis Year to 31 January 2021	£40,000
Overlap profit	2/12 × £36,000	£6,000

Helping hand. Make sure you state the tax years and basis periods as required in the question.

Marking scheme

	Marks
2018/19	
Actual basis	½
Basis period	½
Assessment	1
2019/20	
Current year basis	½
Basis period and assessment	½
2020/21	
Current year basis	½
Basis period and assessment	½
Overlap profit	1
	5

Mock Exam 2

Foundations in Accountancy

Foundations in Taxation (UK) Mock Examination 2

Questions	
Time allowed	2 hours
All questions are compulsory and MUST be attempted	

DO NOT OPEN THIS EXAM UNTIL YOU ARE READY TO START UNDER EXAMINATION CONDITIONS

Section A – ALL 15 questions are compulsory and MUST be attempted

1. Tony is a basic rate taxpayer. On 1 January 2021, Tony rented out a property for the first time. Tony has not completed or received a tax return for many years.

   By what date must Tony notify HM Revenue and Customs (HMRC) of the new source of income to avoid incurring a penalty and what is the maximum penalty he might be charged if his failure to notify HMRC is not deliberate?

   - ○ 5 October 2021, maximum penalty 30% of potential lost revenue
   - ○ 5 October 2021, maximum penalty 70% of potential lost revenue
   - ○ 5 April 2022, maximum penalty 30% of potential lost revenue
   - ○ 5 April 2022, maximum penalty 70% of potential lost revenue **(2 marks)**

2. Betty is an employee earning £28,000 per year. Betty lives in a flat provided to her by her employer. The accommodation is not classed as job related. The employer paid £70,000 for the flat in 1995 and there have been no improvements. The annual value of the property is £4,000. Betty has occupied the flat since 1 October 2020 (when its market value was £255,000) and does not pay any rent to her employer.

   What is Betty's total taxable benefit in respect of the flat for the tax year 2020/21?

   - ○ £4,025
   - ○ £4,000
   - ○ £2,000
   - ○ £8,050 **(2 marks)**

3. Jeremy is an employee earning £40,000 per year. On 6 April 2019, Jeremy's employer purchased a television for £4,000. Jeremy used the television for private purposes from 6 April 2019. On 6 April 2020, Jeremy purchased the television from his employer for £600 when the current market value of the television was £2,100.

   What is Jeremy's total taxable benefit in respect of the television for the tax year 2020/21?

   - ○ £600
   - ○ £2,100
   - ○ £2,600
   - ○ £1,500 **(2 marks)**

4. Nothing Ltd prepares accounts to 30 September each year. It was given notice by HM Revenue & Customs (HMRC) to submit its corporation tax return for the year to 30 September 2020 on 30 November 2020. The return was submitted on 1 December 2021. This was the first late return for the company.

   What is the maximum penalty payable by Nothing Ltd as a result of its late submission?

   - ○ £100
   - ○ £200
   - ○ £500
   - ○ £1,000 **(2 marks)**

5. Abac Ltd was incorporated on 1 May 2020. Abac Ltd began to trade on 1 September 2020 and prepared its first set of accounts for the eight-month period ended 30 April 2021.

   What is Abac Ltd's first accounting period for corporation tax purposes?

   - ○ 1 May 2020 to 30 April 2021
   - ○ 1 May 2020 to 5 April 2021
   - ○ 1 September 2020 to 30 April 2021
   - ○ 1 September 2020 to 31 August 2021 **(2 marks)**

6   Jasper Ltd prepares accounts to 31 December each year. The following information relates to the year ended 31 December 2019 and the year ended 31 December 2020:

	Y/e 31.12.19 £	Y/e 31.12.20 £
Trading profit/(loss)	20,000	(40,000)
Investment income	6,000	15,000
Qualifying charitable donation paid	2,000	0

What is the maximum amount of the loss of the accounting period ended 31 December 2020 that Jasper Ltd can claim to carry back to the accounting period ended 31 December 2019?

- £25,000
- £20,000
- £26,000
- £24,000

(2 marks)

7   **How, and by what date, must capital gains tax on assets other than residential property be paid in respect of capital gains arising in the tax year 2020/21 to avoid incurring interest and penalties?**

- In one payment by 31 January 2022
- In two payments on account by 31 January 2021 and 31 July 2022 based on CGT liability for 2019/20 and a balancing payment by 31 January 2022
- In two payments by 31 July 2021 and 31 January 2022 based on CGT liability for 2020/21
- In one payment by 31 December 2021

(2 marks)

8   Paul purchased a ten-hectare plot of land in May 2008 for £80,000. In January 2021, Paul sold three of the hectares for £36,000 with expenses of sale amounting to £1,000. The market value of the remaining seven hectares of land in January 2021 was £90,000.

What are Paul's allowable costs for computing the chargeable gain on the disposal of the three hectares of land in the tax year 2020/21?

- £24,000
- £23,000
- £23,857
- £22,857

(2 marks)

9   **Which of the following is not true?**

- The value added tax (VAT) return for the three-month period ended 31 March 2021 was due by 7 May 2021
- VAT–registered traders must keep their records for six years
- The use of Making Tax Digital for keeping VAT records and providing VAT information to HMRC is optional for all VAT - registered traders
- A sole trader's VAT registration must be cancelled if the sole trader incorporates the business

(2 marks)

10 A value added tax (VAT) registered trader received an order for goods on 14 August 2020. The goods were despatched on 20 August 2020 and an invoice was sent on 19 September 2020. Full payment was received on 2 November 2020.

What is the tax point (ie the deemed date of sale) for the goods if the trader does not use the cash accounting scheme?

- 14 August 2020
- 20 August 2020
- 19 September 2020
- 2 November 2020

(2 marks)

11 Jessica has been in business for many years preparing accounts to 5 April each year. The tax written down value of her main pool at 6 April 2020 was £12,000. Jessica sold machinery on 10 June 2020 for £11,900 which had originally cost £11,600. She made no acquisitions during the year ended 5 April 2021.

What is the maximum capital allowance that Jessica can claim for the period of account to 5 April 2021?

- ○ £1,000
- ○ £400
- ○ £100
- ○ £72   (2 marks)

12 In the tax year 2020/21, Moeen is an employee earning a salary of £60,000 each year, paid in equal monthly amounts. He is also provided with taxable benefits amounting to £1,500 in the tax year.

What is Moeen's employee Class 1 national insurance contributions (NIC) liability for 2020/21?

- ○ £4,860
- ○ £5,060
- ○ £5,090
- ○ £7,274   (2 marks)

13 Harold owns some shares in Petunia plc. He is thinking about disposing of his shares.

Which of the following statements is correct about Harold's entitlement to business asset disposal relief on the disposal of his shares?

- ○ Harold must own at least 25% of the shares of Petunia plc
- ○ Harold must be a director of Petunia plc
- ○ The qualifying conditions must be met for a period of two years before the disposal
- ○ Petunia plc must be an unquoted trading company   (2 marks)

14 Joker Ltd purchased 50,000 shares in West Ltd for £180,000 in June 2002. There was a one for one bonus issue in July 2010 when the shares were worth £4 each. In June 2020, Joker Ltd sold 60,000 of its shares in West Ltd. Indexation factors are June 2002 to December 2017 = 0.578 and June 2002 to June 2020 = 0.637.

What is the indexation allowance available on the disposal by Joker Ltd in June 2020?

- ○ £68,796
- ○ £145,235
- ○ £62,424
- ○ £131,784

(2 marks)

15 In the tax year 2020/21, Teresa operated a sole trade and had taxable trading profits of £15,000. She was also an employee of Hark Ltd and in 2020/21 was paid a salary of £10,000 and dividends of £6,000.

Teresa joined a personal pension scheme on 6 April 2020.

What is the maximum possible gross contribution to the personal pension scheme that Tereasa can make in 2020/21 on which tax relief will be given?

- ○ £15,000
- ○ £21,000
- ○ £25,000
- ○ £31,000   (2 marks)

(Total = 30 marks)

Section B – ALL EIGHT questions are compulsory and MUST be attempted

16 Roy

Roy is employed by PO Ltd. Roy's annual salary is £120,000. In addition to his salary, Roy received a bonus of £18,200 in May 2020 and a bonus of £19,000 in May 2021.

PO Ltd deducted £38,000 income tax (under PAYE) during the tax year 2020/21.

During the tax year 2020/21 Roy also received the following.

Interest from Savemore Bank Ltd	£1,500
Dividends from Myco Ltd (a UK company)	£2,300
Rental income from letting out a room in his house	£7,800
Lotto prize	£500

Roy makes any beneficial election in respect of the rental income.

Roy paid £3,520 to a personal pension plan in the tax year 2020/21. PO Ltd contributed £2,400 to the same pension plan during the tax year 2020/21.

Required

Calculate the income tax payable by Roy for the tax year 2020/21. Your answer should identify by the use of zero (0) any item which is not taxable. **(15 marks)**

17 PAC Ltd

PAC Ltd is a UK resident company preparing accounts to 31 March every year.

For the year ended 31 March 2021 PAC Ltd had the following results.

	£
Trading profit (Note 1)	1,600,000
Rental income received (Note 2)	30,000
Interest received (Note 3)	25,000
Chargeable gain (Note 4)	70,000
Interest paid (Note 5)	9,000
Qualifying charitable donation (Note 6)	4,000

PAC Ltd has never previously been a large company for the payment of corporation tax.

Notes

1. The trading profit, which is stated before the deduction of capital allowances of £42,000, includes a £1,000 profit on the sale of a car and deductions for:

	£
Depreciation	27,500
Fees relating to the purchase of shares	4,000
Overseas customer entertaining	2,500

2. The rental income includes an amount of £1,000 for the month of March 2020 and a total amount of £3,000 received in advance for the months of April and May 2021.

3. The interest received is the total amount receivable for the year ended 31 March 2021 in respect of a loan made to a supplier.

4. The chargeable gain resulted from the disposal of an unwanted factory.

5. The interest paid is the total amount due for the year ended 31 March 2021 in respect of loan stock issued to provide finance to purchase additional shares in XP Ltd.

6 The qualifying charitable donation was the amount paid in February 2021.

Required

Calculate the corporation tax payable by PAC Ltd for the year ended 31 March 2021 and state the due date of payment. **(15 marks)**

18 QBC Ltd

QBC Ltd had the following transactions in plant and machinery for the nine-month period ended 31 March 2021.

Purchases:
14 July 2020   A machine was purchased for £120,000.
17 August 2020   Thermal insulation (a special rate pool item) was purchased for £756,250.
12 December 2020   A car with a CO_2 emission rate of 90 grams per kilometre was purchased for £18,000. This car is used 20% privately by the managing director.

Disposal:
18 January 2021   A machine, which had originally cost £8,000, was sold for £6,000.

The tax written down value of the main pool as at 1 July 2020 was £240,000.

Required

Calculate the maximum capital allowances that QBC Ltd can claim for the nine-month period ended 31 March 2021.

Note. Ignore value added tax. **(10 marks)**

19 Janet

Janet acquired the following shares in PLD Ltd:

2 August 2005	2,000 shares for £3,000
19 May 2008	4,000 shares for £7,800
15 September 2020	3,000 shares for £9,000
1 October 2020	500 shares for £1,200

Janet sold 4,500 shares for £27,000 on 15 September 2020.

Required

Calculate Janet's total chargeable gain on the sale of the PLD Ltd shares on 15 September 2020.

(10 marks)

20 John

John owns a cottage in the UK, which he rents, furnished, to members of the public.

Required

(a) **State three conditions, relating to rental periods, that must be met in the tax year 2020/21 for the cottage to qualify as a furnished holiday let.** **(3 marks)**

(b) **State two income tax advantages of the cottage qualifying as a furnished holiday let.** **(2 marks)**

(Total = 5 marks)

21 Jack, Peter and Colin

Jack, Peter and Colin have traded as a partnership for the last ten years. Colin decided to retire on 30 September 2020.

The partnership prepares accounts annually to 31 December. The latest set of accounts show a taxable trading profit for the year to 31 December 2020 of £108,000.

The agreed partners' salaries and profit sharing ratios were:

	Up to 30 September 2020	From 1 October 2020
Annual salaries:		
Jack	£10,000	Nil
Peter	£20,000	Nil
Colin	£20,000	Nil
Balance of profits:		
Jack	40%	40%
Peter	40%	60%
Colin	20%	Nil

Required

Calculate the partnership profit allocated to each partner in respect of the year ended 31 December 2020.

(5 marks)

22 Margaret

Margaret is a sole trader, preparing accounts annually to 31 March. During the year to 31 March 2021 Margaret's turnover was:

| Standard rated sales | £72,000 (inclusive of value added tax (VAT)) |
| Zero rated sales | £18,000 |

Margaret's purchases, which were all standard rated, amounted to £24,000 (inclusive of VAT).

Margaret had registered for VAT many years ago but only joined the flat rate scheme on 1 April 2020 and, thus, this is not her first year of VAT registration.

The normal flat rate percentage for Margaret's trade is 9%.

Required

Calculate the value added tax (VAT) payable to HM Revenue and Customs by Margaret for the year to 31 March 2021:

| (a) | If Margaret had not joined the flat rate scheme; and | **(3 marks)** |
| (b) | As a result of Margaret joining the flat rate scheme. | **(2 marks)** |

(Total = 5 marks)

23 Zephyr Ltd

Zephyr Ltd had the following results for the year ended 31 March 2021:

	£
Trading income	810,000
Chargeable gain	58,000
Trading loss brought forward (made in accounting period ended 31.3.20)	16,000
Qualifying charitable donation	3,000

Required

Complete boxes 155 to 315 inclusive (where relevant) on the following extract taken from the corporation tax return (CT600). **(5 marks)**

Company Tax Return
CT600 (2020) Version 3
for accounting periods starting on or after 1 April 2015

Tax calculation
Turnover

145 Total turnover from trade £

150 Banks, building societies, insurance companies and other financial concerns –
put an 'X' in this box if you do not have a recognised turnover and have not made an entry in box 145

Income

155 Trading profits £

160 Trading losses brought forward set against trading profits £

165 Net trading profits – box 155 minus box 160 £

170 Bank, building society or other interest, and profits from non-trading loan relationships £

172 Put an 'X' in box 172 if the figure in box 170 is net of carrying back a deficit from a later accounting period

CT600(2020) Version 3   Page 2   HMRC 04/20

Income - continued

175 Annual payments not otherwise charged to Corporation Tax and from which Income Tax has not been deducted £ _____.00

180 Non-exempt dividends or distributions from non-UK resident companies £ _____.00

185 Income from which Income Tax has been deducted £ _____.00

190 Income from a property business £ _____.00

195 Non-trading gains on intangible fixed assets £ _____.00

200 Tonnage Tax profits £ _____.00

205 Income not falling under any other heading £ _____.00

Chargeable gains

210 Gross chargeable gains £ _____.00

215 Allowable losses including losses brought forward £ _____.00

220 Net chargeable gains - box 210 minus box 215 £ _____.00

Profits before deductions and reliefs

225 Losses brought forward against certain investment income £ _____.00

230 Non-trade deficits on loan relationships (including interest) and derivative contracts (financial instruments) brought forward set against non-trading profits £ _____.00

235 Profits before other deductions and reliefs - net sum of boxes 165 to 205 and 220 minus sum of boxes 225 and 230 £ _____.00

Deductions and reliefs

240 Losses on unquoted shares £ _____.00

245 Management expenses £ _____.00

250 UK property business losses for this or previous accounting period £ _____.00

255 Capital allowances for the purposes of management of the business £ _____.00

260 Non-trade deficits for this accounting period from loan relationships and derivative contracts (financial instruments) £ _____.00

CT600(2020) Version 3   Page 3   HMRC 04/20

Deductions and Reliefs - continued

263	Carried forward non-trade deficits from loan relationships and derivative contracts (financial instruments)	£ . 0 0
265	Non-trading losses on intangible fixed assets	£ . 0 0
275	Total trading losses of this or a later accounting period	£ . 0 0
280	Put an 'X' in box 280 if amounts carried back from later accounting periods are included in box 275	☐
285	Trading losses carried forward and claimed against total profits	£ . 0 0
290	Non-trade capital allowances	£ . 0 0
295	Total of deductions and reliefs – total of boxes 240 to 275, 285 and 290	£ . 0 0
300	Profits before qualifying donations and group relief – box 235 minus box 295	£ . 0 0
305	Qualifying donations	£ . 0 0
310	Group relief	£ . 0 0
312	Group relief for carried forward losses	£ . 0 0
315	Profits chargeable to Corporation Tax – box 300 minus boxes 305, 310 and 312	£ . 0 0
320	Ring fence profits included	£ . 0 0
325	Northern Ireland profits included	£ . 0 0

Tax calculation

Enter how much profit has to be charged and at what rate

330	Financial year (yyyy)	335	Amount of profit	340	Rate of tax %	345	Tax	
330		335	£	340		345	£	p
		350	£	355		360	£	p
		365	£	370		375	£	p
380		385	£	390		395	£	p
		400	£	405		410	£	p
		415	£	420		425	£	p

Corporation Tax total of boxes 345, 360, 375, 395, 410 and 425 430 £ .

Marginal relief for ring fence trades 435 £ .

Corporation Tax chargeable box 430 minus box 435 440 £ .

CT600(2020) Version 3 Page 4 HMRC 04/20

Mock Exam 2:

Answers

DO NOT TURN THIS PAGE UNTIL YOU HAVE
COMPLETED THE MOCK EXAM

Section A

1   5 October 2021, maximum penalty 30% of potential lost revenue

A taxpayer must notify HM Revenue and Customs within six months of the end of the tax year in which a new source of income arises. Although the penalties for failure to notify are not quite the same as for the penalties for errors in the Tax Rates and allowances in the exam, you might guess what the maximum penalty for a non-deliberate failure might be.

2   £2,000

The taxable benefit is calculated as the annual value multiplied by the number of months the flat is occupied by Betty during 2020/21. Therefore the benefit is £4,000 × 6/12 = £2,000. There is no additional benefit as the cost did not exceed £75,000 (despite the house being worth more than £75,000 at the date Betty occupied the property and there being more than six years between acquisition and Betty's occupation).

3   £2,600

The benefit for use in 2019/20 was £4,000 × 20% = £800.

The benefit in 2020/21 on acquisition by Jeremy is £2,600, being the **greater** of:

			£
(a)	Market value at acquisition by employee		2,100
	Less price paid		(600)
			1,500
(b)	Original market value		4,000
	Less taxed in respect of use		(800)
			3,200
	Less price paid		(600)
			2,600

4   £100

There is a £100 penalty for a late return which is submitted within 3 months of the due date (here 12 months after the end of the period to which the return relates ie 30 September 2021). This rises to £200 if the delay exceeds three months. These penalties become £500 and £1,000 respectively if a return was late (or never submitted) for each of the preceding two accounting periods.

5   1 September 2020 to 30 April 2021

The first accounting period started when the company began to trade on 1 September 2020 and finished on the last day of the period of account on 30 April 2021.

6   £25,000

Jasper Ltd must make a current year loss claim against total profits if it wishes to make a claim to carry a loss back. The amount to carry back is therefore £(40,000 – 15,000) = £25,000. This is less than the total profits for the year ended 31 December 2019 of £(20,000 + 6,000) = £26,000.

7   In one payment by 31 January 2022

Capital gains tax (CGT) is due in one payment by 31 January following the end of the tax year (except CGT on the disposal of residential property). Payments on account are not required. Therefore for the tax year 2020/21, CGT is due on 31 January 2022.

8   £23,857

The amount of the cost attributable to the part sold is:

$$\frac{£36,000}{£36,000+£90,000} \times £80,000 = £22,857 \text{ plus the expenses of sale } £1,000 = £23,857$$

9   The use of Making Tax Digital for keeping VAT records and providing VAT information to HMRC is optional for all traders.

Making Tax Digital for VAT is only optional for traders with taxable supplies below the registration threshold (ie those who are voluntarily registered).

10   20 August 2020

The basic tax point is the date on which the goods were made available (20 August 2020). This is not displaced by the invoice date (not issued before the basic tax point nor within 14 days after it) nor the payment date (not before the basic tax point).

11   £400

The pool after deducting the disposal (limited to cost) is £(12,000 − 11,600) = £400. This is a small pool since it is £1,000 or less so the writing down allowance is equal to the unrelieved expenditure.

12   £5,060

Moeen's employee Class 1 NIC liability is £((50,000 − 9,500) × 12% + (60,000 − 50,000) × 2%) = £5,060.

13   The qualifying conditions must be met for a period of two years before the disposal

Harold must own at least 5% of the shares in Petunia plc. He must be an officer or employee of Petunia plc. Petunia plc must be a trading company but can be a quoted company.

14   £62,424

The number of shares after the bonus issue is 50,000 × 2 = 100,000 but the cost of £180,000 remains the same. The cost of the shares disposed of was therefore 60,000/100,000 × £180,000 = £108,000 and the indexation allowance (frozen to December 2017) was £(108,000 × 0.578) = £62,424.

15   £25,000

Teresa can make a gross contribution equal to her net relevant earnings which are £(15,000 + 10,000) = £25,000. Dividends are not earnings for these purposes.

Section B

16 Roy

Roy – income tax payable for the tax year 2020/21

	Non-savings income £	Savings income £	Dividend income £	Total £
Salary	120,000			
Bonus – receipts basis May 2020	18,200			
Employer pension contribution (exempt benefit)	0			
Employment income	138,200			
Property business income (Note 1) £(7,800 – 7,500)	300			
Bank interest (BI)		1,500		
Lotto prize		0		
Dividends			2,300	
Net income	138,500	1,500	2,300	142,300
Less personal allowance (Note 2)	nil			
Taxable income	138,500	1,500	2,300	142,300

Notes

1. Election made for alternative basis under a rent a room relief so only excess rent over £7,500 taxable.

2. Adjusted net income is above £125,000 so no personal allowance is available.

Increase in basic rate limit: £37,500 + (£3,520 × 100/80) = £41,900

		£	£
Tax payable:			
Non-savings income:	basic rate	41,900 × 20%	8,380
	higher rate	96,600 × 40%	38,640
Savings income:	nil rate	500 × 0%	0
Savings income:	higher rate	1,000 × 40%	400
Dividend income:	nil rate	2,000 × 0%	0
Dividend income:	higher rate	300 × 32.5%	97
Tax liability			47,517
Less tax deducted at source: PAYE			(38,000)
Tax payable			9,517

Helping hand. Did you remember to show that the payment by the employer to Roy's personal pension plan was an exempt benefit?

Marking scheme

	Marks
Salary	½
Bonus	1
No adjustment for employer pension contribution	½
Property business income: rent a room alternative basis	1½
Bank interest	½
Lotto prize	½
Dividends	½
Personal allowance	1½
Increase in basic rate limit	2
Tax payable on non-savings income at basic rate	1
Tax payable on non-savings income at higher rate	1
Tax payable on savings income at nil rate	1
Tax payable on savings income at higher rate	1
Tax payable on dividend income at nil rate	1
Tax payable on dividend income at higher rate	1
PAYE	½
	15

17 PAC Ltd

PAC Ltd – corporation tax for the year ended 31 March 2021

	£
Trading income (W1)	1,591,000
Property business income (W2)	26,000
Interest income £(25,000 – 9,000)	16,000
Chargeable gain	70,000
Total profits	1,703,000
Less qualifying charitable donation	(4,000)
Taxable total profits	1,699,000

Corporation tax
£1,699,000 × 19%   322,810
Payable by 1 January 2022 (Note)

Note. Quarterly payments are not due as this is the first time that PAC Ltd has profits in excess of the profits threshold of £1,500,000 and these profits do not exceed £10,000,000.

Workings

1   Trading income

		£
Trading profit		1,600,000
Add:	depreciation	27,500
	fees on purchase of shares	4,000
	overseas customer entertaining	2,500
Less:	profit on sale of car	(1,000)
	capital allowances	(42,000)
Trading income		1,591,000

> **Helping hand.** All customer entertaining is disallowable for corporation tax. The distinction between overseas and UK customer entertaining is only relevant for value added tax.

2   Property business income

	£
Rent received	30,000
Less: owed for March 2020	(1,000)
(taxable in accounting period (AP) ended 31 March 2020)	
received in advance for April and May 2021	(3,000)
(taxable in AP ended 31 March 2022)	
	26,000

Helping hand. Property business income for a company is taxed on an accruals basis, not a receipts basis.

Marking scheme

	Marks
Trading income (in main computation)	½
Property business income (in main computation)	½
Interest income	2
Chargeable gain	1
Qualifying charitable donation	1
Corporation tax	1
Due date	1
Working 1	
Depreciation	1
Fees	1
Overseas customer entertaining	1
Profit on sale of car	1
Capital allowances	1
Working 2	
Rent received	1
Late receipt	1
Payment in advance	1
	15

18 QBC Ltd

QBC Ltd – capital allowances for the nine-month period ended 31 March 2021

	AIA £	Main pool £	Special rate pool £	Allowances £
TWDV b/f		240,000		
Additions qualifying for AIA				
Thermal insulation (Note 1)	756,250			
AIA £1,000,000 × 9/12	(750,000)			750,000
	6,250			
To special rate pool	(6,250)		6,250	
Additions qualifying for AIA, but not given AIA				
Machine		120,000		
Additions not qualifying for AIA				
Car (Note 2)		18,000		
Disposal				
Machine (Note 3)		(6,000)		
		372,000		
Writing down allowances				
£372,000 × 18% × 9/12		(50,220)		50,220
£6,250 × 6% × 9/12			(281)	281
TWDVs c/f		321,780	5,969	
Total capital allowances				800,501

Notes

1. The annual investment allowance is allocated to the special rate pool expenditure in priority to the main pool expenditure as this is more tax efficient due to the lower rate of writing down allowance in the special rate pool.

2. The private use by the director does not affect the company's entitlement to capital allowances.

3. The proceeds figure is the lower of the original cost and the selling price.

> **Helping hand.** Be careful where there is a short accounting period. The annual investment allowance and the writing down allowances need to be scaled down.

Marking scheme

	Marks
TWDV b/f	½
Thermal insulation acquisition	1
Annual investment allowance	1½
Transfer balance to special rate pool	½
Machine acquisition	1
Car acquisition	1
Machine disposal	1
WDA @ 18% × 9/12	1½
WDA @ 6% × 9/12	1½
Total capital allowances	½
	10

19 Janet

Janet – chargeable gain on the sale of PLD Ltd shares

First match the disposal with the acquisition on the same day:

	£
Proceeds $\frac{3,000}{4,500} \times £27,000$	18,000
Less cost	(9,000)
Gain	9,000

Next match the disposal with the acquisition in the next 30 days:

	£
Proceeds $\frac{500}{4,500} \times £27,000$	3,000
Less cost	(1,200)
Gain	1,800

Finally, match the disposal with the shares in the share pool:

	£
Proceeds $\frac{1,000}{4,500} \times £27,000$	6,000
Less cost (working)	(1,800)
Gain	4,200
Total gains £(9,000 + 1,800 + 4,200)	15,000

Working

	No. of shares	Cost £
2 August 2005 Acquisition	2,000	3,000
19 May 2008 Acquisition	4,000	7,800
	6,000	10,800
15 September 2020 Disposal	(1,000)	(1,800)
c/f	5,000	9,000

Helping hand. It is important to use the two-column standard layout for the share pool.

Marking scheme

	Marks
Same day purchase	
Proceeds	1½
Cost	1
Next 30 days purchase	
Proceeds	1½
Cost	1
Share pool	
Proceeds	1½
Cost	3
Total gains	½
	10

20 John

(a) **Rental period conditions**

- The property must be available for rental to the public generally for at least 210 days in a tax year.
- The property must be let for at least 105 days in a tax year.
- The property must not normally be occupied for longer-term occupation (more than 31 consecutive days to the same person) for more than 155 days in a tax year.

(b) **Income tax advantages**

- The income counts as relevant earnings for pension contributions.
- Capital expenditure on furniture can be deducted when incurred instead of replacement relief (or capital allowances on furniture can be claimed if the accruals basis is used).

Helping hand. To qualify as a furnished holiday letting, the property must usually be let for at least half of the days it must be available for rental to the public generally.

Marking scheme

		Marks
(a)	1 mark per condition	3
(b)	1 mark per advantage	2
		5

21 Jack, Peter and Colin

Jack, Peter and Colin – share of partnership profit in respect of the year ended 31 December 2020

	Total £	Jack £	Peter £	Colin £
1 January 2020 to 30 September 2020				
Salary (9 months)	37,500	7,500	15,000	15,000
Balance (40:40:20)	43,500	17,400	17,400	8,700
	81,000	24,900	32,400	23,700
1 October 2020 to 31 December 2020				
Profits (3 months) (40:60)	27,000	10,800	16,200	0
Total	108,000	35,700	48,600	23,700

Helping hand. A common mistake would be to forget to scale down the salary of each partner for the part of the period of account which is nine months long.

Marking scheme

	Marks
1 January 2020 to 30 September 2020	
Salaries	1½
Balance	1½
30 September 2020 to 31 December 2020	
Profits	1½
Totals for the year ended 31 December 2020	½
	5

22 Margaret

(a) **Value added tax (VAT) payable if Margaret had not joined the flat rate scheme**

	£
Output tax £72,000 × 1/6	12,000
Less input tax £24,000 × 1/6	(4,000)
VAT payable	8,000

(b) **Value added tax (VAT) payable as a result of Margaret joining the flat rate scheme**

Total VAT inclusive supplies £(72,000 + 18,000) = £90,000

VAT payable £90,000 × 9% 8,100

Helping hand. The flat rate percentage applies to both standard rated supplies and zero rated supplies. Therefore, it is unlikely to be beneficial to traders with substantial zero rated supplies.

Marking scheme

		Marks
(a)	Output tax	1
	Input tax	1
	VAT payable	1
		3
(b)	Total VAT inclusive supplies	1
	VAT payable	1
		2
		5

23 Zephyr Ltd

Zephyr Ltd – Corporation tax return for the year ended 31 March 2021

Box 155	810000
Box 165	810000
Box 210	58000
Box 220	58000
Box 235	868000
Box 285	16000
Box 295	16000
Box 300	852000
Box 305	3000
Box 315	849000

Marking scheme

	Marks
½ mark for each entry	5

Tax rates and allowances

Supplementary instructions

1. Calculations and workings need only be made to the nearest £.
2. All apportionments should be to the nearest month.
3. All workings should be shown when answering section B.

Tax rates and allowances

The following tax rates and allowances are to be used in answering the questions.

Income tax

		Normal rates	Dividend rates
Basic rate	£1 – £37,500	20%	7.5%
Higher rate	£37,501 – £150,000	40%	32.5%
Additional rate	£150,001 and over	45%	38.1%

Savings income nil rate band	– Basic rate taxpayers	£1,000
	– Higher rate taxpayers	£500
Dividend nil rate band		£2,000

A starting rate of 0% applies to savings income where it falls within the first £5,000 of taxable income.

Personal allowance

Personal allowance	£12,500
Income limit	£100,000

Where adjusted net income is £125,000 or more, the personal allowance is reduced to zero.

Car benefit percentage

The base level of CO_2 emissions is 55 grams per kilometre.

The percentage rates applying to petrol cars (and diesel cars meeting the RDE2 standard) with CO_2 emissions up to this level are:

51 grams to 54 grams per kilometre	13%
55 grams per kilometre	14%

A 0% percentage applies to electric-powered motor cars with zero CO_2 emissions.

For hybrid-electric motor cars with CO_2 emissions between 1 and 50 grams per kilometre, the electric range of a motor car is relevant:

Electric range

130 miles or more	0%
70-129 miles	3%
40-69 miles	6%
30-39 miles	10%
Less than 30 miles	12%

Car fuel benefit

The base figure for calculating the car fuel benefit is £24,500.

Company van benefits

The company van benefit scale charge is £3,490, and the van fuel benefit is £666.

Pension scheme limits

Annual allowance	£40,000

The maximum contribution that can qualify for tax relief without any earnings is £3,600.

Approved mileage allowances: cars

First 10,000 miles	45p
Over 10,000 miles	25p

Capital allowances

Plant and machinery
Main pool	18%
Special rate pool	6%

Motor cars
CO_2 emissions between 51 and 110 grams per kilometre	18%
CO_2 emissions over 110 grams per kilometre	6%

Annual investment allowance
Rate of allowance	100%
Expenditure limit	£1,000,000

Commercial structures and buildings
Straight-line allowance	3%

Corporation tax

Rate of tax	19%
Profit threshold	£1,500,000

Value added tax (VAT)

Standard rate	20%
Registration limit	£85,000
Deregistration limit	£83,000

Capital gains tax

	Normal rates	Residential property
Rates of tax – Lower rate	10%	18%
– Higher rate	20%	28%

Annual exempt amount	£12,300
Business asset disposal relief – Lifetime limit	£1,000,000
– Rate of tax	10%

National insurance contributions

Class 1 Employee	£1 – £9,500 per year	Nil
	£9,501 – £50,000 per year	12%
	£50,001 and above per year	2%
Class 1 Employer	£1 – £8,788 per year	Nil
	£8,789 and above per year	13.8%
	Employment allowance	£4,000
Class 1A		13.8%
Class 2	£3.05 per week	
	Small profits threshold	£6,475
Class 4	£1 – £9,500 per year	Nil
	£9,501 – £50,000 per year	9%
	£50,001 and above per year	2%

Where weekly or monthly calculations are required the Class 1 limits shown above should be divided by 52 (weekly) or 12 (monthly) as applicable.

Official rate of interest (assumed)

2.25%

Standard penalties for errors

Taxpayer behaviour	Maximum penalty	Minimum penalty – unprompted disclosure	Minimum penalty – prompted disclosure
Deliberate and concealed	100%	30%	50%
Deliberate but not concealed	70%	20%	35%
Careless	30%	0%	15%

Bibliography

Bibliography

Her Majesty's Revenue and Customs (2020) *Corporation Tax: Company Tax Return (CT600 (2020) Version 3)* [Online] Available from: https://assets.publishing.service.gov.uk/government/uploads/system/uploads/attachment_data/file/869810/CT600_2020.pdf [Accessed on 17 July 2020]

Her Majesty's Revenue and Customs (2020) *Self-Assessment Tax Return Form (SA100)*. [Online] Available from: https://assets.publishing.service.gov.uk/government/uploads/system/uploads/attachment_data/file/874083/sa100_English_Form.pdf [Accessed on 17 July 2020]

Her Majesty's Revenue and Customs (2020) *Self-Assessment Tax Return Form Capital Gains Summary Page (SA108)*. [Online] Available from: https://assets.publishing.service.gov.uk/government/uploads/system/uploads/attachment_data/file/876796/SA108_English_Form_2020.pdf [Accessed on 17 July 2020]

Her Majesty's Revenue and Customs (2020) *Self-Assessment Tax Return Form Partnership (Short) Pages (SA104S)*. [Online] Available from: https://assets.publishing.service.gov.uk/government/uploads/system/uploads/attachment_data/file/873018/sa104S_-_English_Form.pdf [Accessed on 17 July 2020]

Her Majesty's Revenue and Customs (2020) *Self-Assessment Tax Return Form Self Employment (Full) Pages (SA103F)*. [Online] Available from: https://assets.publishing.service.gov.uk/government/uploads/system/uploads/attachment_data/file/874594/sa103f_English_Form.pdf [Accessed on 10 July 2020]

FOUNDATIONS IN ACCOUNTANCY FTX FOUNDATIONS IN TAXATION (11/20)

REVIEW FORM

Name: _____   Address: _____

Date: _____

How have you used this Practice & Revision Kit?
(Tick one box only)

☐ On its own (book only)
☐ On a BPP in-centre _____
☐ On a BPP online course
☐ On a course with another college
☐ Other _____

Why did you decide to purchase this Practice & Revision Kit? *(Tick one box only)*

☐ Have used complementary Interactive Text
☐ Have used BPP Interactive Texts in the past
☐ Recommendation by friend/colleague
☐ Recommendation by a lecturer at college
☐ Saw advertising
☐ Other _____

During the past six months do you recall seeing/receiving any of the following?
(Tick as many boxes as are relevant)

☐ Our advertisement in *ACCA Student Accountant*
☐ Our advertisement in *Teach Accounting*
☐ Other advertisement _____
☐ Our brochure with a letter through the post
☐ ACCA E-Gain email
☐ BPP email
☐ Our website www.bpp.com

Which (if any) aspects of our advertising do you find useful?
(Tick as many boxes as are relevant)

☐ Prices and publication dates of new editions
☐ Information on Practice & Revision Kit content
☐ Facility to order books
☐ None of the above

Have you used the companion Interactive Text for this subject?   ☐ Yes   ☐ No

Your ratings, comments and suggestions would be appreciated on the following areas

	Very useful	Useful	Not useful
Introductory section (How to use this Practice & Revision Kit)	☐	☐	☐
'Do You Know' checklists	☐	☐	☐
'Did You Know' checklists	☐	☐	☐
Possible pitfalls	☐	☐	☐
Questions	☐	☐	☐
Answers	☐	☐	☐
Mock exams	☐	☐	☐
Structure & presentation	☐	☐	☐
Icons	☐	☐	☐

	Excellent	Good	Adequate	Poor
Overall opinion of this Kit	☐	☐	☐	☐

Do you intend to continue using BPP products?   ☐ Yes   ☐ No

Please note any further comments and suggestions/errors on the reverse of this page.
The author of this edition can be emailed at: learningmedia@bpp.com

REVIEW FORM (continued)

Please note any further comments and suggestions/errors below